Election 2016

Election 2016

THE GREAT DIVIDE, THE GREAT DEBATE

Mark Jabbour

Library of Congress Control Number: 2018913265
ISBN: Hardcover   978-1-9845-6473-3
                         Softcover   978-1-9845-6472-6
                         eBook   978-1-9845-6471-9

Print information available on the last page.

Cover photo by the author
Interior photos and illustrations by the author

1. Election 2016
2. Donald J. Trump
3. Evolutionary Psychology
4. Personality
5. Memoir
6. Fiction

Rev. date: 11/19/2018

To order additional copies of this book, contact:
Xlibris
1-888-795-4274
www.Xlibris.com
Orders@Xlibris.com
782364

Contents

List of Illustrations

For my father
Colonel Nicholas Jabbour, USAF
1920–2016

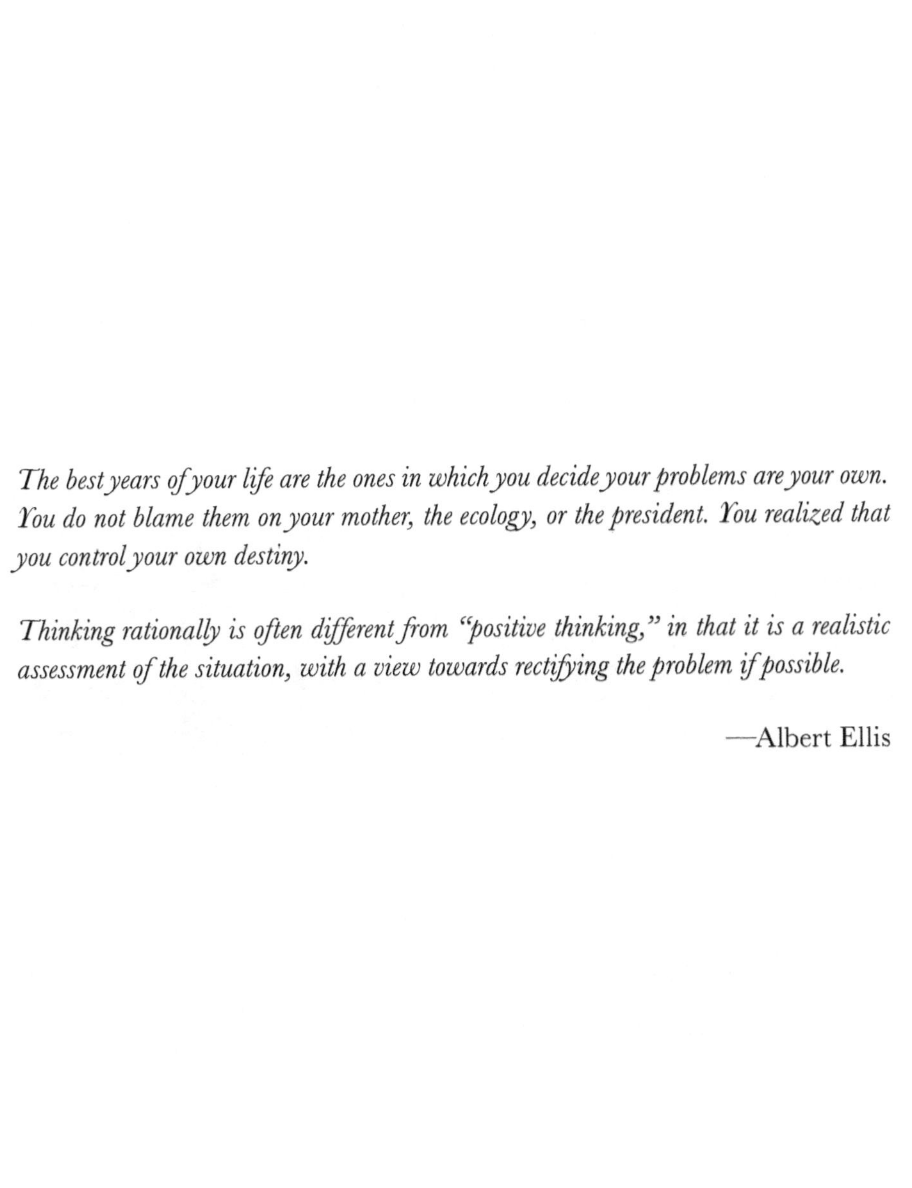
The best years of your life are the ones in which you decide your problems are your own.
You do not blame them on your mother, the ecology, or the president. You realized that
you control your own destiny.

Thinking rationally is often different from "positive thinking," in that it is a realistic
assessment of the situation, with a view towards rectifying the problem if possible.

—Albert Ellis

Preface

Election 2016: The Great Divide, the Great Debate is a collection of essays, comments, and shorts written in real time, reacting to and predicting the emergence of Donald J. Trump as a viable and then winning candidate—interrupted periodically by fictional analysis from myself and fictional characters, like Dr. Sigmund Freud in chapter 6 and again in chapter 24, a therapy session with Horace (possibly the missing link in human evolution), demonstrating the psychological aspects of the campaign regarding the American psyche. The chapter "The Real Mr. Trump and the Solution" is also fictional. Max is a fictional composite of real people I've had conversations with, online and face-to-face. In addition, there are fictional futuristic happenings, speculations about what *could* happen. Also, there are quite a number of footnotes—some cite sources, some are explanatory, and some are updates of relevant subject matter—as the process of writing this book has taken a great deal more time than I imagined.

The great divide seems only to have widened, now fourteen months plus into the Trump administration. There is no bridge, no coming together, and certainly no evolved consciousness. Instead, we (Americans) seem to be on the brink of another civil war, another war between the states. The electorate now appears to be sorting itself out geographically. The internet, specifically the social media, looks to have, rather than connecting people in friendly ways, augmented and exacerbated their differences to the point of not only hostile speech but behavior as well. This election, more so than any other event since that war, begs this question: Who *are* we? Obviously, that question wasn't settled then, and remains open today.

The time right after the attack on New York city and Washington, DC, on September 11, 2001, may have been the closest the nation has ever been to "the United States of America, one nation under God, with liberty and justice for all."[2] The words "under God" were added to the pledge, by Congress, in 1954, at the suggestion of then president Dwight D. Eisenhower. I, like Donald Trump, grew up starting each school day facing the flag and reciting the pledge, with my hand over my heart. At some point in our nation's recent history, that requirement was removed from the school's daily schedule, and that seems to represent "the divide" as well as anything—we no longer pledge (anything) as a nation. Are we "one nation under God," or are we something else? Are we no longer a nation defined by physical, spiritual, and cultural boundaries (as discussed in the chapter "Boundaries") but by a vague notion of inclusive compassion encompassing the whole world? Like some sort of postmodern, New Age spiritualism that touts evolved consciousness? Are we no longer a country, a territory, but an abstract idea open to all and anyone regardless of allegiance? That seems to be one side of the debate. Does the oath "Swear to tell the truth, the whole truth, and nothing but the truth, so help me God" have any meaning whatsoever?

If *one world* replaces *one nation* in the meaning of "liberty and justice for all," what word or idea or belief replaces God when one "swears to tell the truth"? Is it karma? Buddha? If you don't tell the truth, the whole truth . . . are you going to get some bad stuff coming down on you? Is that it? The world will punish you, never mind the courts. Is justice levied by a higher power ("Vengeance is mine, saith the Lord"), not the legal system, not God, but some vague karmic force? Therein seems to be the divide. But I don't think that's the whole story, not by a long shot. I think the divide/debate is about power—who has it and who gets to exercise it. In other words, it's who decides.

When America, as we've come to know it, the second America perhaps, was becoming a nation, the frontier spirit defined America and its people. This was a character (in real life, I think the words *character, personality,*

---

[2]   This is from the Pledge of Allegiance to the flag of the United States of America (1954).

and *soul* all have a similar or close-enough meaning) of strength, rugged individualism, self-reliance, and personal responsibility. Former President Barack Obama's speech on July 13, 2012, while it sounds wonderful and soaring, is really an insult to this notion. He said, "If you've got a business—you didn't build that. Somebody else made that happen." These are words that could only have been spoken by a man who never built anything.

Of course, the frontiersman didn't manufacture his rifle or his traps or the settler forge his own saw and plow, but seriously, everyone knows and understands that those men—and yes, they were mostly men—overcame great odds and hardships to carve out a civilization from a hostile, chaotic natural world. For an American president to disparage the spirit, the character of the self-made man is disgraceful.

What is *power*? In essence, it's the ability to compel another, others, or things to obedience or to make them/it submit to your will. It's about control. Control over what? Behavior and action and resources (food, water, shelter, education, territory, money, and yes, healthy, fertile females). It's about protection from harm. And the one who can *provide* it, that person/entity has power! In a nutshell, power is about survival. In this country, this nation, legal power is awarded to those who win elections. They determine the laws and how to enforce them. Who wins is determined by a vote. Who votes is determined by laws, persuasion, will and willingness, and also, some unsavory practices (lying, bribery, coercion, etc.) by those wanting to gain power.

That is what this book is about and why I wrote it.

This book is a personal account, a personal journal, of the presidential election of 2016. I didn't intend to write it; I was just recording my thoughts on paper as I've done most of my life. I have been keeping a record of who I am, if you will, and then somewhere in time, I thought (given my background in anthropology, psychology, and social work), *This should be a book, a record of the election. That might have value.* Others had that same thought, professionals namely Mark Halperin,[3] John Heilemann, and Mark McKinnon of MSNBC TV, Bloomberg Politics, and Showtime. They began a video documentary, a big-league production called *The Circus*. (You can watch it on Hulu, and I strongly recommend you do.) It's a real-time document of the 2016 election, just like this book. With an open

---

[3]   Halperin is now in a sort of literary/journalistic limbo, having been accused and admitting to sexual misconduct during the course of his career.

mind, I invite you to compare them. I admit to my bias (for Trump and my subjectivism) and to taking creative license with the insertion of fiction ("Freud on Trumpism," "Debriefing Horace," "The Real Mr. Trump and the Solution," and so forth). You'll notice that the first few chapters have no mention of Trump or the campaigns. It's not until September 2015 that I begin to put what's happening into a national/global context. I became fascinated with the campaigns and the media's coverage. I began to pay serious attention, and it became more and more interesting with each day.

You'll notice quite a difference though between the professionals' account and mine: they all got it wrong and I got it right! Without going into detail of how that is possible, some things are obvious. One is that this whole Russian obsession is ridiculous and dishonest! Two is that just how sleazy and smarmy both politicians and journalists are. Take notice of who gets the most face time in *The Circus*. Answer: the three creators. Their preference for Bernie Sanders and John Kasich is also apparent. Just as I do as a writer, in choosing my words and the events I cover, they choose the shots they shoot, the scenes they cover, what goes into the show, and what lands on the cutting room floor.

In this story, I've titled a chapter "Despicable Democrats and the Media." There, I lay out an argument stating that what looks like benevolence and compassion is really just another way to take power. Why not lie if lying works? Who holds you to account? God? Karma? Persuasion and influence are all just manipulation and deceit, and much of that involves self-deception.

To be clear, I am an atheist, and also, I don't believe in karma. If I believe in anything, I lean toward the law of attraction. I lean toward "You earn your fate," except when other forces more powerful than you intervene. What is *so* obvious in the Showtime documentary is that Trump *earned* his win! No one helped him, foreign or domestic. He took no counsel. He was pure Trump, 100 percent, right from the beginning and up until now. His triumph was unprecedented and historic, and he should be given credit. (But that's not the case, is it?) He embodies that frontier spirit—the can-do attitude and confidence that forged this country.

I hope that this book can make some sense of all that. If you choose to buy it and read it, you might learn something, not just about the election, politics, the media, etc. but also about yourself and the human condition.

Sometimes, we are just unlucky. But, and this is important, I *respect* those who believe in a moral code dictated by God. I understand that need and desire to believe in a higher power, in God—the creator. I understand the need and desire to believe in life after death, an eternal soul, and that there is something more than just a struggle to live another day and breed. Understanding leads to compassion. Compassion is not learned in a classroom or in books; it is acquired through observation and experience and, yes, via narcissism. What if it were *me* who was suffering? Empathy, I think, is just narcissism in disguise—dressed up in a raincoat, hat, and dark glasses.

Is the ability to imagine unique to the human species? I don't know.

At the beginning, I really knew nothing of Trump. I'd never seen one episode of *The Apprentice*. I *had* been a supporter of Obama in 2008, in fact, a delegate, one of the 2,200-some who gave him the nomination over Hillary Clinton. I believed in him. I voted for him again in 2012. And *then,* what happened? Not much, as it turned out. America seemed to be in decline (until Trump won).

I've looked out my window, interacted with people, taught a writing class at a community college in Colorado, and thought, *We are going in the wrong direction, headed for extinction, maybe. Other people, Americans, my people, are sick—and the rest of the world's populations are engaged in primitive power struggles. Deceit is king. Something's got to change.* And then I began to pay close attention, very close attention, to the campaigns and the media's coverage of them.

From the onset, the reporting was all wrong. Trump came down the escalator in Trump Tower and said that Mexicans were rapists and murderers, some of them anyway, and that we need protection—a beautiful big wall. And then the campaign was on. Trump was a racist and xenophobe and, soon to be added, sexist. Not investigated, at that time, was a news story of the missing girls of Juárez. Look it up. The link was not reported because it did not fit the narrative as presented, because the media had predetermined Trump as a joke. The media were *dishonest* from the get-go and then did everything in their power to justify their actions! And they continue to do so!

To understand Trump is to be Trump—impossible, of course— which is why I injected fiction into this story. I had a conversation with Sigmund Freud and went on a road trip with *the* Donald Trump. I used my imagination in the hope of gaining an understanding of what the hell is going on.

February 26, 2018
North Westminster, Colorado

Acknowledgments

I wish to acknowledge the following people for their support, encouragement, and love: my father, Colonel Nicholas Jabbour; my brother, Jack J. Jabbour; and my son, Jake L. Jabbour.

I wish also to acknowledge the following friends for not abandoning me when most others did and for providing me with feedback while at the same time challenging me, respectively: Marco V. Morelli, Michael Keane, and William Alexander Sheare.

In addition, I thank Dr. Leslie Hannon, whom I entrusted with my life and without whose professional ear, guidance, intervention, and unconditional positive regard, I never could have seen this project through. (She could double her fee, and it'd still be a bargain.)

And I thank all the professional help and encouragement from the team at Xlibris Corporation, especially Ms. Le-Ann.

Gods, Heroes, and Men

JUNE 16, 2015

From the beginning of man's time here on earth, there has been a need to worship. Some have said man (humans) has a religious gene. Some would claim this need is couched within a hierarchy of needs.[4] Others claim that God created man and the earth and provided man with everything he needs to survive his time on earth. My position is that this need (love and belongingness/affiliation) stems from worship. The roots run deep, and the roots are truth, in other words, reality or that which doesn't go away even if you don't believe it.[5]

First, as a child, man worships the mother and the father (and competes with his siblings for attention from the object[s] of his wonder) and more so with the father because his father is all-powerful.

The mother also worships the father because she needs him desperately. Her world is a frightening place. She needs to believe that her mate can provide and protect her and her children.

---

[4]   See Abraham Maslow's motivational theory, the hierarchy of human needs, wherein I would classify the need to worship within the construct of belongingness and love needs.

[5]   This is attributed to author Philip K. Dick.

The father worships the king (the leader of the tribe). The father needs the king because the king is all-powerful and determines if he lives or dies.

The king knows he needs the people to service and protect *him*, and so he conjures up gods who cannot be seen and speak only to him, the king. And the king worships and listens to the declarations of the gods, which are (in practice) thoughts that emerge in his vainglorious brain because he is all-powerful. (Or so the king believes.) In essence, the king worships himself but is also very superstitious because he knows, deep down, that he knows nothing—nothing but the fact that he got to be king by his strength, cunning, will, and desire.

The king is smart, and so he develops rituals. The rituals help control the frightened, desperate, and credulous people. They believe what he believes, and together, the king and all the king's men conjure up collective rituals in the form of dancing and chanting and drumbeating (i.e., music). Music bonds the tribe together. The people work themselves into frenzies and shout out to the gods their fear and fury and joy and gratefulness. They scream for blood, for the thrill of the kill and sacrifice, for the meat that sustains them, for the glory of triumph, and for the continuation and perseverance of life. (Think rock concert. The lead singer/guitarist is the king/god, and the *sacrifice* needed to score tickets.)

Hail to the king. The king collects the strongest and most powerful men and forms an army of warriors to hunt and fight and to raid, rape, steal, and dominate all who do not submit and worship as he does. (The narcissistic tendency goes way back.) All this so he may remain king. The warriors become heroes in the eyes and minds of the people. The heroes get to mate with the choicest of women who adore them.

Hail to the heroes.

Worship is the glue that binds people together, that they can triumph in a world rife with strife, suffering, and struggle. The ritual becomes a spectacle and a means by which all can participate and be a part of the force that triumphs. If you are here now, it is because what you have done has worked, so you repeat it. If it fails you, you must not have done it right, not well enough. But because the king and the gods love you and are benevolent if appeased, they have given you another chance. Try harder. Work harder. Dance better. Cheer louder for your heroes, your king, and your gods. Next time you will triumph. To the victor go the spoils. Scream louder.

So here we are today in the twenty-first century. But really, some two million, not six thousand, years passed the first man and the primal hoard. Some forty to fifty thousand years passed was the beginnings of art and worship. Fifty thousand years or two thousand generations of modern man we are.

We are here now, self-declared postmodern, and yet some think we have made no progress. We men, goes the argument, are still governed by the same basic, primitive needs and desires that allowed for us to be here now: strength, power, force, and cunning. And of course, the worship of such via ritual and spectacle.

So we attach to a team, the home team, the team of our youth, and root, root, root for the home team. But what we are doing is that which we have always done. And as the saying goes, "If you do what you've always done, you'll get what you've always got."

The root of sport is worship and triumph. At the root of worship is participation in ritual/superstition. At the root of ritual is attachment/affiliation, love, and belongingness. At the root of attachment is survival, because the child is helpless without the father—the protector.

In the year 2015, the new kings are the CEOs of corporations who—with the aid of modern, new warriors, the *madmen* (the designers of ritual and of worship)—cajole the people into believing that by *participating* in the triumph of sport and by *ownership* of product, you, as an individual and as a member of the team, actually matter.

Go, team.

The question is, Is it real? Does it matter who wins the game? The game (whatever the game might be) is proxy for war. Does it matter if you die so long as you die in the service of the king? The king grants you eternal life in the afterlife—in the other world beyond this one. Have we, men, progressed beyond the need for war, for dominance, and for triumph? Can we triumph over primitive needs and desires? Is beauty enough? Is one finite life enough?

We will always compete and compare—that's who we are. Childhood decides. The child is father to the man.[6] Who are you for, King James or

---

[6]   This is from William Wordsworth's poem "My Heart Leaps Up" (1802). I'm stretching the meaning/interpretation here to say that early man is the father of modern man and that our habits, behaviors, emotions, feelings, and needs remain the same. Moreover, that early man most likely felt the same as Wordsworth and you or me when looking up in the sky or to the horizon and seeing a rainbow.

the upstart hipster Stephen Curry? USA or Russia? Roll Tide or go Ducks? Jesus or Muhammad? Jew or Arab? Democrat or Republican? Yankees or Dodgers? Dodgers or Giants? Marilyn or Jackie? iPhone or Android? Apple or Microsoft? Ford or Chevy? New York or LA? Whose side are you on?

The Peopled-World Map

JUNE 30, 2015

The peopled world is made up of now (2015) some seven billion different souls or characters/persons—personalities, but they are knowable and categorical. The figure below illustrates that and is adapted from Lorna Smith Benjamin's *Interpersonal Diagnosis and Treatment of Personality Disorders* (1996). All people have a personality, regardless of whether or not it is known to the self or others. We discern a person's personality by his or her actions or behaviors. Everyone can be located on the illustration / figure / visual aid / whiteboard map. The map is divided into four quadrants or two halves, with each half again divided in two. The four headings are hostile, friendly, differentiation, and enmeshment.[7] The two halves are friendly/hostile and differentiation/enmeshment. The four quadrants (clockwise from top left) are hostile differentiation, friendly differentiation, friendly enmeshment, and hostile enmeshment. An individual (character/

---

[7] *Differentiation* is the process of becoming an individual separate and apart from one's parents and/or parental-like persons or a group's influences. *Enmeshment* is a state of being entangled with another person or group, wherein the boundaries between the self and other(s) are unclear. It is closely related to contagion, groupthink, and codependency. See also the chapter "Boundaries."

soul/person) will fall into one of the four quads. The inner open-spaced square represents 70 percent of the population, with each quad containing approximately 17–18 percent.

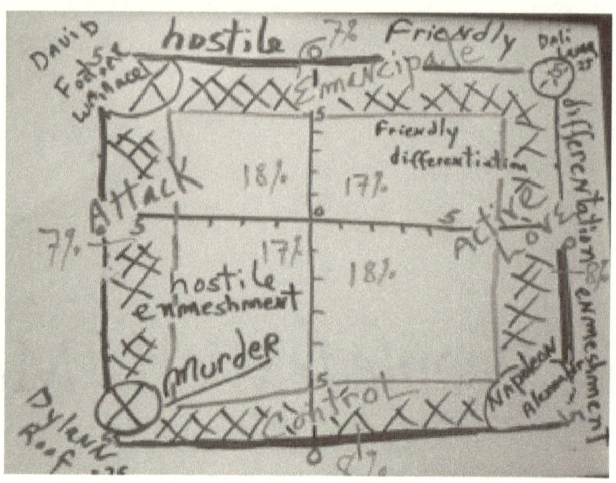

The peopled-world map

The crosshatch-marked outer space bordering the inner square represents 30 percent of the population. These are the individuals who shape the cultures, the societies, people live in. They are the leaders/kings/ chiefs. They make the laws. They are the leaders because they are unusual and dynamic. They have power. They are the ruling class, the elites [1] (See the numbered list at the end of this chapter for clarification and detail.)

At the extreme nexus of the lower-left quad, that of the hostile enmeshment, I have placed Dylann Roof, the young man who murdered nine people in the famous Charleston church massacre (June 18, 2015). He was waging (hoping to incite) war for a cause he believed in but could be diagnosed as having a personality disorder of the extreme. His avatar in a Hollywood film might be Michael Corleone, the coldhearted assassin, leader of the Corleone family in *The Godfather*, who sits down and shares a meal with adversaries before shooting them all. (We cheered and admired him in the movie.) Opposite Roof, again in the extreme outer reaches, this time of the friendly differentiated quad, I placed the Dalai Lama, the Buddhist monk who practices unattached love or love without touch or distinction. At the upper-left extreme, I placed David Foster Wallace, the literary genius and cultural analyst/reporter/critic who hung himself in

2008, at the age of forty-six, who practiced detached, objective observation. [2] At the lower-right extreme, I placed the emperor Napoleon and his adversary, the tsar Alexander. (Or you could put Donald J. Trump). He is the benevolent king whose behaviors and emotions are tangled up with his subjects. He feels their pain, or is it his?

The world is made up of opposites. The opposites exist on continuums. Active love has its opposite attack. The opposite of emancipate (being free) is control. Roof's action can be understood as an act of extreme attack and control (i.e., murder). Benjamin states, "Murder is judged . . . at the endpoint of the attack and the control dimensions." Forgiveness, expressed by the victims or survivors, can be understood by murder's opposite— extreme emancipation and love. "The Tibetan Buddhist who successfully meditates on total detachment from an enemy while intensely loving the enemy is given a complex label: active love plus emancipate or *reactive love* plus *separate* or active love plus *separate* or *reactive love* plus emancipate, depending on the nature of the meditation." [3] We might think that only such a person as the Dalai Lama could pull that off. We might be wrong.

The point is this: All the public chatter I've heard is mere distraction. [4] Only on the margins does what happened in Charleston have anything to do with flags or guns or religions or mental illnesses or even races. Those are all symbols, manifestations, and tools of personality—the greatest taboo. These are things no one wants to talk about, except on a superficial level: "I'm an introvert" and so on. Roof has an *extreme personality disorder*, which went undetected, undiagnosed, and untreated and which resulted in the murder of nine persons—targets of his rage and hostility, of his enmeshed, hostile personality. [5]

So the question that follows is, How does this happen? This is really four questions. How does personality form? Can a personality be manipulated? Are such extreme personalities simply a consequence of being human? Is there anything that can be done without unintended, harmful consequences, or will we just make things worse? Those are questions and subjects we ought to be discussing—having a conversation about.

What is obvious is that Roof's desire (to start a race war) will not be the result of his action. In fact, the opposite will happen. People will be brought together, united, in a collective desire to fight this kind of horror, just as what happened after the terrorist attack by Osama bin Laden.[8] Bin Laden can be placed at the extreme lower right, along with Napoleon and Alexander, the benevolent king personality.

But look! Where are we now? We are worse, farther apart, for all our coming together after 9/11. From the perspective of oppressed, attacked, dominated Muslims, bin Laden was a loving and benevolent leader, one who would fight and free them from the nonbelievers and imperialists. The people merely just had to submit to Allah's will and direction via bin Laden's interpretation. He was a hero, not a villain. He did not start the war(s); the Russians, the Baathists, and the Americans did. His war was holy—to force invaders and occupiers out of his holy lands. It was justified (in his mind), an abreaction.

Dylann Roof (in his own words) felt he had no choice. [6] He, too, felt justified. The "progress" and coming together of people (races) that was being forced on him (via the new, open, postmodern world) *forced* him to act—to kill. The more connected and equal *we* became, the more alienated, enmeshed, threatened, and hostile Roof became. He had to take *control* and *attack*. And no one intervened, or saw it coming, or took him seriously. He was closed-minded, introverted, disagreeable, and neurotic. [7] No one cared enough to notice or, if they did, to act.

I am not being sympathetic, or empathetic, (well, maybe a little);, but I am attempting to shed light on this question: How does this happen? From understanding comes compassion is the natural course of intelligent thought, behavior, and emotive response, [8] which is the truest meaning of education—to learn about the human condition and personality.

Look at the map (picture) above.

Where would you place yourself? Everyone is there. I know it's uncomfortable to think about it—personality—especially in this "we are all together, kumbaya" world we are told we live in, but *who we are* is reality. We are not all the same; we are different in many ways. At the same time, we are alike in many ways (we have 98.6 body temp, we laugh, we cry, we feel pleasure, we feel pain, we eat, we drink, we breathe, we eliminate, we

---

[8]   This collective response of uniting under a common threat can be explained via the amity/enmity complex, best composed by Robert Ardrey in his book *The Territorial Imperative* (1966, p. 269). This concept was first put forth by Charles Darwin, Alfred Russel, and Herbert Spenser; and I contend that it changes everything. I'll discuss it in greater detail in later chapters.

sleep, and we dream. We share the same physiological needs and right on up Maslow's hierarchy) [9].

Without knowledge and understanding, we will do what we've always done because we *are* the same, and we *won't* change because we have stopped the evolutionary process of natural selection. If put another way, we have been so successful and dominant as a species, with our adaptation to environmental threat via our technology, that there is no longer any hazard we can't defeat. As a species, we won. Contrary to the postmodern worldview, we have not evolved past our modern selves. We are self-conscious, adaptive, tool-using, competitive, comparative, sexual, language-using bipedal animals. We will fight (by any means) or run away (escape), or hide (freeze) because we all live in fear of oblivion and wish to reproduce. Most of us anyway.

We are all diagnosable. We are all knowable despite what the experts tell you. I don't diagnose so as to find fault in you; I diagnose to know you better, to understand you. We all want to be seen, be noticed, be recognized, and validated, but not known or watched. We want to be loved, but not exposed. We want affirmation and affiliation without disclosure or submission. We want security *and* freedom! But still don't understand what freedom means or is.

"It's not my fault! I don't want to be judged. I want to be forgiven and live forever." [10] Except for the extreme personality, who doesn't fear death and oblivion. You are at the mercy of the movers and the shakers—the players—the fearless and the aggressive, the strong and the twisted.

1. The percentages here are arbitrary, not based on any data, but they could be accurate. We'd like to think that murderers and miscreants are very rare, that most people are good, solid citizens and well-adjusted. But that's likely not the case. We must make laws, we think, because we think without laws—people can't be trusted to behave in good faith. People may or may not be trustworthy, meaning they will not harm you. Look at the leaders the people elected to represent us. Look at the people we admire. Look in the mirror. Be honest. Listen to the lies we tell ourselves.

2. Not so dissimilar to Roof would be Wallace's character Randy Lenz, in *Infinite Jest*. Lentz is a killer too, who gets off on lashing out in anger for relief. This is what Freud might call an unsupervised abreaction, the "There! Take that!" expression/manifestation of

behavioral explosion of intense anger and rage of a person with a personality disorder.

3. The *Interpersonal Diagnosis and Treatment of Personality Disorders* (1996) by Lorna Smith Benjamin (Guilford Press, New York, p. 63–64) states that the different designations are dependent upon how one is perceiving the meditation as an actor or a recipient.

4. Include President Obama's leading mourners in the singing of *Amazing Grace.* It's a short-term feel-good exercise and means nothing in the long run, but it provides good entertainment and scores political points.

5. People will find targets for the repressed frustration, anger, rage, and hatred until and unless they can accept reality as to who and what they are and what can be done or not done about that.

6. The most important question is, Does choice really exist? We need to believe it does to give us agency/power/control, to give life meaning, but it might not. Free will might be a collective delusion. Did you choose where you were born? Did you choose your parents? Did you choose your religion? Did you study them all—places, people, religions—and try them all out? Did you choose who you fell in love with? Did you try them all out? Or did you choose between Coke and Pepsi? Not really a true choice at all. Did you choose your personality? By the time you might have had a choice with regard to anything, it might be too late. I don't know.

7. How do you help someone if they don't ask for or want your help?

8. Emotions and feelings also exist on a continuum with bipolar extremes. At one end is despair; at the other, joy. The midpoint is between boredom and contentment, which are close together. You cannot get from one extreme to the other normally. You have to move up or down the continuum in sequence. (Manic depression is called a bipolar disorder for good reason. It's a very unstable state of being.) The grieving process is also, normally, sequential: shock, denial, anger, bargaining, then acceptance. And it, too, comes and goes, like all feelings and emotions.

9. We all do these things and experience these things, but to different degrees and have different preferences, which form who we are— our personality, our behaviors.[9]

---

[9] See Abraham Maslow's *Towards A Psychology of Being* (1968) and *Motivation and*

10. Everything is labeled a disease, and there is a pill you can take. Can't sleep? Here's a pill. Can't focus? Here's a pill. Can't stop eating? Here's a pill. Can't make up your mind? Here's a pill. Feeling down? Here's a pill. Feeling anxious? Here's a pill. It's not your fault; it's your chemistry. You can't help it; you were born that way, or so we're told.

Personality (1970) and Hans Eysenck's *The Inequality of Man* (1973).

Immigration, Some Thoughts

AUGUST 19, 2015

Immigration, okay. Everyone is in a snit now that *the* Donald did what they asked and got specific with a "position paper." He's right if you think out into the future and not just about winning the Hispanic vote or being politically correct. Here's why: In 1970, the US population was 220 million; now it's 330 million. The world population is now 7 billion, projected to be 9 billion by 2050 and 11 billion by 2100. The real problem, not the surface one but the deep-rooted one, and the truth of the matter is that the planet cannot sustain that many people, especially at a consumption level of the US middle class, which is everyone's aspiration (viewed and known by all now because of the internet and the phone).

We in the United States (the wealthiest country) can't take care of the people we have: 30–40 percent is at or below poverty and 70 percent is overweight or obese. You don't need studies or research to know this; you've only to go out among the populace, open your eyes, and pay attention. The roads and bridges are potholed and crumbling, and the highways are jam-packed. There are ghettos of poverty in every city and homeless people begging and sleeping on the streets and in the parks. People, from coast to coast, hate people who are different. And that's here, in the best place in the world to live, the United States of America.

People can't live together when they're crowded together in abject poverty—without food, water, shelter, and access to health care (basic physiological needs), peace (safety and security), and meaningful work (dignity and self-esteem) in any sense of purpose and pride. People under such pressure/hazard are . . . Well, people are different. Some will manage, but for most, it's an ugly situation. Some will thrive, and some will die. There will be winners and losers. The adventurous ones, the extroverted ones, the tough-minded ones will migrate and head out for a better life.

America, the USA, was founded and built by these types of people. But most people just go along to get along, hoping to live another day, doing whatever it is they have to do, trying simply to stay alive. To pretend this isn't the case, that everything will turn out fine, is pie in the sky. Maybe that lets you to sleep at night. I call it denial.

Is it possible what Donald J. Trump has put forth in his paper? Most likely not all of it. I suspect he knows that, but he's got people talking honestly about a problem that's only going to get worse. Rival candidate Jeb Bush said, "We've got to fix the broken problem." (Meaning immigration.) A problem broken *is* fixed. The guy's so confused he can't even talk or write a good speech. And Hillary Clinton? Please! If she weren't a woman and former First Lady, she'd have maybe three people in her camp. Clinton keeps extolling, "You don't understand!" Truth is, she doesn't. She lives in a world of her own—paranoid, where everyone is out to get her. Yet she knows how to get things done? She wants us to believe. She's made the "hard choices" (banking $13 million for a book no one reads), globe-trotting and playacting as a statesman while her husband collects huge speaking fees because he was once president and *knows* what's what. He's got the key? What nonsense! She's done nothing but laugh, dance, smile wave, scream, complain, and nod like a mindless bobblehead.

How do we fix our problems? The first step, as everybody knows, is to accurately identify them—to name them.

The problems are that there are

1. too many people,
2. too much consumption,
3. too much depletion and destruction of the natural world,
4. too many weapons,

5.   too many nuclear warheads,
6.   too many cars,
7.   too many dogs,
8.   too many cows,
9.   too many chickens,
10.   too many restaurants,
11.   too many channels,
12.   too many books (that's right!),
13.   too much entertainment,
14.   too much spectacle,
15.   too many faux choices (Coke or Pepsi?),
16.   too many charlatans,
17.   too many myths,
18.   too many pipe dreams (not nearly enough realism),
19.   too many lies, and
20.   too much political correctness.

I do have some ideas but I'm no politician. I think it's possible to think about people living together on the planet in peace (Peace being people living side by side without assaulting or killing one another, no war, and of course, allowing for the usual amount of deceit—I'm being realistic) well into the future. But it's going to take some real radical, critical, outside-the-box thinking and truth telling. (The truth *will* set you free, but not before it's finished with you.) Otherwise, life on this planet will get worse for most people, while others live behind gated, heavily fortified walls.

Westminster, Colorado, where I live, is a lovely, modern city—beautifully landscaped with golf courses, playgrounds, lakes and ponds, bike paths, green spaces galore, and wide streets with all wires, water, and sewage underground and out of sight.

There is every convenience nearly on every corner, but there are too many people—unhealthy, old, alienated, shut up in their huge homes and apartments bought with money they inherited from their parents and invested in "the market." They are all trying to be oblivious or is it anonymous? Some are wannabe writers writing trite mommy blogs and/or memoirs of abuse and neglect, dreaming of hitting the big time, *the show*. There are also the legal immigrants—the smart ones—from places in the East, who start high-tech companies and stash gizmos in closets and bathrooms, overcharging for work that they really don't understand. (Who does?)

I've watched this now for five years, and new huge single-family homes are being built on every open swath of land. Drive north and look! All the land is being consumed by huge homes, hospitals, senior villages, box stores, and mixed retail. And there are the brown people (there are few black faces here) who speak only in hushed tones, in Spanish, with earbuds in their ears, and live in squeezed-in trailer parks over on the "other side," down the hill toward Denver, mowing the lawns, trimming the trees, blowing the leaves, building the new homes and apartments—working for peanuts. They are strangers in a strange land, trying hard to survive by shoveling snow, paving streets, building houses, and picking up garbage (working for chump change). And then there are the young white adults who live with their parents in huge homes, in basements, and in back rooms, surfing the internet, looking for love and a life swiping left and right, and playing games. Some work in the box stores (you'll get your fifteen dollars an hour, your living wage, if you vote for HRC) or care for the sick and old, smoking the glass pipe (legally) and getting high, dreaming their dreams.

This is America, the land of opportunity. The people will keep coming and coming. The land is so, so beautiful; the mountains so majestic. The politicians and bankers and corporate CEOs will find a way to shoehorn them in (more people means more consumers, more taxes, more money for those at the top), giving them a little something to keep them from rioting and revolting. America—land of the free (if you are so free, why is it nothing is your fault? Reconcile that) and home of the brave.

Go ahead and call Trump a joke, smoke your dope, go see your doctor or your therapist (you've got your Obamacare now), take your legal drugs to help you sleep, lose weight, smile, or be quiet. Feel no pain. Nothing can be done, right? Enjoy your spectacle, watch your shows, read your books, dream your dreams, eat your meat, or not. Drink your designer coffees (there's a coffee shop within a mile of your house), meditate, have your glass of wine (or two) after dinner. Relax and don't forget to teach your children how to be PC (politically correct).

PS. I suspect I've offended just about all my friends (on Facebook) with this post. I *was* born on the Day of Contentious Conviviality. I can't help it. It's not my fault. Donald was born on the Day of Gutsy Confrontation. (It's not his fault either.) We are who we are.[10]

---

[10]	Gary Goldschneider, *The Secret Language of Birthdays: Personology Profiles for Each*

A Citizen Primer

AUGUST 27, 2015

There are fifty separate states (determined by men some time ago) in the USA, the lower forty-eight and two that are detached. The forty-eight states are bounded by two oceans, one on the eastern border and one on the western, and two sovereign countries, Canada, along the northern border, and Mexico to the south. The southern border is marked by the Rio Grande River and some desert cacti and the north by some blazes on some trees. Each US state is made up of x number of counties, which are lines drawn on a map (determined by men some time ago) that divide the state into administrative districts for the purpose of local governance. Colorado has fifty-six counties. I have lived in six of them. Each county is further divided into smaller and smaller units—districts and then finally precincts. Colorado is a caucus state, and each district has a caucus for the purpose of electing delegates to represent the people (other citizens) with regard to the things that matter (i.e., governance of society and social order).

(In the election of 2008, I was a delegate for House District 49, precinct 4154935405, Larimer County, in the state of Colorado, USA.)

Day of the Year (1994).

Any citizen may go to their caucus (usually in a public building, like a church or school) and speak to other citizens of their precinct on the matter of being chosen to represent them, regarding the upcoming local, state, and national elections. Everybody (from the precinct who's there) then votes whom *they* want to represent them when all who have chosen to speak have spoken. Those delegates then go on to the next event, the county convention. (Mine, in 2008, was at Rocky Mountain High School in Fort Collins.) There again, citizens as well as candidates can get up and speak concerning the current issues, persons seeking office, and then vote on a party platform.

Again, delegates are chosen to go to the next event, the state convention. Each party, Democratic and Republican, have parallel processes going at the same time. Some districts and/or counties may have only one delegate, such as Jackson County in Northern Colorado, which, by the way, had only three registered citizen Democrats.

In 2008, the state Democratic Party convention was held in Colorado Springs in May. This is when the party gets really serious and the real partying begins. Deals are made in the back rooms of bars, hotels, and bedrooms. Big-time speakers and politicians show up, and the final delegates are chosen. Colorado has nine (9) delegates who then get to go to the national convention, which, in 2008, was in Denver. (I didn't make the cut.) Some of those nine are fixed (super)—the governor, the mayor of Denver, and the two state senators. Others go around and campaign for votes.

The author at the Colorado caucus for Barack Obama,
House District 49, precinct 4154935405, 2008

In the final election, the national general election, the president of the United States is voted by all the citizens of the country. (But in reality, the number who vote is closer to 65 percent rather than *all*, which is why turnout is *so* important.) Voting is voluntary. (It's a free country.) Each state, all fifty (plus the District of Columbia) is awarded a number of delegates based on population as declared by the current US census data. California has the most delegates (55), followed by Texas (38), then New York and Florida (29 each); Wyoming has the fewest (3). There are a total of 538 delegates, the electoral college. It takes 270 votes (delegates) to win the election. All but two states have a rule in place that says the delegates must vote according to the popular vote of the citizens of their state. For instance, if (say 2020) in Colorado the popular vote is 1,249,000 for Joe Biden and 1,250,000 for Donald Trump, Trump wins! All Colorado's nine electoral votes must then be cast for Trump. To carry this further, let's say at the end of the election of 2020—Wednesday morning, November 7—forty-nine states are in. Biden and Trump are tied at 261 votes each, and then Colorado's vote outcome (too close to call, so every vote must be counted and recounted) will determine the next POTUS. With this scenario, one vote, perhaps *your* vote, can mean war or peace. (Recall the election of 2000.)

All this is to say that it *does* matter who gets to vote (i.e., who is and is not a citizen). And so politicians—those who want to get themselves elected and have a say in the making of laws, in the governance of the nation, in matters of war and peace, life and death—will do all manner of things to determine *who gets to vote*. A politician will try to stack the votes in his or her favor by promising things to voting *blocks/communities/constituents* so that they, the voters, feel/think compelled to vote for the said politician. Typical blocks of voters are seniors, males, females, youths or African Americans, Hispanics, white southerners, evangelicals, Catholics, Jews, college educated, the working poor, and so on. Non-citizens and felons (criminals convicted of felonious crime) and citizens under age eighteen are not allowed to vote.

In the beginning of this country (as determined by white men who emigrated from Europe), only white landowners could vote. The voting population has gradually grown because politicians are trying to win the favor (votes) of new blocks of voters—white women, blacks, young people (voting age was lowered from twenty-one to eighteen because of the Vietnam War in 1971), new immigrants, and so forth. All manner of tricks are tried and executed: redistricting, passing voter ID laws, expanding this group or that, determining birthright citizenship, pandering to this group or that, handing out money (in the form of tax breaks and social services), and making all kinds of promises and deals. All this, in the final analysis, is in the quest for power and status and, of course, money.

My idea is, in order to vote, to become a citizen of the USA, with all the legal rights and protections that come with that, one ought to have to pass a written exam of the above process and an essay test on Tolstoy's *War and Peace*.

Trump's Problem

SEPTEMBER 3, 2015

Trump's problem is, How do you get yourself elected when your constituency is maybe, at best, 10 percent of the population—some from whom you want to take away money? I don't like the fact that people are linking Donald Trump to being racist, sexist, xenophobe, misogynist, and the most hateful, vile label, white supremacist. I don't like that folks might think I am one of those things because I endorsed him. There is not one shred of evidence that he is any of those things. I have read many articles depicting Trump as such. Sorry, they are full of erroneous arguments, start at the beginning when he spoke of the problem of illegal immigration. His statement has been so distorted. He was referring to this article: http://www.huffingtonpost.com/.../central-america-migrants-ra. (The origin of the article is Jorge Ramos's network.) In a follow-up to his statement, Trump said, "Well, someone is doing the raping."

He was also referring to the missing girls of Juárez, which had just been in the news. His comments were twisted into Trump calling/thinking all Mexicans are rapists and criminals. *That's crazy!* There is *no* evidence he thinks or believes that. But there is a great deal of evidence he doesn't. Take the *Boston Globe*'s research or any unbiased research. He's been around for forty years. No one can find any evidence that he harbors any of those hatreds attributed to him. The only slur that might have credence is that he is not a true conservative. He's not. He's a businessman who loves competence and intelligence (and beautiful women, ooooh, what a crime).

The Jorge Ramos incident is revealing. He did not have him ejected. Ejection is a violent event. It happens with fighter pilots and riders who are not belted in, in cars. It might be applied to bouncers in bars back when "America was great." In the late 1970s and early 1980s, there was a doorman (bouncer) in a nightclub I tended bar in, whom we called Buffalo. The club was always packed, shoulder to shoulder, and the cocktail waitresses had to almost fight or stiff-arm their way through the crowd. They were also and always very, very attractive women. Sometimes, customers would get fresh or rude (grab them by the waist, arm, butt, and yes, pussy).[11] So the waitress would signal me, the bartender, and I would signal Buffalo. Buffalo would take the offending client/costumer by the arm firmly (just as you saw in the video with Ramos) and move the offender toward the exit, the front door, and then Buffalo would slam the jackass into the doorjamb, say sorry, and hurl the jerk out into the parking lot. That's an ejection! And so it was back in the day when America was great.

---

[11] "Women may dress and act provocatively or allow themselves to be touched sexually. Essentially, the bar is a place of *license*, that is, acceptable deviance, where 'out of line' behaviors are permitted and even encouraged. For those who play within the rules, there is ample opportunity for unleashing libido and partially satisfying a host of unmet need. Not only can patrons shirk their ordinary social roles, they can also dissociate from 'being naughty' once they leave the barroom setting." Harvey B. Milkman and Stanley G. Sunderwirth, "The Great Psychiatric Tavern," in *Craving for Ecstasy and Natural Highs* (2010), 78.

Freud on Trumpism

SEPTEMBER 7, 2015

Dr. Freud: Methinks the liberal and progressive factions of the population doth protest too much.

Me: Indeed.

Dr. Freud: Such protestations exhibit an intense psychic conflict, an egotistic defense mechanism—repression, specifically that of a reaction formation.

Me: Which is . . .

Dr. Freud: Simply, you hate that which you fear you need.

Me: Ahh, the strong father.

Dr. Freud: Precisely. The conflict is the desire for, and at the same time, the anger toward the strong father. In this case, it is represented not by the wolf in the wild, the alpha male of the pack, or the psychoanalyst. No, it's Mr. Trump. Mr. Trump has tapped into a very primal thing here. Those who hate Trump also exhibit envy and jealousy for what they lack and have lost or fear that they may lose—power. That and/or this. The accusations of racism, sexism, xenophobia, and misogyny are manifestations of unmet childhood emotional, psychological, and physical needs in addition to possible sexual and/or physical abuse, neglect, and then the resulting trauma. They resent the abandonment by their birth father and view Mr. Trump as a manifestation of that man. Moreover, those unresolved issues have then festered within the individual, congealing into a self-destructive mass of goo that—

Me: I'm sorry to interrupt, but *goo*, is that a new clinical term?

Dr. Freud: A layman's term for something thick and sticky, unseen, residing in the brain, the unconscious. It is undetectable, even by modern brain scans, that only the most sensitive and receptive analyst can uncover. It clogs up the healthy actions of neurotransmitters, hormones—one's basic emotions. You see, it's the result that leads to complex patterns of behavior that can be roughly described as complex post-traumatic stress disorder. Those unresolved conflicts are compressed within the organism, and when they find an outlet, well, the explosion is quite terrific. It's, to use a common cliché, a perfect storm.

Me: Oh my god! That sounds awful. Can anything be done?

Dr. Freud: One can drink. Hahaha, just kidding . . . Cocaine, now that was a drug with miraculous healing power.

The coyotes yowl, running free on the adjacent golf course. Sigmund sips from his snifter of brandy, relights his cigar. I take a long pull from my bottle of beer and then throw down a shot of whiskey.

Me: Dr. Freud?

Dr. Freud: Yes?

Me: What is Trumpism?

Dr. Freud: Trumpism is simply the art of the deal. Not the deal as in a game of cards but the deal as in a contract or treaty—a negotiation. Trump wrote the book on it. Well, he put what it was and is into words. Trumpism has always existed in the animal kingdom. Trump is, well, trump, the prototypical alpha male. Do you play bridge, Mr. Mark? (*I nod.*) Yes, very good then. Trumpism is winning. It is going into battle without weapons, tools, and artifacts, save for your wits, your presence, your body—your body language, if you will. You see, it is fighting without death. You do not kill your rival but discourage him, convince him that he cannot win and he'd be better off to retreat and live, to survive, than to stay and fight and die. Does that make sense? (*I lean forward in my chair, tilt my head slightly, and lift my chin and brow.*) You see, if rivals of the same species did battle to the death—

Me: Doctor. Rivals? Who and what for? If you don't mind.

Dr. Freud: Yes, of course. It, the competition, would be for resources, territory, mates. For all resources are contained within the territory. The planet is finite, you know. We humans have divided it up with lines on maps, which we call borders, into countries with names. But they are really territories. And so are the resources, finite, unless we are wise, which, so far, we have shown that we are not: food, land, fertile land, water, woodlands, fuel, coal, oil, grasslands, minerals. You must know this on some level, yes? (*I nod.*) People, too, are resources. Labor, laborers, workers, soldiers, and now, consumers, buyers of products. But most important are mates—the females. The strongest men, the smartest men, the most cunning men are really competing for the females so as to reproduce, to keep the line going. It's simply life driven by the desire to live. It's not that complicated really. Yes? No? (*I shrug.*)

So where was I? Ah, Trumpism. So the trick is, the art of the deal is to convince your rival that you and him are both better off if you win and he settles for less. In that way, everybody wins. Everybody lives. Everybody gets to reproduce, to eat, to drink, and to be merry. This is nothing new. Now you call it what? Nonzero sum, something silly like that. There is no need for bloodshed. For if there is death and dying and killing, eventually there will be no one left to do the work that needs to be done. It is far better if everyone lives. But, and this is where the rivalry comes in, all men cannot mate with the same woman, the choicest of the females. Only one can. The big dog, so to speak. The fittest, if you will, meaning the strongest, smartest, and cleverest selects the finest female, the fittest, again, if you will, meaning the healthiest, which is determined by first sight. Thus the male gaze and then smell and taste, and touch, poking and prodding and finally mounting. And then . . . well, this does go on and on. And we don't have time, do we?

(*I glance out the window. The light is fading. I shrug.*) It is the way of things. The defeated rivals disperse and take with them what they can, the lesser women, and find vacant territory to inhabit or use what they learned in defeat and try and force others to move out to take over some other's territory. It is endless. But now the world seems full—full of people. There are too many people. An explosion is coming. There is too much compression, too much pressure. The planet has become a pressure cooker. Haha. Sorry. Yes, Trumpism is . . . And so how is this determined? Who is the fittest? By battle, yes, of course. That is the brutes' way. But we humans developed language, or language evolved because it led to less death. You, anyone, can see the evolving of this if you study the animal kingdom. Our closest relations, the great apes, the silverback gorilla, rises up and pounds his chest, shows his fangs, and charges if he must, all to intimidate his rival, to say without words, "You cannot win. You cannot defeat me. You cannot have her. Go away. Go away out of my sight, out of my territory. This is mine and these are my women, my children, my tribe, my land." Trump Tower, if you will. Trump's name is everywhere. He has captured not by battle but by the art of the deal—negotiation—much of the prime real estate, the prime territory. The best locations are in the best cities, like Manhattan, Miami, Las Vegas, San Francisco, and others. Prime properties are along the coasts, along the great rivers, where he builds resorts and golf courses. Everywhere where people want to be, there is Trump.

And so he charges people to live and play and work where they most want to because he captured them/it by his wits and his cunning and his strength. He is a mutant. He is *Trump*! Everyone knows this. They have no chance. But they have to try to make an effort, yes? To try and save their self-respect, their self-esteem, and the respect of others for themselves. Everyone can see this. Everyone knows now. And so they will do everything and anything they can to take him down, to make him retreat. They are . . . (*Freud takes a long drink of his brandy*) they call him names and say what an awful man he is, that he is not nice. Ha! As if the territory were awarded to the nicest man and not the strongest. As if there were a vote. Ask your women who they would prefer. Ach, a useless exercise. Never mind. It's no wonder he calls his rivals losers and weak.

(*Sigmund pauses for a puff on his cigar, blowing the smoke out slowly, as if to make his point. I almost expected him to blow smoke rings. I take a drink of beer.*) Ah, back to the history of things . . . So the human now has language. He no longer has to beat his chest and show his fangs—he negotiates. And sooooo the negotiation is just a substitute for the physical intimidation, which is a substitute for actual combat. What the rivals are doing is trying to convince one another who is the stronger, and this is done by bidding, an auction, if you will, as in the game of bridge. The strongest possible bid ever is seven no-trump, which means that the bidder person is saying that he will take every trick, every single one, without a doubt. He is holding all the high cards, all the aces, all the kings, all the queens, and so on. This almost never happens. The winning hands are hands that are usually strong in one suit—spades or hearts, diamonds or clubs. But no one really knows, so you must play the game. You make your bids, your opponent or rival makes his, and then you see who gets the contract. You may bet against the contract that is made. There is some luck on the cards you are dealt, but in the end, it is how you play the hand that matters. That determines the winner. If you play your cards right, if you play from strength, if you have a long suit, you will start to trump even your rival's aces, kings, and queens. Trump is trump and cannot lose. Ah! I get lost in the game, thinking of when I won. Perhaps we should take a break.

The sun has now set completely, and darkness has taken over the sky. The coyotes yell and yowl to one another, announcing to all who is where and what is what. We move to the balcony and listen for a few moments. We go back inside and resume the interview.

Dr. Freud: So you see, Mr. Mark, nothing has really changed. We are who we are. Primitive creatures are still battling between ourselves and within our own selves, trying to resolve conflict either by fighting or running away. But Mr. Trump has mastered a new way—yes, in some ways, an old way—combined with our great (*for a second, I thought Dr. Freud was going to signal air quotes*) evolutionary feat of language and become better than anyone else at it. He is the fittest, Mr. Trump. He can win without killing. The diplomat, the politician, tries to win with flattery and bribery, which everyone knows is untrue, and falsely promises the voter whatever he wants—money, food, education, or job. Trump threatens to flatten you, which might very well happen. He is the strong father who can command the child to obedience with just a look. When push comes to shove, as it will with overcrowding, hoarding, compression, and pressure, well, we shall see, won't we? (*Did Dr. Freud just wink at me?*) It might be that your friends, Mr. Mark, with all their repressions, will thwart his drive to become president, which would be a shame. Mr. Trump might be, with his Trumpism, the one man who can save the world from the horrors of global war or nuclear war.

Me: But, Dr. Freud!

Dr. Freud: Stop, it's getting late. I am an old man and need my rest. It is all only a cosmic joke, you know. You know that, don't you? Evolution "thought" it had created a master species, but in the end, really, it is just a neurotic, self-conscious creature driven to self-destruction because it cannot master its own unconscious. I tried. I did. But what did you do? You wouldn't listen. You did not understand the unconscious . . . or your dreams. You took to that fool Jung, that traitor. He was a third-rate analyst, not even one of my best students. A pervert, really. You didn't know that?

Me: No, sir . . . I thought maybe, he, Jung, had a few good ideas . . .

Dr. Freud: *Pffft.* So repressed. A second-order loser with his glasses— his granny glasses—trying to look smart, hip. The glasses just a ruse to lure young girls . . . *Pffft.* Have you any more brandy? Maybe something from the top shelf? A bottle I could take with me?

Me: Sir, Doctor? Ah, well, your daughter, err, Anna . . .

Dr. Freud: *What!*

Me: No, I mean, I just mean . . . I had this dream, and well, there was this girl—

Dr. Freud: Sit down! Not now. Not like this. Write it down. Maybe, maybe, we'll talk tomorrow. Maybe I can schedule you in.

Me: No. I'll be okay. I think I've got enough. I think I've figured it out. (*Dr. Freud gathers himself and begins to exit, his hand is on the doorknob, and I can't stop myself.*) See you tomorrow?

Dr. Freud: Yes, sure. Of course. I'll call you. Good night.

Debate Prep

Debate prep for the viewer—Psych 4.0: language and classification. Nomenclature influences perception, as does confirmation bias. It works like this: *Yellow Volkswagen* will prime you to notice yellow Volkswagens, and then you will notice them, whereas before, you wouldn't have, which will lead you to think about a whole bunch of things related (in your mind and memory) when you see one that will incline/induce you to *confirm* whatever you already thought or believed or were taught to believe about whatever *it* was (antithetical to critical thinking and using your mind to figure things out). Listening to others is fine under some circumstances but can be a hindrance to independently thinking and/or being your own person and/or making up your own mind. As a result, when a so-called authority calls Donald Trump a shallow buffoon, clown, sexist, racist, xenophobe, whatever, you will tend to agree because despite what the scoreboard (the facts) says (Trump has been successful in many endeavors for decades and is *in fact* a billionaire), it makes you feel good to believe he's a fraud and doesn't deserve his fame and fortune. Whereas, if the said authority would call him a real estate tycoon or business mogul, your perception and confirmation bias might be different. But no one in authority has used tycoon or mogul as a description of Trump. And yet many people *are* gravitating to Trump—people of all different classifications: smart *and* not so smart people, tolerant people and prejudiced people, educated and uneducated, rural and urban. There is something going on.

Well, I missed much of the debate as my dad called, and I was talking and listening to him. He is ninety-five, and conversations with him require my full attention. But my sense of the debate is this: three hours is too long. Eleven people on stage are too many. And I thought the moderators were awful. It seems to me that the "expert" journalists and news personalities have oversized egos just like the professional politicians and act as if the debate (TV show) were more about them as it is a service to the voters. Trump, on a call in the morning, nailed it. He said CNN increased the debate from two to three hours to make more money selling ads. TV now is all about the ratings and money generated by the selling of advertisements. Of course, those in the business deny it and say they are providing a public service. I'm not buying it. Money contaminates everything damn near, but it's how we humans keep score (as well as with likes and clicks, which also generate advertising dollars).

Can you imagine being attacked by a dozen people on a stage for three hours with millions of people watching? That wasn't a debate. Trump did okay. He's a tough dude. I loved his response when asked what his Secret Service code name should be. "Humble," he said. The guy has a sense of humor.

Another One Bites the Dust

Click on YouTube, and enter "Another One Bites the Dust" while reading. (Life needs a soundtrack, except when it doesn't.) Who will be next? I offer free analysis and odds. I would take book, but I think that's illegal, and I am a man who respects and fears the law.

From most likely to quit to least: Pataki, Graham, Gilmore—no odds (or bets) accepted.

1:2 = Santorum: "I won eleven states last time," a proven loser

2:1 = Jindal: damaged by circumstance and personal history, abortion obsessed

3:1 = Paul: the curly-haired son of the grand master of the political revolution, trumped by Trump

4:1 = Kasich: a pock-faced politically / not politically correct, wishy-washy governor from a crucial battleground state, doesn't sell well

5:1 = Carson: a soft-spoken, marbled-mouthed, mumbling Muslim doubting former brain surgeon; a typical narcissistic, repressed, holier-than-thou doctor

6:1 = Huckabee: a fatuous, formerly fat, Bible-thumping former Baptist preacher (see Carson above)

7:1 = Cruz: a jut-jawed, government-hating senator from Texas (see Carson and Huckabee)

8:1 = Fiorina: damaged, crooked-faced, and stiff; a failed big-time CEO with a big chip on her shoulder

9:1 = Christie: the "no salad for me," jolly, bombastic traffic cop governor of New Jersey; a formidable politician and a huge force

10:1 = Rubio: young, fresh, smooth-faced, thirsty and hungry, bilingual, informed former senator with Cuban roots

11:1 = Bush: stoop-shouldered and repressed, the bumbling brother and son of former presidents, heavily burdened with family baggage

So if I were to take book, it would work like this: Let's say you think Santorum is the next to quit the race and you bet one dollar. You'd win fifty cents. But you'd have to pay me ten cents for making the transaction. Not worth it, obviously, except for the fact that you were right, which is worth something. A lot, maybe. There is a record, a proof that you were right for once in your life (because I would keep records, although I wouldn't because the activity is illegal). So you would know you were right! And it would make you feel good and so on and so forth. Maybe you think Rubio is least likely to quit, but you want to take a chance for the simple reason you need money and are a risk-taker. So you bet ten dollars that Rubio'll be the next to quit, and he will! You win a hundred dollars, less the vig.

This is, like I said, illegal, so we won't do it. But it's still fun to think about, and having fun is important. I stayed up and watched Trump on *Colbert* last night, and what I saw was a man, Trump, who had a wonderful smile, sense of humor, and yet was disciplined and dignified, meaning he had fun without being foolish or pandering. And then this morning, as I watched the pomp and circumstance with the pope and the president (on C-SPAN, i.e., no commentary), I tried to imagine Trump there instead of Obama. And I thought it would have been great! It would be less pomp and much more authentic. Fun.

These are what happened:

Kasich (4:1) hung on until May 4.

Cruz (7:1) dropped out the day before.

Rubio (10:1) quit two months before Kasich and Cruz after failing to win his home state of Florida in March.

Jeb Bush (11:1) quit after the third primary, South Carolina's, in late February.

Christie (9:1) said no more after the second primary, New Hampshire's, in early February.

Obama's UN Speech

SEPTEMBER 29, 2015

What a week for speeches and interviews! We had the 3Ps = the pope, the POTUS, and Putin. And there was also Trump. How to separate the fact from fiction? Obama's speech at the UN was so sad, so full of contradiction, almost moment to moment. The reason is, he's a humanist, i.e., believes that humans are born basically good despite all evidence to the contrary, which is why his policies and presidency have been such a big fail. I fell for it, wanted so much to believe in humanism and hope. I'm afraid it's not true. Freud was right about the pleasure principle and the reality principle. It's in his book *Civilization and Its Discontents*. "The truth will set you free, but not before it's finished with you."[12] Trump is the id and the ego (*das ich*) unburdened by the superego (*das uberich*), as is Putin to a lesser degree. The pope, well, got all his bases covered, having forsworn sex, the root of life and the living.

Oh no, I think I just heard Bill Clinton explain his sexual/not-sexual relationship with Monica Lewinsky, as a manifestation/expression of his genes. He said, I think/believe I heard, that he is or his genetic makeup

---

[12] "You have been snared by something untrue. You are deluded." David Foster Wallace, *Infinite Jest* (1996), 389.

is "4 percent Neanderthal," and so he is not responsible for all that which happened back then when he was president in 1998. (And apparently, HRC bought that.)[13]

This is the essential excuse, that it is—whatever it is—not one's fault but the consequence of circumstance beyond one's purview, unless, of course, the something that happened is believed to be good. Then the question is how much credit belongs to you, your team (parents, siblings, pastor, teacher, therapist, coach, friends, mates, partner), your luck, and/or God.

---

[13] This is from a live interview of Bill Clinton in *Erin Burnett OutFront* on CNN.

In a Nutshell

OCTOBER 1, 2015

What is wrong?

The USA's secretary of state, John Kerry, spoke before the United Nations' gathering in New York city recently and said that what started the chaos that is Syria today—which borders on a catastrophic World War III, seemingly irresolvable, except perhaps by that which ended World War II—is a peaceful civilian protest because of the scarcity of jobs/employment (money, which equals security for most of the world's population) for young men who, as always, want only to show off and display their power/prowess by providing for the means of staying alive for themselves, their mates, and their children (potentially). In other words, there is no work, which is the sense of dignity for men. Work provides value not only for society/community but also for the individual. It is what makes a man a man—providing value for his family and community/society/nation. Of course, all this sensing is hierarchal, from son to father to leader to God to heaven to eternal life. And so a protest is to question the authority and therefore must be resolved, but if the hierarchy is false (that is true) and cannot be resolved, one must use force, because *everybody knows* that might makes right, despite what those atop the hierarchy say. When push comes to shove, he who pushes hardest wins (true).

Set that aside for the moment and return to the concept and question of work. Work is labor, and labor produces *something* that is necessary for survival—be that food, clothing, or shelter. And there also is the energy, which is work and working. Emotion is energy in motion or the manifestation of that which motivates a human to work. One works because it makes one feel good about him or herself. Work provides satisfaction emotionally as well as practically. A man without work is worthless, which, to a person, feels like failure. In other words, a man without meaningful work feels as if he were a waste, useless, which is intolerable. So a man must work to work. Get it? Man must work to have purpose, to be of value to himself and to a potential mate and to his children. To work is to live, to be alive!

So why is there no work for young men not only in Syria but also all around the globe, including in America? A book could certainly be written, but let me instead use a personal example.

There was a time in my life when I built furniture—fine, handcrafted, solid-wood furniture—not only beautiful but also that which would last for lifetimes, maybe forever if properly cared for. And yet there was not enough market for it to make a living. Why pay *x* amount for a table or a bookshelf or a bed, whatever, if one can drive to a box store and buy the same thing (functionally) for a fraction of the cost? Artists, for the most part, cannot make a living. Why/what does it, art or quality, matter when one can save money? When one saves money, that frees up money for more important things, yes? Who needs a craftsman and a relationship with the corner store/shop when one can drive a few miles to a box store and buy a bookshelf/bed/table, even a house? On credit! Nothing matters but one's immediate gratifications and those then in comparison to one's rivals/ neighbors. All is relative today. All is to *display* one's worth and value, a mirage. The internet and the adjoining addiction to screens have amplified the obsession with keeping up with the Joneses. All becomes an illusion and delusion. The truth cannot set you free when it has become relative and subject to anyone's interpretation and manipulation.

Cognitive Dissonance

NOVEMBER 14, 2015

Cognitive dissonance is a feeling of discomfort / ill ease caused by inconsistent and/or incompatible thoughts/beliefs/feelings with one's understanding of the way things are. So what do we humans do when cognitive dissonance rears up out of the pumpkin patch that is our life, our comfort zone? We seek relief—relief from the discomfort by *many* different methods. One size does not fit all because we are different. When one discovers a method that works, one will do it again and again. It becomes a habit. In short, rewarded behavior will be repeated. The behavior becomes entrenched and fine-tunes our sense of who we are, our self-identity.

In the round table discussion on Friday (November 13, 2015) on *Morning Joe*, an esteemed journalist stated a proposition and then asked a question regarding Dr. Ben Carson's thinking and beliefs, in effect, his worldview. The said journalist wanted to know that given that Carson's mind has been, apparently, infected with "bad data" (the Egyptian pyramids were built to store grain), would it be possible to replace the bad data with good data? That's the essence of cognitive dissonance, and sadly, the answer is probably not. It takes a highly open mind to change one's thinking or belief, one's *knowledge*, especially once it becomes fixed and when one's personality is set, along with one's thought processes and beliefs.

"I, Dr. Ben Carson, am a brilliant man, saved and gifted by God the Creator. This is true." The evidence of this thinking is the mansion he lives in, the adornments and accents, and society's high esteem for his work. If you think Trump has an over inflated sense of self, you haven't seen anything until you've seen Ben's home. Ben's not going to change his mind. It happens, changing one's mind, but it's rare. Therapy doesn't always work even if you could get the person into therapy. Drugs sometimes work to actually change the brain. But then what? Can a closed-minded person's mind be altered to make it open? Closed-mindedness is the essence of prejudice—the act of prejudgment. An example would be "I know Donald Trump is a despicable person. He's a racist, a sexist, a bigot, a loudmouthed blowhard, and a privileged white supremacist, who wouldn't be anything if he hadn't inherited money from his father. He was born on third base and thinks he's the greatest man on earth." I have heard that over and over again from people who ought to know better but don't. They just *know* it, regardless of contrary evidence. The evidence is right before their eyes, in his accomplishments, if they could see beyond their prejudice. "I am an open-minded, liberal, progressive person," they say. "I'm tolerant," they say.

And then I offer proof, evidence, that that is *not* the case. They are, in fact, demonstrated by their behaviors and words, not so open-minded. But they don't change their mind. Instead, they harden, dig in, and defend their beliefs. Instead, they change their opinion of me. "Mark is a pigheaded, arrogant, narcissistic, unfiltered jerk. I knew it. I never did like him. I hope he gets help." (This is another real-life example of cognitive dissonance.)

With Trump, the evidence is his company, his buildings, his properties, his family, his children, his assets, his bank account, his workers, and his employees—all of which point to excellence, competence, mental acumen, toughness, fairness, compassion, and the ability to get things done "ahead of schedule and under budget." What he has accomplished could not have been done without a great ability to work with people, those he doesn't like, as well as those he does. That is called diplomacy or the art of the deal. He turned a small/large fortune into a *huge* fortune. Not a paper fortune as some have done but a real one—one of property and people and love. He owns and manages some of the best and finest buildings, resorts, hotels, and golf courses in the world, which are located in the most prime spots! He has created thousands of jobs! He even owns a winery in Virginia. He's a grower of grapes! His children love him! His children are successful!

What else is there? His hair? It's real, it's his, and he loves it. Ask Mika Brzezinski; she's run her fingers through it! His sometimes misbehaviors with women? (See Pussygate, October 17, 2016, for a more detailed discussion.)[14]

I'm not a politician. I *can* be jerk, a punk. I'm retired. I'm no longer a laborer, an employee, a businessman, a bookstore owner, a manager, a homeowner, a home builder, a carpenter, a cabinetmaker, a teacher, or a husband. I'm just a psych major, a philosopher, a reader and a writer, and a son and a father.

---

[14]   See also footnote 7. The culture back in the 1950s right up until, frankly, now was quite different, not exactly caveman-like but close.

Syrian Refugees

With the recent escalation of the war—the war of ISIS, a Muslim cult of fundamentalists (convert or be put to death)—versus all nonbelievers, there is a vociferous and emotional debate in the United States on whether or not to give sanctuary and refuge to some Syrian people fleeing the conflict, anywhere from ten to two hundred thousand people. There is a concern that embedded within the refugee population could be ISIS soldiers, with an intent to kill nonbelievers and are trained to deceive all measures of detection. All sorts of loaded, emotional language (meant to invoke strong feelings) is being used by all parties to put forth their positions. My wish is for the safety, peace, and prosperity of the Syrian people, as well as everyone else. The process to come into the USA as a refugee takes, at the present, eighteen to twenty-four months. So the refugees, said to be four million, of a population of at least fourteen million, are now in holding camps (fenced territory crowded with people, tents, and minimal sanitation) or on the move.

Let us take a fourteen-year-old girl, fleeing the war zone, and call her Diane. While she's waiting in a camp, she catches the eye of a sixteen-year-old boy, Jack, and falls in love. These things have a way of happening, especially under harsh, threat laden conditions such as war. Such a happenstance is called the misattribution of arousal.[15] Now the boy, Jack, has become radicalized during all the upheaval, turmoil, and war; but he's cool. Jack and Diane flirt, and right before they are to be processed into the USA, Diane becomes pregnant, unbeknownst to her but intended by Jack, who is now eighteen. The refugee status of Jack is pulled and he's not allowed into the US. Someone doesn't like the look of him. But Diane processes through and winds up in a home in North Dakota, delivers her baby, and gets a job at a diner in Bismarck, working the night shift. Jack and Diane keep in touch via an app hidden within a game they play on their iPhones. Diane tells Jack of their child, a boy, Jacquin. Jack goes on to join the fight and is killed several years later by an MI6 special agent at a World Cup soccer match. Diane learns of this on CNN, as Jack became quite famous, posting videos on YouTube. Diane never told anyone who the father was, just made up a story, ashamed of what had happened to her. She went on to college at Northwestern and was deemed a sort of American success story. She majored in religious studies/philosophy and felt compelled to tell Jacquin about his father. At fourteen, Jacquin became radicalized himself. To him, his father was a martyr, a hero. It is

---

[15] Some evidence for heightened sexual attraction under conditions of high anxiety. D. G. Dutton and A. P. Aron, *Journal of Personality and Social Psychology* 30 (1974): 510–517.

The crux of this is, in situations of high anxiety that produce *sensations of arousal* (weak knees, high heart rate, dilated pupils, and increased awareness and alertness) can be misinterpreted by the person/subject, if in close contact with a person of the opposite sex/object, as attraction. In social psychology, this is called the fundamental attribution error. If true, this can explain so much of the phenomena of "bad love," which leads to all sorts of unpleasantness: hurt/anger/frustration, conflict, child abuse, divorce, rape, murder, war, and so on. The FAE may be the single biggest reason/cause for all that is amiss in the peopled world—in other words, cognitive dissonance, or in other words, that which you think/believe is true and real turns out not to be. It's a mismatch between your expectations and what actually happened.

If said another way, you have been deceived, misinformed, and/or ill-educated! Sometimes even by your own interpretation of events, or stimuli. (See *Educated: A Memoir* (2018) by Tara Westover regarding how education (formal and informal) can, and often does, teach one what to think rather than how to think.) Gaslighted. Whose fault is that? Certainly not yours. ("It's not my fault!" may, in fact, be true sometimes.)

now 2035 and Jacquin is boarding a 757 jet airliner headed for London, England, where his father had been gunned down in a firefight fourteen years earlier. Jacquin has joined an ISIS cell in England, and they have made murderous plans.

That's one story. Here's another.

America decides, as a country, not to take any Syrian refugees and instead decides to join forces with France and Russia to crush ISIS. The allied army simultaneously negotiates with Saudi Arabia to house the refugees in a manufactured city in that country, a country fully one-quarter the size of the USA but with one-twentieth the population, and then begins an invasion of Syria. Neither event takes that long actually. After ISIS has been destroyed (all fighters killed or surrendered) the allies divide Syria into three zones, running west to east, with each allied power running one, until local populations can form a government. Relative peace and prosperity reign in Syria for the first time in centuries. There's lots of work rebuilding. Meanwhile, in Sand City, inside Saudi Arabia, Jack sees what is happening in his home country, likes the looks of things—and loves the look of Diane. They return to the northern portion, their home, and begin an apricot and peach farm . . . and live happily ever after.

What didn't happen was, Jack didn't get radicalized. Diane wasn't displaced, forced eight thousand miles from her home, didn't have to learn a new language and culture, and so on and so forth. This all happened because the American people had the good sense to elect Donald J. Trump as president, and he was able to persuade France and Russia of the soundness of his war plan, as well as to successfully negotiate a deal with the Saudis to build Sand City. There was much cooperation, jobs, and general well-being for all.

These are two stories that involve the same couple but with vastly different outcomes. In the first story, what is well-intentioned turns out to have negative, unintended consequences; and in the second story, what seems harsh and uncaring at first glance turns out very well for the couple.

The road to hell is paved with good intentions.

Gobbledygook

NOVEMBER 20, 2016

Gobbledygook is a pompous official jargon or political speak.

Yesterday I watched and listened to Hillary Clinton give a speech, then an interview, then take questions at the Council on Foreign Relations (a New York City think tank). She has been hailed as being "substantive, credible, experienced, and qualified" to be the next POTUS. You've been hoodwinked. Here's what she said:

> Break down bureaucratic barriers, work with our partners, form coalitions and comprehensive programs, share intelligence, earn the trust of communities, difficult challenges, put partisanship aside, generational struggle, network security, necessary resources, consolidate authority, most qualified. I fully respect . . . [everyone, anyone?]

This is what she has learned as First Lady of Arkansas, First Lady of the United States (1992–2000), US senator of New York (2001–2006), candidate for POTUS (2008), and US Secretary of State (2008–11). The thing is, it's gobbledygook, and any semismart person can learn it. You put a lot of serious-sounding words together in phrases; throw in some nouns, pronouns, verbs; learn public speaking, and voila. You can get yourself elected. Now you've got your next POTUS. The fact that she's a woman would be a first, a real feel-good thing for folks, just like electing Barack Obama, the first African American president. And just like Obama, she'll likely be all talk, no action.

Bernie Sanders's America

DECEMBER 3, 2015

It's spring of 2017, and Bernie Sanders has had a great first hundred days. He pushed through and passed a fifteen-dollar minimum wage effective immediately. The Affordable Care Act has been strengthened and implemented nationwide, forced onto small businesses. Taxes have been raised on the rich—the evil rich men, and also as a consequence of raising the minimum wage and the strengthened ACA, the CaliFame hat and apparel maker of Carson, California, in business since 1977, has had to close its doors, no longer able to make a profit. The company had a boom in 2015–16 when it made the now-collector's hats of Donald J. Trump's sabotaged presidential campaign, "Make America great again." The company employed one hundred workers, mostly legal immigrants from Mexico, and was even able to give them Christmas bonuses in 2015 and 2016.

Brian Kennedy, the owner, sold the company to Mitt Romney's company, who paid Kennedy ten cents on the dollar for the appraised value of CaliFame, and then sold the machinery, equipment, inventory, and client lists to a wealthy Mexican man in Mexico City. Made out like a bandit, Romney did. The former workers left Southern California and went back to Mexico and reclaimed their old jobs, working now for three dollars an hour with no health benefits. They wished for their old life back, back in beautiful Southern California. They weren't getting rich but were making a living then, and their children had good schools to go to, getting an education and maybe the chance to make a better life for themselves. That's all gone now.

Romney sold the building to Trump, who razed it and built sparkling, luxury apartments. The apartments sold quickly to wealthy American athletes and wealthy jet-setters from Saudi Arabia, China, Russia, India, Brazil, and the like. All the buyers were men who consider Los Angeles a playground, mostly because of the beautiful young white women who work in the high-end escort business. The women flock to LA from Vermont and Connecticut and upstate New York, hoping to make it in the entertainment business, becoming stars in TV ads and shows like *True Detective* and *Homeland* and *Mad Men* ironically. Of course, most of them don't become successful. Some of them go home, go back to school, thinking incorrectly that they'll become famous writers; but many stay and become "party girls." The money is good but doesn't last that long—ten, fifteen years at most. There are always younger, fresher girls waiting to take their place.

Some of the women save their money, invest it in the market, and then move to the country and open up a small organic farm or an antique shop and wait for a tall, dark, and handsome stranger, preferably a widower, to come by and fall in love with them and start a family. The dream is still alive for some of them—a cottage house with a porch, picket fence, flower garden, two kids and a dog, a fishpond, and green grass. Widowers are preferred because they've been broken in (tamed) or broken down. They are sad, lost, lonely men without a wife, the wife having died prematurely of cancer or in a car wreck or gunned down by a terrorist or a crazed, sad, lonely, jobless, angry young man. These widowers tend to be sensitive men, thrilled for any female attention.

And then of course, there are the drugs. The drugs pour over and under the border from Mexico—cocaine, heroin, prescription painkillers, and party drugs. And there are the guns—protection is necessary to move about the city lest what is yours is taken by bandits. LA has become not the city of angels but the city of sex—Sex City, a city of drugs and money, private jets, pimps, and bandits. The politicians are all on the take and the cops too. It's best to keep your head down and take what trickles down from the men who live in high places. The USA now resembles Mexico.

Decent people have fled, selling their homes to the rich foreigners for whatever they could get, moving east to the desert and living mostly in manufactured homes, double-wides made in Mexico, and playing bridge and bingo in community buildings with big fans on the windows. They live on Social Security, but for how much longer? No one knows. Water, electricity, and gasoline are rationed. The retirement villages resemble refugee camps after the wars. What are you going to do when the money's all gone? We could've been great again, but faux self-esteem and political correctness, idealism, and wishful thinking got in the way. Reality was ditched for rainbows and unicorns. People just wanted so much to believe in what the wild-haired socialist was selling—everything for free, a politically correct world where everyone loved everyone and competence and toughness was subsumed by feel-good platitudes and a well-disguised culture of narcissism—except for the evil rich men who took over the world.

How Did We Get Here?

This is a brief recap.

Sometime around 1990, Saddam Hussein detected and/or suspected that Kuwait had been stealing Iraq's oil via diagonal drilling. Not only that, but Kuwait was also making forays over the border and stealing Iraqi women, taking them back into Kuwait and using them as sex slaves. (This is from FBI Special Agent George Piro's one-thousand-hour interrogation of Saddam in 2006.) So Iraq invaded Kuwait for the purpose of enacting retribution and revenge. Osama bin Laden, fresh from victory over the Russian invasion of Afghanistan, approached the Kuwaiti and the Saudis and said, "Let me handle this. I drove the Russians from Afghanistan, and I can drive the Iraqi from Kuwait."

"No," said the Arabs, "we'll get the stupid Americans to do it."

George H. W. Bush, then president of the USA, said, "Sure, no problem." To do so, Bush had to put American (infidel) bases and soldiers in the Muslim holy land. (They are still there.) The US military quickly drove the Iraqi military out of Kuwait, and Bush made the decision not to proceed forward and drive Hussein from power in Baghdad. Instead, he encouraged the southern Iraqi Shiite to do it. Bush said he'd help. He lied.

Saddam Hussein crushed the Shiite uprising. These events further enraged Osama bin Laden and his followers, the fighting mujahideen.

Shortly after, in 1993, the World Trade Center in New York city was attacked via a truck bomb, and from time to time, other US targets were attacked. In 1996, Osama bin Laden issued a public fatwa demanding the US military withdraw from Saudi Arabia. He was pooh-poohed by those in positions of power. In 1999, then US president Bill Clinton tried to kill bin Laden with a cruise missile attack, but it failed. The missiles missed the always-moving, mindful, militant Muslim leader. On September 11, 2001, as we all know, bin Laden attacked NYC again. He succeeded, and the Twin Towers came tumbling down. At the same time, the Pentagon was struck. The second president Bush declared war on bin Laden and Al-Qaeda. This ushered in the War on Terror.

In March of 2003, Bush launches "shock and awe" bombing attacks on Iraq's capital, Baghdad, in Gulf War II, or Operation Iraqi Freedom, under the guise that Saddam and Osama were buddies and that Hussein just might give weapons of mass destruction (a.k.a. WMD) to his pal, the Muslim terrorist or freedom fighter, depending on where you sit with regard to war and peace and all that matters. All that, the rationale, however, was false.[16] Subsequently, the US military destroyed the Iraqi Army and captured Saddam, who then was tried and hung by the new leaders of Iraq on New Year's Eve 2006.

But (big *but*) an insurgency rose up almost immediately, led by Sunnite Jordanian Abu Musab al-Zarqawi, a very vicious killer. In addition to attacking American soldiers, Zarqawi attacked Shiite Iraqis. Zarqawi was soon killed by a US bomb strike in June of 2006, but now there was a war within a war—a civil war within an international war. The international war ended in December of 2011 when the now/new, antiwar young African American US president Barack Obama withdrew the last of the US military forces. But (big *but*) the civil war reignited because of the American withdrawal. Zarqawi's group had morphed into something called ISIS, or the Islamic State of Iraq and Syria. The civil war between Shiite and Sunnite Muslims had expanded and now was a regional conflict about ideology, theology, and territory. ISIS began to capture Syrian and Iraqi cities and oil wells, killing anyone in their path who did not join them. This war was like the old wars back in the day—very brutal and very

---

[16]   https://www.youtube.com/watch?v=pNRR8jS7R58

vicious, sparing no one. President Obama, however, wasn't much interested in that (he had other things on his mind) and just gave minimal help to the Iraqi Shiite central government in Baghdad, as well as issuing disingenuous threats to the Syrian central government in Damascus.

Now, 2015, begins the US presidential campaign for a new commander in chief after what has been, in effect, twenty-five years of stupid and weak US leadership and foreign policy. The world is at war. Europe, Asia, and Russia have been sucked in. *And* the war has come back to America, the homeland, with ISIS-inspired terrorists/jihadists/mujahideen, whatever, bombing, gunning down, and murdering everyday American citizens at sporting events and Christmas parties. No one feels safe unless their heads are buried in sand, floating up in the clouds, or maybe in books.

Enter billionaire real estate mogul, world-class businessman Donald J. Trump, who has been watching the incompetence of the US presidential leadership for the past twenty-five years. He says he wants to "make America great again" (back to the roaring '80s, in his opinion), and so then *the* Donald throws his hat, and his famous hair, into the ring (after consulting with his wife and children). DJT launched his campaign in June 2015, in grand style, as is his wont. And despite all the elites and experts dismissing him as a carnival barker, a clown, a buffoon, a racist, a sexist, a xenophobic fascist, Trump captured the hearts and minds of the largest percentage of Republican voters, soundly beating his sixteen opponents in almost all the polls for six straight months running. Trump (a.k.a. *Trump*) stands to be the Republican nominee for the general election for president of the United States come November 2016. The elites, experts, reporters, media, and also the Liberals and Democrats are freaking out! Some want to "eat glass."

I am loving it. I love *the* Donald! I believe he may be the last honest man of power in the United States. I recently watched a rally of his (he is drawing huge enthusiastic crowds) live on YouTube. Then I watched it again the next morning. What follows is my report of what I saw.

Trump Rallies' Winners and Losers

RALEIGH, NORTH CAROLINA, FRIDAY NIGHT, DECEMBER 4, 2015

There was a raucous, and rowdy, typical Donald J. Trump's campaign event / speech crowd—you might have heard or read about it/them. But so here's what really happened. I watched it twice, once live for fun (all Trump events are streamed live on YouTube) and then again the following morning to take notes. Trump rallies are that first—fun! People come for a good time and because you never know what's going to happen. His speeches are just roughly and loosely outlined so he can speak to the moment. This night, there was an organized (on Facebook)[17] protest. There were to be ten planned interruptions, spaced five minutes apart, and there were. The protest went off as planned and scheduled. Trump didn't know

---

[17] Was this a part of the Russian espionage campaign "fake news" that has now been exposed to disrupt, sew chaos, and undermine America and Americans—pitting them against one another? To create a civil war in America?

about the plan before the event, which plays right into DJT's strength. One scheduled protest was a person who rose and shouted, "Stop the hate. We make America great!" The crowd turned at the commotion and then began its own chant—"USA, USA, USA!"—until the protesters were "gently" removed. That was how the night went. A protest would erupt, and the crowd (8,000–10,000) would react with jeers and/or chants.

Sometimes, Trump would keep speaking louder (his voice became hoarse by the end of the night). Other times, he would comment or make jokes, which the crowd loved. And finally, Trump made a short speech to the protesters, in general, be they Democrats, Liberals, or whatever, suggesting that if he could gather them all together, he could persuade them to join the movement to "make America great again." The supporters, thousands, would roar with delight at Trump's quips. The protesters did, in fact, add to the festive atmosphere. The folks came expecting a party, and a party is what they got. (These rallies resemble more a rock concert.)

Behind Trump, seated on the grandstand were some very, very attractive women dressed in red and black Christmas party cocktail dresses. Two special guests were in the crowd, and when Trump spotted them, he brought them up to the stage—American as pie and Diamond and Silk.[18] They were internet sensations! The girls broke into a spontaneous riff for the cameras and crowd who roared! The back half of the event was devoted to the audience's questions. There are no plants in Trump events; you and he never know what will come up. He answers them all, usually adroitly pivoting to his main themes and ideas. But sometimes, the questions are really far-out, as in very extreme. Like the one where a woman asked what he thought all those big, tough, strong young refugee men would do once they got into the country (implying that the fate of native, naive young American women could be at risk). Trump said, "I'm not gonna even go there."

Often, the question would invoke an eye roll, twisted lips, and/or an appeal to the crowd as in "Can you believe this? Whaddaya gonna do?" One joke that got the largest laugh was at Hillary's expense. The subject was trade deals and negotiations and how Obama and Kerry were the

---

[18]   They are known as Diamond and Silk, black conservative women who have become a presence on Facebook and now victims of Facebook's liberal bias censorship—deemed "unsafe to the community." CEO Mark Zuckerberg, when questioned by a house congressional committee (April 11, 2018), said the censorship of conservative points of view was a "mistake."

worst and that's one of the things he, Trump, does best—make deals. He always wins, which is perhaps his main appeal (that and that he gets things done and can't be bought by special interests or lobbyists, which drives both liberal and conservative elites crazy). The crowd roars! (The proof is in the pudding, right before your eyes. He reminds everyone to loudly applause.)

And then Trump added that maybe Hillary would be worse than Obama because she lacks the stamina and energy to function as commander in chief. He said, "She gets up in the morning, puts on her pantsuit [huge laughter and applause], then does an event, and goes back home to sleep. And you don't see her for five days." Bahahaha. (Even Hilary cracked up when showed the clip.) Everyone had fun, except the protesters who, I think, just moved more voters into the Trump column.

Here's another joke: A questioner stands and asks, "I was wondering what you would say to President Obama [very respectful, this young man]—"

Trump interrupts, "You're fired." The crowd erupts, and Trump gets very animated. My prediction is, Trump will win the Republican nomination and then win all fifty states in the general election. The popular vote will be 70/30.[19]

Don't, don't believe what you read or see via clips and commentary on the TV. As the late great, genius Michael Crichton said, "Everybody has an agenda, except me."

---

[19]   I was wrong on that account, which still baffles me. I find it hard to believe people are so stupid, but they are. Our schools don't generally teach students to think critically, and certainly, parents don't—it's all about obedience to authority, obeying the rules. Trump's main appeal to me was and is that he doesn't. He beats all the odds. Did *it* his way and won, which is, or was, the American creed (cue Sinatra).

Political Correctness

DECEMBER 25, 2015

Political correctness (**PC**) is the speech and/or behavior practiced so as not to offend or disturb another person or group of people and/or practiced so as to make oneself more likable—that's where the political comes from. Politicians, more than anyone, need to be liked to gain votes and get themselves elected so they can do good things for the people who elected them. I think most people by now understand that that is not true—the part about doing good things (for you).

That's the facade that is falling down after years and years of being proven false by virtue of being witness to reality. What politicians are, are really good liars. They first deceive themselves by not understanding themselves, their true motives (why they do what they do), and then they lie to us. (Not all of them as some lie knowingly.) But all that's not so different than any other person. It's a part of the human condition. We deceive ourselves so as to feel good or better about ourselves, than reality or truth dictates. It's human nature, a part of what makes us so resilient.

What has happened, however—after years and years of people trying hard to be politically correct, to be good, to be liked, to do the right thing—is that we have gotten ourselves so far away from the truth and reality that we are about to crash or destroy ourselves by vicious and ruthless conflict and combat because we have denied who we are, both collectively and individually. We are not the children of God (any god); we are not special creatures. Humans want to believe we are not animals, not divine, not machines, but something unique and special, something worthy of eternal life. But that's not true; it's just something we invented to make ourselves feel good and/or to control others, to elevate ourselves above others and everything. We are, in fact, animals (primates), products of evolution subject to the laws of nature, to the laws that govern all animals— the laws of population density and resource distribution and consumption, within controlled and patrolled territory, the hunting ground. We just have different tools, the means by which to manage the distribution of resources (meaning air, food, water, shelter, sex, children, and labor). We have managed in our "wisdom" to pollute (meaning to poison) all our resources, to include our children, who grow up believing they are entitled to whatever it is they want, while all the while becoming more and more unhealthy, unable to even manage their own health and well-being.

Briefly, this is a first-person account of how stupid, thoughtless, and also self-serving political correctness is.

Before I was a creative writing instructor, a fiction writer, a bookstore owner, a graduate student, a child mental health counselor, a bartender, a carpenter, I was a fine woodworker making custom furniture and cabinetry (I know, dumb) and art gallery operator, which was an attempt to do something other than tend bar. As such, making ends meet was next to impossible, so one thing I would do is to exhibit and sell my stuff in local fairs or shows. (There is actually a summer circuit with a show every weekend in a different town/city in the state.) There were three big ones in the community in which I lived—one before Christmas and two in the summer. One, at summer's end, was quite prestigious, a judged affair that drew artists from all over the state. (I once took home the red ribbon in the fine woodworking category.) Unfortunately, big items did not sell at these events (the shows were more about name recognition and future prospects, i.e., marketing events or promotions), but small, up-to-twenty-dollar items would, like picture frames, little boxes, and rubber band guns, and swords. I would make these from scraps and leftovers from large pieces. The guns and swords were huge sellers and could have been a livelihood all their own. (But that would have been boring, mass-producing them.) Anyway, the sale of them covered expenses and maybe dinner out. They sold out quickly, the guns and the swords.

Everybody loved them, except the PC council members of the prestigious event. "No, no, no. You cannot sell those weapons at our show," they said. "They are against our values of peace and kindness. Those weapons engender and promote violence in children." Give me a break! The community was rural mountain where many (not everyone) hunted. Some in the community were what were known as tree huggers and against all that was part of the natural world, except the aesthetic. It was the late '80s. These folks were my peers, baby boomers, who grew up in the '50s, '60s, and '70s and had sold out for big paychecks, big houses, big cars like SUVs, and innumerable gadgets to make their lives easier *and* for feel-good therapy—so as to feel good about themselves as purveyors of all that is good (also known as the therapeutic narcissistic culture or the me generation or boomeritis). They adopted positions of political correctness regarding animals (such as cats have to be declawed to save the birds) and child-rearing (everyone gets a trophy, has a right to huge parties, a pony, good grades, and therapy or drugs, all in the service of becoming your best self and making the world a safer and more equitable place).

To make a long story short, I had to quit fine woodworking and go back to bartending. My wife divorced me, and I eventually turned into a cranky, cynical, aging, antisocial alcoholic writer and paleobehaviorist philosopher.

Now to bring these thoughts up-to-date with the current cultural corrosive consequences of political correctness, there is this—regarding the contemporary campaigns for president of the United States. A pollster, one Kyle Dropp, conducted research regarding who is the preferred candidate for POTUS, and he found that a substantial percentage of people, enough to swing an election, preferred Donald J. Trump but would not say so publicly either to real people (their friends), pollsters, or robots (Google algorithms or Russian trolls). Those people—fearing ostracism as a result of political correctness, but were better educated and wealthier than most— were "embarrassed to have another living soul know they support Trump." Dropp explained, "In part to 'social desirability bias' in which respondents answer questions in a manner they believe will be viewed favorably by others."[20] In other words, people are lying not for the good of the country,

---

[20]   This is from Jonathan Capehart, *Washington Post*, December 21, 2015.

not for the good of their children, but out of a sense that they *will be better liked* if they conceal their true thoughts and beliefs! This is not good.

There is a false narrative being disseminated by the PC faction of liberal and conservative elites (the well-educated and well-spoken) and rivals of Donald J. Trump that he is a sexist, racist xenophobe and a lying, two-bit, self-promoting carnival barker who would destroy the very fabric of America. And if you vote for him, *you* are also a sexist, racist pig. *Full stop!* Neither of which are true by the way. Neither Trump nor you or I, necessarily, are such. But we have the need to feel righteous about ourselves and/or to conform to thoughtless and mindless politically correct standards of what some self-serving persons determined to be true and good (which it is neither) for their own advancement.

First, there was passive aggression—a way in which an individual can make a rival feel bad (guilty) without overtly attacking them, thus gaining an advantage. And now there is microaggression, where a person can *accuse* a rival of being anything from insensitive to out-and-out sexist, racist, whatever, in order to bring the target person, the rival, their competition, down. Both mechanisms, passive aggression and microaggression, are power plays by weak people. The former is mostly an unconscious behavior, an egotistic defense mechanism (now used as a character slur, as in "she's passive aggressive"); the latter an overt character attack.

Hillary Clinton is expert at both tactics knowingly, which makes it so very surreptitious. (Trump has likened her to a snake, the archetypal representation of evil, which could be the most accurate description of her.) Hillary portrays herself as a victim of sexism and misogyny and also as a fighter and champion for other victims (of the patriarchy and white privilege). Snake as victim (very clever, perhaps too clever, which might be why many people despise her) could have the deleterious and ironic effect of ruining this country and generations of people and maybe even forcing the country into war all because a man—a coarse, blunt, narcissistic man—to be sure, dared to tell the truth about what is what with respect to the human animal and who would, without apology, bring a club to a knife fight. Trump would eat your young if it came down to it to protect his own. When Trump said that Barack Obama had schlonged Mrs. Clinton in the 2008 nomination fight, what I interpreted he meant was that the black man bitch-slapped the white woman. And you want this person, this loser, who can't stand up to her husband or boss to be your president? To go up against Vladimir Putin, the Chinese, the Iranians, the ISIS, the North Koreans?

To be honest, Mrs. Clinton has made a career out of "victimology," meaning claiming victim status rather than taking responsibility and fighting back, which is, I thought, the American ethos. Her tricks just won't work in the real world (apart from the PC world).

I want to stand and shout, "What is wrong with you people? You can't be that stupid!" But I know that's not true. People are not stupid but ignorant. Well, maybe stupid—to be *so* deceived by politicians and the PC police, the postmodernists. On the other hand, it has worked for many of you, for many of us, humans, until now when our success at reproducing has produced so many of us that we're running out of resources, contained within very real, natural boundaries and territory. But then what does it matter? We're special, capable of eternal life in another dimension beyond the natural world, right? Beyond the world of animals and machines and tools, of blood, war, and death, of nature's tooth and claw. We're special. We're special! You just have to believe and be kind to one another. Right.

One last note about what political correctness has done to the real world—it hasn't changed it for the better, just distorted it so as to make a sane man mad. (Yes, it's true. Read Trump's *Crippled America*.) The state of information has gotten so bad that every source of news and history is an advertisement for an ideology or a person, both now "brands." And the advertisements are false, skewed to direct your thinking and decisions to a faux narrative, a myth, a fiction, that serves the interests of the storytellers and their backers.

I can no longer trust anything I hear, see, or read except perhaps that which is in peer-reviewed scientific journals where I can check the methodology of the research. *But* those always end with the caveat "more research is needed." And no one replicates research anymore because *that* doesn't pay. So maybe the study was flawed. It's no wonder that escape is what many (most) people opt for. Here are a few words about what I mean when I say *escape*. Escape from reality can take many, many forms—from illness, both mental and physical, to the many varied means of addiction, say, pornography to food to drugs [legal and illegal] to shopping and hoarding, to name but a few. And then there is actual stellar and planetary escape, the idea that we humans can, having successfully poisoned this planet, move to another. Then there is intellectual escape, where we imagine we can time-travel to another dimension. There has always been spiritual escape. And of course, there is the ultimate escape—suicide.

All these mechanisms of escape are simply different manifestations of flight, driven by the fight-or-flight reflex shared by the entire animal kingdom. It is the survival instinct, an evolutionary adaptation that has determined behavior for eons, for creatures with means of motion and aggression. Hide, run, or fight? The instinct is now being taught, here in the year 2015, to the general public, by experts, as a means to stay alive when attacked. Ha! Because the people are too busy staring into their screens to see the threat coming! But then that has the ironic effect of simply perpetuating that which is the mythical narrative of the elites, which is, of course, in their best interest. It seems that there is no way out—no true escape. There are more guns! Ban guns! Oh wait, there might be an alternative, but that would require we start all over again, back at the beginning, when men and women were hunters and gatherers. And knowing what we now know, this time we tell the truth? [21]

---

[21] It's worth mentioning that I sent Mr. Trump my essay on Syrian refugees and got a prompt reply, thanking me. I also got, not one but two, Christmas cards from Trump, and so I retuned the gesture (as a general practice, I don't send out Christmas cards or a Christmas letter), telling Team Trump to "keep your head up and your heart strong." There were only a handful of people, at the time, working on the campaign, battling great odds.

Crippled America (2015) by Donald J. Trump

BOOK REVIEW BY YOURS TRULY
WEDNESDAY, JANUARY 6, 2016

In 2008, I caucused in Colorado for Barack Obama. I was a delegate representing the Democrats of Larimer County. I voted for President Obama again in 2012. I just switched (January 4, 2016) my party affiliation so I could caucus for Mr. Trump in 2016. This book, as Trump says on the jacket, is "my blueprint for how to make America great again." It is exactly that. The book is a detailed forty-thousand-word discussion on what and how Mr. Trump plans to do that, why it needs to be done, and why he is uniquely qualified to get it done. It's a compelling argument. In fact, if you read this book and are void of bias and prejudice, you just might agree.

One thing that stood out to me was how fast he wrote the book, with no coauthor, and also how up-to-the-minute it was. Released in November, the book includes many of the events of the first three/four months of the campaign. In other words, he wrote it while campaigning—a nonstop, relentless process of rallies, town hall meetings, position papers, press briefings, debates, and interviews, not to mention nonstop tweeting—covering some twenty states. The man is nearly seventy years old and hardly sleeps, maybe four hours a night! He works nonstop, which he has done since he began working for his father in the early '70s. His mind never stops observing and thinking—*big*—about what he can and will do.

At the back of the book, he posted his financial statement (his net worth is over eight billion dollars) and a list of the seventy (70) properties he owns (commercial buildings, condos, apartments, residences, resorts, golf courses, hotels, airplanes, and even a winery) in nine countries around the world. What he is, first and foremost, is a developer, and now he wants to develop or redevelop America. Many of the properties he owns he bought in various states of rundown-ness, which some might say is the state of America, and he renovated them and turned them into first-class, world-class properties. In doing so, he created thousands, hundreds of thousands of jobs: temporary (construction) and permanent (service and managerial). In the process, he also improved the local communities (i.e., upgraded the community) and, in so doing, increased property values, which has a ripple effect: improving schools, education, and the overall quality of life. What Mr. Trump wants to do is do for the country what he did for his company and name (brand). He is the opposite of what most politicians are—all talk, no action.

Basically, the book is what you'll hear if you watch one of his rallies on YouTube, but with a lot more detail. He answers the questions you might have. His writing style is like his speaking style—direct, authentic, and honest—even with his sense of humor coming through. In the chapter "Our Infrastructure Is Crumbling," there is this: "The Chinese build new cities over there in about 12 minutes, while we take years to get the permits to add a dormer window to our own homes." Funny, true in the abstract, and exaggerated to make his point, which is the way he rolls. But of course, the media and his rivals would call him out for being untruthful (four Pinocchios) if not out-and-out lying. He's very critical of the media and also politicians, but he tells you why they do what they do, which is good to know because then you see how it all makes sense.

Trump is very big on the values that we all aspire, but he practices them without exception—honesty, straightforwardness, love of family, fiscal conservativeness, flexibility, and self-discipline. Don't lie, steal, or cheat or tolerate those that do! Ha! He's the exact opposite of many (most) people. The status quo is frightened of him, no doubt about that, because he is not beholden to them. All his life he's been told "You can't do that!" (even by his father). And yet he does, and he succeeds to the benefit of all. He is the epitome of the unfiltered leader, meaning he wasn't groomed by the status quo (to fall in line and do their bidding) but finds his own way. Again, this *is* the American mythos. He is the traditional masculine male.

At the end of the book, there is the "About the Author" blurb, which is funny because the whole book is about the author. This (quote) blurb (unquote) is seventeen pages and has four thousand words, just in case you missed it. It includes a bullet point list of his properties and begins "Donald J. Trump is the very definition of the American success story . . . He is the archetypal businessman—a dealmaker without peer."

I strongly recommend reading this book before voting. All profits are going to charities, I think he said. At this writing, his social media followers have increased by four million, and he has risen to 42 percent in the national polls, more than tripling his closest rival, making fools of all the "experts."

The Week the Election Was Won

JANUARY 12, 2016

This past week was the week that the US stock market had its worst opening in history. David Bowie returned to whence he came; the Mexican drug cartel kingpin, El Chapo, was captured again; *and* the Wild Card Weekend of the NFL Playoff was crazy! There were indeed some wild games—the winner losing at the very last moment and the loser winning when they should have lost—but none of those were the most significant event of the week. No. This was the week that the 2016 US presidential election was won, and everyone, all the experts and the pundits and the establishments' candidates—the Republican's man Bush and the Democrat's woman Clinton (all who had thought it was a done deal)—were beaten! They were all so sure they had this thing in the bag from the get-go, and then along came Donald J. Trump, whom they (word of the year) all called a clown, a carnival barker, a buffoon, a sexist, a racist, a bigot, and a xenophobe. Now they know.

They have lost.

In back-to-back speeches on Saturday in Ottumwa, Iowa, and Sunday in Reno, Nevada, Donald J. Trump nailed down the presidency of the United States with two incredible, extraneous, improvisational, brilliant closing arguments.

(I'll wager there never has been such a performance in the history of the world.)

In Ottumwa, Saturday morning, he started out as he usually does, reciting the latest poll numbers that show him leading in every state and in every category (the only polls he ever cites). And then something strange happened—he broke out of his usual routine and went completely *improv* with all new material and then picked up speed and got totally silly, as in unbelievable! The crowd was almost breathless. The closest thing I've seen to it was Robin Williams at his comedic best, and to be truthful, Trump's performance blows that away.

And then on Sunday, Trump flies into Reno, the Biggest Little City in the World, and gives what Jenna Johnson calls "one of his most memorable" speeches. Johnson is on the campaign trail with Trump, assigned by the *Washington Post*, to keep readers abreast of the politically incorrect billionaire real estate mogul's campaign theatrics, performances, events, and speeches. She tries, but sometimes, she can't keep up with Trump's 757 jet airliner, helicopter, police-escorted limo rides, and/or his frenetic pace. (She's left to fly commercial and drive rental cars through traffic.) Trump, in general, doesn't like the media's coverage of him and always calls them out at events as being dishonest (they are mostly) and, in the beginning, "scum and sleazebags." (This is "the art of the deal.") But Johnson, a former Olympic swimmer, is hanging in there. Some of the others have had to quit—they being too neurotic and Trump being too intentionally tough on them.[22] In fact, it seems to me that Jenna, a Clinton supporter, is warming up to him. What Trump did Sunday was give the most brilliant closing argument I've ever heard. He hit all his main points on all the issues, all his policy positions—the whys and hows and whos and what's what. My

---

[22]   Trump's war with the media may, in the final analysis, prove to be his undoing. He's won over a few, but most have dug in their heels and have shown they will go to any length to try and save their self-esteem and reputations, as truth tellers and experts, even if it means lying and distorting (cherry-picking, misinterpreting, omitting, etc.) the facts. The reporters have weaponized their pens.

favorite line, a new one, was (speaking of and for the big banks and bankers) "When you [Trump] walk down the sidewalk, I get the shakes."

Trump replied, "I beat the hell out of the banks." The crowd roars!

He left no doubt and took no prisoners. He crushed it, slaughtered his competition, both Republican and Democrat, as well as all the other world playas. This, my friends, is how you make an argument, how you persuade. And then he smiles! Though rare, it is beautiful.

Trump makes *me* smile.

Truth be told, he likes the press. He calls them out, belittles them, mocks them, but knows he needs them (it's a host/parasite relationship) and truly thinks, with good reason, that he can win them over the same way he eventually wins over all who deal with him. (He's a flirt.) He is relentless, tough, brilliant, appreciative, and so very funny.

He is *the greatest show on earth!*

Watch those two speeches back-to-back on YouTube (all his events are streamed live by multiple TV outlets and other channels) and see if you aren't won over. And you know (I know), it isn't "all talk, no action" because his name, his brand, his buildings, and his properties are everywhere around the globe. He makes deals with everyone!

Trump closes with this:

> "We're going to make America great again. Better, even. We're going to win so much you're going to get sick of winning. You're going to beg me, 'Please, Mr. Trump, I'm sick of wining. Can we just lose once?' Never! We're never ever gonna lose!"

So, my college-educated friends, pop some popcorn or heat up some chili-cheese nachos, smoke some weed or do whatever it is you do to relax, kick back, and enjoy the show. This will never ever come again, and you're fortunate to live in these times. If you don't watch those two speeches before you vote, you should be forced to forfeit your vote.

Mr. Donald J. Trump's Platform 2016[23]

Mr. Trump opposes all talk, no action.

Mr. Trump supports ahead of schedule and below budget.

Mr. Trump supports lower taxes and fewer regulations.

Mr. Trump opposes all wastes, frauds, and abuses.

Mr. Trump supports small business.

Mr. Trump supports competency.

Mr. Trump supports quality.

Mr. Trump opposes incompetence.

Mr. Trump opposes corruption and cronyism.

Mr. Trump opposes lying, stealing, and cheating.

Mr. Trump supports smart and tough.

Mr. Trump opposes strong and stupid.

Mr. Trump supports merit pay for all workers.

Mr. Trump supports workers' hard work and opposes social and worker loafing.

Mr. Trump supports free and fair trade and opposes bad trade agreements.

---

[23] I made this up but based it on reading his books and watching his interviews and all his campaign events live.

Mr. Trump supports the right/best person for the job, regardless of race, gender, creed, or religion.

Mr. Trump opposes bloated bureaucracy.

Mr. Trump supports deal-making on the golf course.

Mr. Trump opposes poverty.

Mr. Trump supports clean air and clean water and opposes pollution.

Mr. Trump supports beauty in architecture, design, and development.

Mr. Trump opposes ugliness.

Mr. Trump supports cleanliness and opposes filth.

Mr. Trump supports a strong military and all military veterans.

Mr. Trump opposes war except for national defense.

Mr. Trump supports keeping Gitmo open and enhanced interrogation.

Mr. Trump opposes criminals and terrorists and their activities.

Mr. Trump supports legal immigration and opposes illegal immigration.

Mr. Trump supports building a wall on the southern border.

Mr. Trump supports eminent domain for the improvement of society.

Mr. Trump supports the XL pipeline but thinks the USA should get some of the profits.

Mr. Trump opposes space exploration until that time when more pressing issues are well on the way to resolution.

Mr. Trump supports clean, viable energy.

Mr. Trump supports the law and law enforcement.

Mr. Trump supports local control of education and opposes common core.

Mr. Trump supports good teachers and opposes bad teachers and teaching.

Mr. Trump supports lowering the cost of higher education.

Mr. Trump supports the Second Amendment and concealed carry.[24]

Mr. Trump supports lower health-care costs and basic health care for everyone.

Mr. Trump supports mental health.

Mr. Trump supports women's health.

---

[24] At present (February 21, 2018), there is a debate about whether or not teachers should be allowed/required to have guns (concealed) within reach in schools to protect students/children in gun-free zones. President Trump has (currently) invited all parties to the White House to hear what they have to say. My position is, sure, if the teacher is qualified. Not required but allowed, which is in agreement with the spirit of the Second Amendment. Citizens always have the right to protect themselves and their family from harm. The fact that *any* person may be armed deters assault. I've no doubt of that.

Mr. Trump opposes abortion.

Mr. Trump supports medical marijuana.

Mr. Trump opposes addiction.

Mr. Trump supports strong families.

Mr. Trump opposes free stuff.

Mr. Trump supports protecting Social Security and Medicare.

Mr. Trump supports children and old people.

Mr. Trump supports the power of positive thinking.

Mr. Trump supports thinking big.

Mr. Trump supports flexibility and maximizing options.

Mr. Trump supports knowledge and information and using leverage.

Mr. Trump supports the use of psychology and promotion.

Mr. Trump supports fighting back when attacked by a factor of ten.

Mr. Trump supports winning and opposes losing.

Mr. Trump supports honesty.

Mr. Trump supports hamburgers, fried chicken, and french fries.

Mr. Trump supports having fun.

Mr. Trump supports joy.

Mr. Trump calls Americans to action to make America great again and make it a place where our grandchildren can live safely and to pursue the American dream of peace, love, work, health, and happiness.

The Independent Bookstore and the Decline of Society

There is much chatter about books—the writing, reading, selling, and keeping of them and the teaching of writing—here now in the middle of the second decade of the twenty-first century. I have a perspective being a lifetime reader, a builder of bookshelves and a bookstore, as well as a bookseller, and a writer of novels, and finally, a teacher of writers and writing. But mostly, this essay will be about the independent bookstore, the Indie, and how it is vanishing and the impact that it has on society. It is true that there are more books being written and published today than ever before, five times as many as when I owned my bookstore back at the turn of the century, and that access to them is easier than ever before, because of the internet and new technologies. Why, you can learn of a book, read reviews of it, buy it, and then start reading it in just a few moments. That process is literally "in the palm of your hand" and can be done from almost anywhere. Wow! So who needs a bookstore, one of bricks and mortar and shelves and dirty money and cash registers and lines and people and cars and parking and traffic and just all that hassle, anyway? Aren't we, the introverted reader and writer, better off without all that anxiety-producing, overwhelming stimuli, that crap? Well, in a word, no.

Each independent bookstore was/is a unique place, if not experience. Each shop, even if located within spitting distance of the other has a distinct personality, which is a reflection of the owner, even if the shop is a franchise, like a Walden bookstore. (At its peak, there were 1,216 Walden bookstores. The company began liquidation in July of 2011.) Now it has been reported that there is a resurgence of independent bookstores, up 25 percent since 2007 to the sum of 2,094, but still far less than before. And that's a good thing, but I submit that those stores are being supported by a hardcore group of readers, the 20 percent of readers who read 80 percent of the books. What is missing is the ubiquitous store—on every main street in every town and in every shopping center in every suburbia. It is into these shops that a traveler, a visitor, and/or one of the other 80 percent of the reading population and even some nonreaders would and did wander into, killing time perhaps, because everybody knows you can do that in a bookstore without being assaulted by salespeople and pressure. Or maybe just to use the bathroom? And then lo, the things that one might learn and experience, that they could and would do, are not available in any other way. Minds would be exposed and opened by a random chance. In other words, this opportunity of mind-opening and knowledge-gaining happenstance is gone, and that cannot be a good thing for society.

Two of my favorites, both gone now, were Earth Song in Del Mar, California (the model for my own bookstore, Stories: A Bookstore in Bergen Park, Colorado) and Black Swan in Newport, Oregon. The Black Swan was an old Victorian-style home converted into a restaurant and bookshop. Dining took place in the varied rooms, with bookshelves lining the walls. I used to play bridge there with friends between peak hours. We would meet and have lunch, the staff would clear the table, and then we would play cards and chat. The Earth Song was a shop that my father discovered when he moved to Solana Beach in 1974 after retiring from the US Air Force. When I'd visit him, it was something we always, *always* did together. He was one of the 20 percent, knew the owner well, and introduced me. The owner was the one I sought out first for counsel before opening my own shop. We always left with books, music, and sometimes, gifts. Then of course, we'd have lunch at one of the local, independently owned cafes, taverns, or restaurants and chat. With a beer or two, of course.

The author with his father at Stories: A Bookstore, Evergreen, Colorado

The Campaign

JANUARY 29, 2016

Campaign is a series of military operations with a particular objective in a war, as in electing a candidate.[25]

Can we stop, as Sarah Palin said, "pussyfooting around"? At the root of all human behavior is sex—or more accurately—reproduction, manifested in a competition for a mate or war between rivals to select the best possible person or candidate for the job of reproducing oneself.

One (any human/organism) wants to select the best possible person available of the opposite sex to reproduce with, so as to give one the best possible chance to continue one's genes. It doesn't matter if *you* are a virus, a tree, an insect, or a human—that is the goal of life.

In essence, eternal life is equal to reproduction/replication.

So we find ourselves now, in the midst of the 2016 US presidential campaign, at the apex of evolution regarding the human animal, and people are freaking out! There *is* a candidate who invokes the primal in all of us—Mr. Donald J. Trump.

---

[25]   *Webster's New World College Dictionary*, 4th ed. (2001, 2000, 1999).

Trump exposes that which is basic instinct in everyone and what *has* been denied, except in the finest of psychoanalysis (and rock and roll)—a desire for power and control or, as Nietzsche said, "The will to power."

And so what is, is that the reporters of the news, the finders of facts, the disseminators of what is, are fighting against their instincts. Attractive females are hired by powerful men (see Megyn Kelly, the Fox News superstar) in positions of influence to attract viewers, to perpetuate and continue their power (see Roger Ailes), or in essence, to reproduce himself. All this, of course, is denied and operates on the unconscious level of human motivation.

Recently, I read an article by a female professor in psychology who wanted you to believe that she knew what she was writing about. She said, "Oh, Trump is nothing but a sexist, denigrating women so as to advance his aspirations for power and control over all that is." Furthermore, she said (I'm paraphrasing) that that would be to the detriment of America because other powerful men (Putin) and also domestic rivals would see and know that and then hire attractive females to distract Mr. Trump (are you getting the sense of the James Bond movie plot thing here?) and then take advantage of his weakness ("Penchant for sexism," Hillary Clinton said) and his vulnerability to beautiful women. Really? Seriously! Trump is so hip to all *this* it is actually funny watching it all unfold. These women (TV reporters, so called journalists) are hired not with respect to anything other than their attractiveness, ability to speak well and fast, ambition, and also, a modicum of intelligence (i.e., a four-year degree from a college or university). Trump knows this and plays with them. To suggest that he could be manipulated by sex is, maybe, an indication of *the problem*, meaning denial of that which is reality that the campaign reflects.

The Case for Trump

AUGUST 6, 2015

Donald J. Trump for president 2016. Yes, hear me out. For years and years now, ever since the 2000 election was stolen, America has been in a downward spiral. Theft may be the most humiliating and debilitating thing that can happen to a person. It is akin to murder——soul murder. I'm not talking of petty theft but real thievery——a home invasion, where your home is you, your body and soul, your personality, your personal reality. I am not being over dramatic, trust me. Maybe it *is* karma because America's people and politicians are so full of themselves with *it* (American exceptionalism and/or intersectionality) and institutional cognitive dissonance that America and its people have got what's coming to them.

However, I'm not a karma guy. I'm a law-of-attraction guy. In other words, you are actually, really, and truly responsible for what befalls you, including bad things. (I've heard that expressed as "there are no victims, only volunteers"). But of course, the counterpoint is, now I'm blaming the victim. Maybe it depends on context. And then an exception could be when there is a conflict between petitioners (say, you and me), meaning what I want conflicts with what you want, which happens more often than not. This is often business, and Trump is a master——one of the best.

Read the scoreboard. Read the billboard. Read the man's name on the buildings. Where's your very own customized 757 jet airliner with your name on it?

I have been in my many lives, many things, and one of which was being a businessman. I understand the game. I won and won, and then I lost and lost again and again. If I were to go to the Trump school of business, I might get a B grade. But in the end, what did me in was that I wasn't ruthless enough (i.e., I cared too much about people and morals and not enough about the bottom line—profit).

So what is *profit*? Profit is progress, which progressives don't understand. Money allows you independence, and if you don't steal it (money or its equivalent), that's about as free as you can be. Trump earned his money, his wealth, and his freedom. Forget the bootstrap-versus-inheritance argument because inherited money is just a grubstake. The question is, What do you do with it? That's it. Trump has maximized his grubstake, and now he wants to "make America great again." Okay, he's a hypomanic narcissist. He might have a mixed unspecified personality disorder. He's not normal, typical, or average. Neither was Obama or Bush or Clinton or Reagan or Carter or Nixon or Kennedy. Bush (the forty-first) and Ford were within the standard deviation of average, I reckon. Jeb Bush calls his father a "perfect man." I don't know about that. Trump is so right on when he describes Jeb as "low energy." He sure looked that way to me with his stooped shoulders. Trump is unique, and he's perfect for the times we find ourselves in. He can get things done, break through gridlock, and persuade people (and nations) to act in his (our) best interest and not theirs.

I implore you to watch this almost two-hour video of Ta-Nehisi Coates's talk about his essay regarding reparations for African Americans because "somebody did something to us, and they owe us" (for the theft of their souls?).

Here is the link: https://www.youtube.com/watch?v=FudYZTM4ens.

At the 46:25 minute mark, Coates says the same thing Trump says, that Obama failed the African Americans because of policies or maybe it was something else. Does it matter? Trump called Obama out on that, and the commentators all deemed Trump racist. No. Trump was speaking truth to power. Trump has said to African Americans, "Give me a chance! What have you got to lose?"

Trump is the benevolent king, and he's on your side.

Update

FEBRUARY 3, 2016

So here we are six months after I wrote and posted the note "The Case for Trump," and we've had the first actual votes cast and delegates awarded. Mr. Trump came in second to Ted Cruz in the Iowa caucus, 24 percent to 28 percent, seven delegates to eight. And the media, the GOP establishment, and all my liberal friends are having a party. They think Trump will fall now finally. Think again, or reconsider your position—consider hopping on the Trump Train. *The* Donald is making his case, the same case he's always made. And mine hasn't changed either.

Now we have some real numbers to factor into the argument. Trump, not a professional politician, got over forty-five thousand votes, the highest number of votes *ever*, in the Iowa caucus, except for Cruz's total. But Cruz may have cheated; he certainly lied to gain the advantage on election night. Maybe he actually paid people to vote for him; I wouldn't put it past him. I'm curious. How much does it cost, your vote? Well, we have some hard numbers. Former Governor Jeb Bush spent $5,200 on each vote he got. Dr. Ben Carson spent $3,100 for every vote. Senator Rand Paul (he dropped out today) spent $1,500 per vote. Each vote cost Senator Ted Cruz $700 (officially). Senator Marco Rubio, $600. Businessman Donald

J. Trump spent only $300 per vote, *and* he spent his own money, which means three things: (1) Trump respects money and knows its value, (2) Mr. Trump cannot be bought, and (3) *the* Donald knows how to get the most bang for a buck.

Think about that. Isn't that the type of management you'd prefer for our country?[26] After all, it's your money that's being spent. What the government does is collect money from its citizens (via taxes) and then spends it. The government also borrows money, spends it, and pays interest on the borrowed money. The country is now $19 trillion in debt, and it's going deeper and deeper every day. Mr. Trump is a businessman. He knows money. He knows how to make deals. He knows how to get along with people without lying and cheating; he's been doing it for forty-some years.[27] He has a record, and try as they do to spin things to make the case against him, there's no evidence that he's *not* a great businessman and money manager who builds things and creates jobs and takes care of the people who work for him. And his children love him.

---

[26]   It's now February 24, 2018, and we're into Trump's second year. The stock market has soared 37 percent, unemployment is at historic lows (for African Americans and Hispanics too), and consumer confidence is high. Yet he still struggles with the working ways of the US legislative process. Politics and government are completely different than business or running a campaign when it comes to management. People might be similar, but the power dynamics (of business versus politics) are not.

[27]   Again, it's not as easy in politics and government as it is in business, as he's finding out. Time will tell. Maybe by the end of his first term, we'll have a better gage on whether or not a businessman can run this country (unless the Democrats win the House and Senate in 2018 and impeach Mr. Trump).

Debriefing Horace

FEBRUARY 9, 2016

This is a summary of our therapy session. Horace doesn't believe in confidentiality, with some exceptions such as sexual behavior—intra- and interpersonal. He thinks that's part of the problem (i.e., secrets). So I asked, and he told me what he thinks about the POTUS election on the day of the New Hampshire primary. Specifically, I asked Horace, "What are your thoughts about the millennials and their overwhelming support for Bernie Sanders? And what of first-wave feminist Gloria Steinem's comments?"

(Some background regarding Horace.) Horace is a very, very, *very* old soul. Sometimes, he hints he might, in fact, be the missing link!) Anyway, Horace says, "Ms. Steinem told the truth, and then of course, she was forced to take it back, to say she was just joking. But that was proof that Freud was right, that there is no such thing as 'I was just kidding,' that that's a cover-up. I say Trump tells the truth. If the Americans have the guts to elect Trump—*whoa zap!*—Katy, bar the door! All hell is going to be unleashed.[28] And then he asked if I had a cigarette.

---

[28] And it indeed appears that it has. The Democrats, liberals, and elites are beside themselves with the success of Trump's presidency, and if they can't impeach him, civil war is a possibility (i.e., all hell breaking lose).

I said, "I've quit thirty-one years ago, but I have some weed if you'd like to puff on something.

He said, "No, I'll manage." He started speaking again, "Because of the sex ratio imbalance favoring females, it was true that women felt pressure, mostly unconscious, to gravitate toward situations where the best possible [unmarried] mates congregated [i.e., Bernie rallies, which is nothing new]."

And then he went off on a flashback, trying to convince me of his omnipotent knowledge. I checked my notes as I scratched my nose. "Remember when you bartended? How you manly men were, off the books, encouraged to buy drinks for attractive girls? Because the owner knew that attractive girls, single or not, would attract men who had money and would spend copious amounts of gold to impress attractive females. Well, you know what I'm talking about, right?" I nodded. "Nothing's changed, except the sex ratio. However, there's something else going on." My eyebrows went up. "Now you've got single older men—lonely men who are divorced, horny, whatever, supporting Sanders because they know that that's popular with younger women. Sanders, that is."

I fell back on the standard response, "Could you talk more about that?"

Horace pulled on his ear and looked at me like I was the dumbest thing on the planet—a rock. "Steinem was right. Older women become more militant/activist/angry . . . bitter . . . because they lose *power* as they get older! Their power is at its peak when they are young and fertile, whereas with men, they get more powerful as they age if they're successful. Thus, Trump appeals with some younger women." There was a long silence. "Look, the most potent vote a woman has is when and with whom she chooses to mate with. It's really that simple. And yet she, the young woman, more often than not, chooses poorly. It's true! Two out of three marriages, including relationships that produce offspring, are disasters. Why? Look here." He pulled a photo out of his . . . whatever, fur? "This is an award-winning photo shot of a woman jumping to her death, killing herself. But now you have all sorts of social safety nets that say 'Don't jump. Don't do it. We'll take care of you and your children.'"

I'm stunned, shocked at Horace's disclosure. I want a drink. I tell Horace our time is up. "We can talk again later after the New Hampshire primary."

His countenance does not change.[29]

---

[29] We never did speak again. I don't know what happened to him.

Thunder Pass

FEBRUARY 27, 2016

So where is it you want to be, a box in place with no way out at the mercy of forces beyond your control, a victim in a simple, easy, and comfortable place with tall seemingly secure walls or a tougher/harder trek where you risk danger and stand a chance of something better, a place where you might survive thunder and lightning and become *something*, some person, altogether different?

On the twelfth of January, I asked/requested/gave my friends an assignment (due on February 29): to summarize, with written words, their position regarding Mr. Trump's candidacy for POTUS.

I got no response from anyone, and yet *they* continue to speak out and complain with certainty, by the way of posting other people's opinions, like supposed experts.

Sometimes, they ridicule my thoughtful arguments and/or unfriend me. I admit, my disappointment is bordering on contempt.

You are going to get, consciously or unconsciously, that which you desire.

The Twenty-First Century So Far

MARCH 7, 2016

We are one-seventh, or 15 percent, through the twenty-first century and smack in the middle of a US presidential election to decide who leads us forward to the quarter-century mark (2025). The candidates have been whittled down to six, from the twenty-two that began the contest back in the summer, the "summer of Trump." The remainders have nicknames. There's Big Don, Little Marco, Lyin' Ted, Crooked Hillary, Crazy Bernie, and Golly Gee Gosh John. Five are career politicians. Three of those five are sitting senators. One is an active governor. And one woman, the liberal and media favorite, is a former First Lady, a senator, a former failed candidate for **POTUS**, and a recently former secretary of state. She is a calculating enabler and denies she's always been thinking and planning about being the **POTUS** for a long time. She's just a girl doing what needs doing for the people, the good of the country, she says. And then there's Big Don, a world-class businessman and real estate developer, a billionaire with his own 757 jet airliner and properties all over the globe.

It has been a rough and rocky century so far. Through the first two two-term executive administrations (2000–2015), one Republican and one Democrat, the R was hailed as a "compassionate conservative," and the D (a subsequent Nobel Peace Prize–winning, African American touting "hope and change") was a man who would save humanity. The verdict is in, and it appears he failed. But the century hasn't been all bad. There have been winners and losers. Look at (in no particular order) the winners and losers of the twenty-first century.

(Yours truly points, with laser beam light, to the big screen and the PowerPoint presentation.)

1. Big business is the winner; small business is the loser.
2. Mass communication is the winner; interpersonal communication is the loser.
3. Gay people are the winners; African American people are the losers. (The audience gasps.)
4. Single women are the winners; children and families are the losers. (There is a murmur.)
5. Money managers are the winners; individual investors are the losers. (There is a scattering of applause.)
6. Terrorism is the winner; world peace is the loser. (There is silence.)
7. China, Mexico, and Vietnam are the winners; USA, Europe, Africa, and Middle East are the losers. (There is a murmur.)
8. Weapons manufacturers are the winners; people are the losers. (There are shrieks.)
9. Health-care providers are the winners; patients are the losers. (There is silence.)
10. Higher education administrators and professors are the winners; students and K12 teachers are the losers. (Again, there is a hushed murmur.)
11. Big-city America is the winner; small-town America is the loser. (There is silence.)
12. Politicians, lobbyists, and consultants are the winners; people are the losers. (There is a loud cheer, which gives me pause. Why?)
13. Big government is the winner; individuality is the loser. (There is another cheer. I'm beginning to think I've a mixed, confused crowd or I'm in the wrong venue.)

14. Professional athletes and their owners are the winner; fans are the losers. (There is silence.)
15. Entertainment is the winner; intimacy is the loser. (There is silence.)

I'm not suggesting there is a zero-sum equation regarding the comparisons, just that they exist and that there is a relationship. After all, isn't everything interconnected, a tapestry?

Here's my takeaway: Stop calling Trump supporters stupid. Maybe they're on to something.

So to summarize (even more briefly), you've got your winners: gays, single women, money managers, terrorists, a few countries (a very few), big business (giant multinational corporations), weapon manufacturers, health-care providers, college professors and administrators, big cities, big government, professional athletes and their team owners, the entertainment industry, the mass media (the internet), and lobbyists, consultants, and politicians. And then you've got those on the losing end: African Americans, children and families, small investors, small towns, most countries, most people on the planet, patients, students, teachers, fans, and generally, people's feelings of belongingness and of affiliation and intimacy, number 3 on Maslow's hierarchy. And I think it actually might come before number 2, safety and security. I think affiliation might be paramount to safety and security (worth a conversation).

So if you're on the winning side, you're probably pretty content with the way things are—vote accordingly. If not, there's only one real choice, one person who brings the chance of changing things, of delivering on the promises of the two previous presidents. And that's the nonpolitician Mr. Donald J. Trump.

Beer and the Wall

MARCH 16, 2016

I went to the corner store, and the owner had rearranged the beer bins, which led me to ask (which is my wont because I'm a curious soul) *why*, which led to a lengthy discussion on beer, business, trade, and Trump.

Briefly, let's say for simplicity's sake, a six-pack of Corona (my preference) cost $10. Well, Corona merged with Budweiser (formally owned by the Busch family), but it is now owned by a multinational corporation. Let's call them the Bud Group (BG). All the big formerly family-owned beer makers in the USA are now owned by multinational corporations, most of which are traded on stock exchanges. But the Mexican government has laws that prohibit a Mexican company from selling a majority of a Mexican company to a foreign company, say, the Bud Group. So the Mexican group must retain 51 percent of the company, which means of my $10, more than $5 goes to the Mexican company, $3 goes to the BG, and $2 stays here in the hands of my friend, a small business owner and employer of three part-time workers. This is a very bad trade deal for us (Americans with, as a country, $20,000,000,000 in debt and growing). Now I could purchase a locally brewed beer, say from Fort Collins, Longmont, or even here in Westminster, and all $10 would stay here in Colorado (except that which is taxed by the federal government)—$2 going to my friend and $8 to the folks in Fort Collins, etc. (the owners of the brewery and all their workers, growers, laborers, brewmasters, truckers, salespersons, and so on).

Enter Donald J. Trump (who understands all this way more than any other candidate or me or you or even my friend who owns the store). Trump says, "Not gonna happen anymore, folks. I'm gonna build a wall, and Mexico is gonna pay for it. They are going to give me $1 of the $5 (20 percent), or I'm gonna tax them $3 to bring their product into our country." (By the way, the Mexican government won't allow the Fort Collins brewery to sell its product in Mexico. In Mexico, you drink Mexican brewed beer or the multinational companies' beer.) So because of the new tax, Corona now costs $13,[30] and I go, "No friggin' way! I'm gonna drink the locally brewed beer," which still only costs $10. The local company will then start to make more money, pay more taxes, employ more people, and so on and so forth. The BG and the Mexican company's sales go down. The Mexicans then want to renegotiate with Mr. Trump, our president, and he says, "Let's talk."

Whatever happens, Mexico pays for the wall one way or the other.

The wall is necessary to keep out desperate people and those who exploit them for profit. The wall is a boundary, a physical barrier that signals (a symbol) to the world that America cannot be taken advantage of or exploited because *we are strong*. All the drugs and sex slaves used to exploit vulnerable Americans are going to cease. To be an American is to be strong, independent, and free. We Americans will take care of our own, our people, our tribe. This is Trump's message and why he will win.

So now what happens?

Well, the multinational groups want to crush my friend and all competition, so they hire smart, sharp, beautiful guys and gals to lobby the politicians whom they have bought and paid for with campaign contributions to allow the large supermarket chains Kroger, Safeway, etc. to sell real beer, wine, and liquor in-store, in place of just 3.2 beer (like it is in California).

These big corporations collude (sort of, but it's really just business) to drive my friend, the small business owner, out of business, as well as the Fort Collins brewery. The multinationals get richer and then reward their stockholders (including most politicians, once they understand the game)

---

[30]   When I wrote this chapter, Corona costs $6.50 at my corner store. It now (May 22, 2018) costs $9. Mexico is ripping us off, and no one cares.

who also get richer. And then the ordinary American becomes a ward of the state, beholding to the state for health care (number 1 on Maslow's hierarchy) and safety and security (number 2), and gradually succumb to loneliness and isolation (number 3) because their self-respect and self-esteem (number 4) has long ago been sapped by the fact of becoming dependent on the state for their basic needs. The average American has become racked by pain: physical, emotional, and psychological. Self-actualization? Forget about it. The only solace comes from escape via alcohol, drugs, sex/masturbation, video games, pain (disease), violence, food, religion, exercise, meditation, and finally, death. All of which is exploited for profit by the rich multinationalists, globalists, universities, politicians, and the state (i.e., those in positions of power).

The multinationals pay a subsistent wage, maybe, or hire immigrants who think $8.25 an hour is a great deal. Then the rich (in every sense/meaning of the word) get richer, and the rest are left without hope but full of delusion and fantasy that somehow they can get enough of the state's benevolence to buy beer, wine, liquor, and drugs to make it through another day. And so it goes. We're pretty much in that condition already.

Bernie Sanders? Give me a break! He hasn't a clue about how anything works, much less how to make a deal. Hillary Clinton? She's part of the game and seriously clueless, having been compromised so, so long ago. My nickname for her was Clueless Clinton.

So what are you going to do? What can you do?

Vote Trump! Tell your friends. Get on board the Trump Train! Me? I'm going to switch to the local breweries and whiskey distilleries.

A = E + h[31]

---

[31]   For A = E + h, see *The Territorial Imperative: A Personal Inquiry into the Animal Origins of Property and Nations* (1966) by Robert Ardrey.

A is equivalent to love, affiliation, friendship, alliances, and coalitions (Maslow's number 3). *E* is equivalent to one's enemy, either a person, a tribe, a clan, a nation, etc. (Maslow's number 2). The last one, *h*, is equivalent to a hazard, say, a natural disaster, like flood, hurricane, wildfire, or global warming. Thus, our friendships and affiliations depend on an external force/entity that threatens our personal survival, safety, and security. All our relationships are an extension of this equation. This is, in essence, the root of much human behavior, which has evolved from mammals, which evolved from reptiles, which evolved from fish, which evolved from water and plants, and so on and so forth. This *is* evolution. In a sense, we *are* all related.

The Hostile Takeover

MARCH 17, 2016

A hostile takeover is what Trump is doing to the Republican Party, where delegates are the shares. In business, a hostile takeover is when an outside buyer starts buying up shares of a public company in an attempt to acquire a controlling majority position. Mr. Donald J. Trump, in 1982, began buying shares of Holiday Inns at fifty dollars a share and had purchased 4 percent before his play was noticed. The stock shot up to sixty-five dollars upon speculation that Trump might be making a run at a hostile takeover. He lays out in *The Art of the Deal* his three options: (1) Keep buying up shares toward a takeover. (2) Sell and take a nice quick profit. (3) Sell back his shares to the company at a premium, taking advantage of their mismanagement and incompetence, to extract the high price just so they, the incompetent management, the current owners of the company, can retain control and save face. (Trump eventually did option 3 at seventy-six dollars a share, and everyone won. Today, Holiday Inn is part of a larger group, a multinational company, and is trading at sixty-five dollars a share, the price doubling from where it had been three years ago).

Let's fast-forward to 2016 and the Republican Party's primary campaign to take over the White House and the presidency of the United

States from the Democrats, who are offering up two seriously flawed candidates. The capture of the White House (by the Rs) is assumed to be easy, so the Republican nomination is a highly sought position. Trump sees (and it has been verified to be true by the RP's oh-so-slow response) the Republican Party is extremely poorly managed, *and* the shares are cheap. He begins his takeover bid by getting the votes of the Wounded Warriors, military veterans, and white evangelical Christians. He's picking off one of the managers of the RP (also a candidate), Lyin' Ted Cruz, share holders. It was easy. Then he went after the heart of the management, Low-Energy Jeb, the believed next-in-line of the Bush family presidential dynasty. Trump picked up more shares, a little more expensive, but still easy pickings. Now the RP is in full panic mode, and it throws all its support behind the new hope, whiz kid, Little Marco Rubio.

Trump keeps buying, and now has got 42 percent of the stock. Cruz has 34 percent; Rubio, 15 percent; and the last-chance candidate, John Kasich, 6 percent. Cruz sees an opportunity and is making a move, a big push to take control of failing Marco's shares as well as Kasich's. The shares have become expensive. The question is, Will Trump's hostile takeover succeed? Can he get 51 percent, or 1,237 shares, before the convention in Cleveland this summer? Or will he fall short and make a deal? (Maybe the contract to build the wall with his name on it?) Or will Cruz cut a deal with Trump for the VP position? Will Kasich or Rubio? The winner will take the White House, the ultimate company, the most powerful company in the world, but one that has been mismanaged for decades. It's definitely the most daring hostile takeover bid in the history of the world—riveting, the stuff of novels.

After Tuesday's primaries (March 15), it looks more likely that Trump will be successful in his hostile takeover play, but it also looks like the Democrat elite are teaming up with the RP's elite to try and derail Trump's takeover move. Why? Because the Democrats fear Trump more than any other candidate. So now it looks like Trump and the American people against both parties and the ruling class of the United States, the super wealthy and their pawns, the establishment media and the establishment's politicians, all who are colluding to stop Trump. I've now seen a TV ad campaign here in Colorado, trying to persuade voters to support and vote for the large supermarket chains' liquor licensure—bad for small businesses and good for the big businesses. It's bad for my friend, bad for us. Vote Trump. Support small businesses. Support your friends and neighbors. Make America great again.

Rachel Maddow Reports

MARCH 18, 2016

No, she doesn't report; she distorts and lies. I was flipping channels last night and caught a part of her show, a 9:38-minute segment called "The Dark Arts." In it, she looped an act of aggression—a man shoving another man at a GOP political event in Michigan—twenty times during the piece. I think she has a violence fetish, because I've observed her doing that before and previously linked her to the violence that broke out in Chicago on Friday. She laughs and giggles, plays the smart, quirky nerd role; but she's really a subversive, using her platform to incite violence. Maddow links violence to Trump, with her videos and commentary, when none really exists. She's trying to scare voters. It's a subliminal message hiding behind her sweet, little-girl-like demeanor. What I've caught her doing is not something *I've* put together—video clips out of context to make her look bad. They are segments that she produces in total. (You can go to her website and watch the segment.) At the end of the segment, she says, "Front-runner Donald Trump *promised* riots . . ." which is a complete lie. He did no such thing. Maddow is dishonest and is trying to frighten you. Why? I don't know. Ratings? Money? *Something* from her past? This I know—she's not a good reporter.

Dishonest Reporting and the Attempt to Derail Trump

MARCH 19, 2016

The link below is one source of Donald Trump's comments about Mexicans and immigration when he first announced on June 16. Asked the next day how he could say such a thing, he answered, "Well, someone's doing the raping." Clumsy, yes. Inaccurate, no. Did the press report the human rights atrocities? No. In addition, to this day, his comments are used to declare him a racist, so as to persuade the Hispanic population to vote against him (a dishonesty by his rivals and the press). In reality, he is a true friend to the migrants, bringing the problem to light, which is necessary to find a solution. The wall *will* help. Smart people understand this. For the sake of women, girls, and children all around the world, don't submit to the lies. Vote Trump.

http://fusion.net/story/17321/is-ra

Trump and Flint, Michigan

There are hearings going on in Congress now, concerning the what, why, and how of the problem of lead in Flint, Michigan's water supply, which has resulted in the lead poisoning of children, leading to problems regarding healthy brain development. This is a problem not just for Flint but also in cities all over the country. Congress is doing what Congress does—grandstanding, pointing fingers, screaming for heads to roll, and so on. But nothing has been done. You want the problem fixed? Call Trump. This is what New York city did back in the '80s, when faced with failed projects (overt government incompetence, fraud, waste, and abuse beyond the usual covering up). Trump is a problem-solver who knows how to get results. Trump, almost single-handedly, brought NYC back to prominence in the early 1980s, with his rescuing of projects gone haywire, the renovation of old buildings, and the construction of Trump Tower. How does he do it? He identifies the problem, calls in the most knowledgeable people, listens, and then hires the best people. He doesn't care if you are male, female, black, white, brown, red, Christian, Jew, Muslim, Buddhist, Atheist, straight, or gay, only that you be a US citizen or legal immigrant and can do the job right—meaning ahead of schedule, under budget, and of high quality. *That's* what Trump means by "make America great again," a flashback to the '80s (*not* make America white again). Trump moved into Manhattan despite his father's advice *not to* and made it a great city! And yes, he got rich in the process. Now he doesn't want money, just recognition and appreciation, validation, and the chance to do the job. *Don't* believe the lies of the suits (the ruling classes) and boots (the terrorists) and cutes (feminists) who fear him because they know their time is up. All you have to do is vote Trump, and then you can say "Trump you!" to all the sleaze, scum, and incompetents who have brought the world to the brink. Yes, Trump is dangerous, as all real men are to those who threaten their family. America, are we or are we not a family?[32]

A New America

The incoming negativity toward Trump has intensified. The negative press reporting and pontificating is relentless and heavy, bombardment coming from all sides and persuasions, and yet Mr. Trump soldiers on, getting stronger, which is amazing. There's never been anyone like him, try as the pundits do to compare him to others.

There is no doubt in my mind that Trump would be the best president ever, regarding policy, both foreign and domestic, if he's allowed to do what he's always done—problem-solving. The man knows what he's doing, and he's written it all down in *The Art of the Deal*. Trump knows and understands that relationships (the essence of human life) are all about understanding people—what they need and what they want (Maslow's hierarchy of human motivation)—and that to get along with them, you must negotiate because "Deals work best when each side gets something it wants from the other" (p. 335). It doesn't matter if it's a marriage, a trade deal, a real

---

[32] February 27, 2018. This section needs an update because here we are again with another national crisis, a recurring one, the school massacre in Parkland, Florida. The results (from Congress) will be the same: nothing will be done that effectively solves the problem—sad, lonely, hurt, angry men who want revenge. The causes of crisis, whatever the crisis, are always a complex and complicated series of circumstances and events. I liken it to a "perfect storm" scenario or reciprocal determinism, and the failures of persons in authority/power are always many. And everyday people will holler, protest, blame, and demand accountability and change and very little will. That's the way democracy and bureaucracy functions, barely. The easy answer is always more money, which Congress is very good at—spending money (other people's). Trump won because he showed he was a problem-solver who could get things done. Unfortunately, he doesn't have a free hand as president, as he did as head of a private enterprise, the Trump Organization. And the nature of humans is one of a competitive species who fights over territory, resources, and power, with winners and losers.

estate transaction, whatever. And that flexibility and unpredictability, perseverance and patience, are tools in your toolbox. This is true. You must understand that once the process starts, any process, there will be unforeseen occurrences and changes, the unknown unknowns. You must adjust. If one thing changes, it affects everything else.

For example, the wall proposed by Trump.

Imagine a new America, one where there are coast-to-coast high-speed bullet trains that crisscross the land (Trump has mentioned such) and the positive impact that would have on the country. What if one train were built along the southern border? (Of course, the wall would have to be built first.) The growth and economic impact would be astounding. Imagine residential and commercial developments being constructed (the kind of thing Trump excels at) on top of bluffs—with great views to the south, over the wall into Mexico. The construction could be passive solar, adobe and brick, cool in the summer and warm in the winter. Spectacular! Water would be brought in via a pipeline from a great lake, part of a flood control project on the Mississippi River. The same type of development could happen on the Mexican side of the wall. Goodness gracious, spectacular! There will be peace and prosperity. There will be jobs, dignity, safety, and security and thriving, mingling populations and cultures. All we need is Trump—a man with vision, experience, and energy and will to get it done—a Congress that cooperates, and a wall.

Trump: The Art of the Deal (1987) by Donald J. Trump with Tony Schwartz

BOOK REVIEW BY YOURS TRULY
MARCH 27, 2016

If you want to understand the phenomenon that is Donald Trump, his candidacy for POTUS, and the man himself, all you need do is read this book. Today (Sunday, March 27, 2016) the experts (political reporters, rivals, pundits, psychiatrists) all seem baffled to explain him, but it's all right here in these pages (367). And all the experts are wrong! So the real questions are about them, not Trump.

Trump is the most consistent person I've ever encountered, as well as the most self-aware. In addition, he understands people, both in general and as individuals, better than anyone I've ever known or read about.

His campaign strategy is all in here—the why and the how, as well as his reasons for running. All you have to do is read this book with an open mind. It becomes apparent that this man, Donald J. Trump, would be the best possible president for the country at this time. He is like a gift from God! The proof is all around you, all around the country, even the world. I don't know why people are so amazed and shocked. Here's a candidate with a record that is empirical. You can read the book or not, obviously. I'm just stunned that more haven't.[33]

---

[33] Here is a link to an interview with the ghostwriter Tony Schwartz at Oxford last November 4, 2016. Schwartz despises Trump; it's obvious. But to me, it's also obvious that Schwartz is an angry man, very conflicted, sad, and pathetic.
https://www.youtube.com/watch?v=qxF_CDDJ0YI

Malpractice, Victimology, and the Greatest Problem

MARCH 29, 2016

When I began reading the attached article, "Is Donald Trump Literally Making Us Sick" by Jean Kim MD, a practicing psychiatrist, I thought it was satire, then I realized the author was serious. http://www.damemagazine.com/2016/03/20/donald-trump-literally-making-us-sick.

After finishing it, I googled her and saw that she is employed by the US government in Washington DC, and obviously, what she says carries some weight. This is, in my opinion, malpractice and exemplifies the greatest problem affecting the health and well-being of the general population of the United States. The problem is the failure "of observers of the world to determine whether their perceptions are genuine and verifiable or whether they are merely the *projections of inner feelings* [emphasis mine]."[34] Said another way: "The single great informing conflict of the American psyche—the conflict between the subjective centrality of our own lives

---

[34]   Michael Crichton, *State of Fear* (2004), 649.

versus our awareness of its objective insignificance."[35] What it is, in essence, is the distortion of reality via one's own perception, so as to make oneself feel better or, in this case, to unscrupulously twist reality for one's own benefit at the expense of others' health and well-being (i.e., malpractice). Kim is, no doubt, a "thought leader" by virtue of her education, standing, status, and employment. And she is so wrong, which is likely not her fault, but nevertheless, it doesn't absolve her of the responsibility regarding the health and well-being of others, given her profession.

No one, not even Donald Trump, can make another person sick. This is important! One's health is, first and foremost, the responsibility of the person, the individual, once they reach maturity—maturity of personality at or around twenty-two years of age. A person then becomes responsible for themselves, their physical and mental health. Kim declares herself to be an expert on PTSD, and her argument is that Trump retraumatizes victims of childhood abuse or war or fathers . . . some thing or some person and, Kim states with all the authority of her position, is making them, at the least, anxious, and at the worst, physically sick. Seriously?

This is victimology at its most profound—telling a person, client, patient, voter that whatever it is that is bothering them is not their fault or responsibility and that they are powerless victims. The cause lies outside of them, and so the remedy is to remove, or change the other, and then everything will be fine. There is so much wrong with this approach to problem-solving, to "helping others," thus my designation of the greatest problem. It simply leads to so many other problems. It is a recipe for disaster! Such crooked thinking causes an escalating spiral of helplessness and misery and, yes, physical and mental problems. It simply compounds the problem. Even Jesus Christ knew this, instructing his followers to not be anxious: "Do not be anxious about tomorrow, for tomorrow will be anxious for itself. Ask, and it will be given. Seek, and you will find. Knock, and it will be opened to you. Whatever you wish that men would do to you, do so to them, for that is the law and the prophets."[36] You reap what you sow, in other words. You earn your life.

The irony is this: Jesus Christ and Donald Trump live by the same rules, though with admittedly different results—Christ being crucified and Trump soaring around in a customized 757 jet airliner. But both got what

---

[35]   David Foster Wallace, "The Suffering Channel," in *Oblivion* (2004), 284.

[36]   This is the gospel according to Matthew.

it is/was they desired. It is as Christ intimated—the law of attraction—a philosophy that Trump was raised on by his pastor, Norman Vincent Peale, who preached the power of positive thinking. Seek, and you will find.[37]

The mature personality is now thought to be best described as a constellation of attributes known by the acronym OCEAN—openness, conscientiousness, extroversion, agreeableness, and neuroticism— or the Big Five. For this discussion, I'll focus on just two, extroversion and neuroticism. Each domain, it's important to understand, contains within it many other traits or characteristics. For extroversion, you'll find friendliness, gregariousness, assertiveness, energy level, excitement-seeking, and cheerfulness.[38] Could there be more descriptive terms for Mr. Trump? So let me designate Trump as a highly extroverted person. It's necessary for understanding that these five domains are each on a spectrum going from very high to very low and, as such, have opposites. Staying with extroversion, it's opposite, or very low extroversion, would be introversion. Under the rubric of extroversion then would be very high extroversion and also very high introversion.

The other domain I want to include in this discussion is neuroticism. Under the domain of neuroticism (negative emotion systems) are traits such as fearfulness, anxiety, shame, guilt, disgust, and sadness.[39] So regarding Trump, it's safe to say that he is very low in neuroticism.[40]

What I'm going to do next is ask you to imagine in your mind a matrix of four squares. Clockwise from the top left is Donald Trump, a very high extrovert who is also a very low neurotic. To the right would be a person who is a very high extrovert and also a very high neurotic. This person could be diagnosed as bipolar or manic-depressive. Below that would be a person who is a very high neurotic and a very low extrovert (i.e., a neurotic introvert). It is that personality that Kim is exploiting— the neurotic introvert. (As do many others in the field of mental health, including Big Pharma and those individuals under their purview). In the

---

[37]   Trump cites this in *Crippled America: How to Make America Great Again* (2015) yet alludes also to the advantages of considering negative outcomes, the downside, thus practicing a more real/accurate/practical form of Peale's positive thinking (*The Art of the Deal*, p. 48–50). This is not *the secret.*

[38]   Sam Gosling, *Snoop: What Your Stuff Says about You* (2008), 43.

[39]   Daniel Nettle, *Personality: What Makes You the Way You Are* (2007), 108.

[40]   Trump is correct when he declared himself a "very stable genius."

bottom left quadrant is a person low in both extroversion and neuroticism. This person is stoic, perhaps a Buddhist.

The good news is that this typology is fairly simplistic and that people or individuals are way more complicated than just a two-dimensional graph. After all, there are three other personality domains, as well as physical appearance, intelligence, and athleticism. In other words, people are very complex. But professionals, like Kim, exploit vulnerable people for their own benefit, consciously or unconsciously. And the effects of that on the overall health and well-being of a society, a culture, or a nation can be devastating.

The Beautiful Woman and the Old Hag

THURSDAY, MARCH 31, 2016

This is a famous picture (beautiful-woman, old-hag illusion) that demonstrates a phenomenon called figure/ground.

The beautiful woman and the old hag illusion, created first by an anonymous illustrator in the late nineteenth-century Germany

I think it illustrates some other interesting things happening now in the current political discourse. Look close. There is a beautiful woman looking away. You can barely see her nose, her ear is under the dark hairline, her jawline is below the ear, and the "slashed throat" is a choker around her throat. She's wearing a coat. Or the ear is the eye, the jaw line is the nose, the choker is the mouth, and the bare neck is the chin of an old hag. It *can* be a Rorschach test, primed by your current mood. You see what you are feeling. But once you see both, you can switch back and forth and see that from exactly the same place or perspective. You can see different things.

Let's take the current Corey Lewandowski (Trump's campaign manager) / Michelle Fields (beat reporter) lawsuit, alleging assault and battery by Corey on Michelle. If you're a Trump hater, you see proof of one thing; if you're a Trump supporter, you see another thing. I've watched the video, zoomed in and slowed down frame by frame, and looked at Fields' history. (She's done this before and has a book coming out.) It looks like Lewandowski is telling the truth. He never touched her, or if he did, he gently put his hand on her back as he squeezed between her and Trump, as you do when you work through a crowd. But that won't stop the Trump haters from seeing and believing what they want, also known as confirmation bias. My guess is that the case won't come to trial. No attorney, after looking at the evidence, will take the case for the accuser. But that won't matter; it's just another shovel full of dirt thrown on Trump's wished-for grave, with all his haters jumping for joy now that he looks to be in trouble and that the stop-Trump movement is working. According to Dr. Jean Kim (see "Malpractice, Victimology, and the Greatest Problem"), this should provide the cure for all those folks who Trump has made sick. What a sad, bad joke our society has become.

Communication

APRIL 3, 2016

Electronic mail, was it effective communication? What *is* the desired result of communicating? Is it to be understood? Is it to get what one wants? Perhaps, at the most basic, it could be to reach an understanding between two people or parties that facilitates a mutual benefit—an agreement that allows for coexistence. With email, there are no cues from the body, facial expressions, or voice inflection (tone) to validate what appears on the screen. There is no handwriting either, not even a signature, only hastily punched characters arranged to represent a paucity of words plucked from thousands, with almost endless possible interpretations. "What did that mean? Where did that come from?" There is no way of knowing. It has been said that communication is 93 percent nonverbal, and with email, even the context of the words is obscure, making the meaning even more opaque. Projection is amplified!

> Email is ripe for cherry-picking and confirmation bias—
> pick what you want and leave the rest. It's so easy with
> email. All a sender can be certain of is the Response / No
> Response. No, even that isn't so. You can't *know* when or
> if your message was read.

With people so busy, the messages tend to be brief. If I respond in-depth, the person will know that I have nothing better to do, no life.

Though brief, the communiqué can be packed with a lot of bits of information, threads. After the Response / No Response indicator, next is what the recipient chooses to respond to, which tells the sender something. But it's never clear what that something is. Nothing can be verified. Nothing can be taken back with a quick "Just kidding" or "I didn't mean *that*" or "I'm sorry" with a gentle touch. But there is a record, documentation, which adds weight to what otherwise might be weightless.

This new attempt at communication is risky, but quick and easy. Is it easy to be careless (bad), or is it carefree (good)? Is it for someone like me with tendencies toward impulse (bad), or is it spontaneity (good)? Is it impatience (bad), or is it intuition (good)? Is it a seemingly uncontrollable compulsion (bad), or is it determination (good)? Is it for provocative queries (good and bad)? Is it dangerous (bad), or is it daring (good)?[41]

There is so much chatter now about communication. What does it all mean? In 1996, I took a class, Therapeutic Crisis Intervention, whose basic tenet was all behavior has meaning (a blend of Nietzschean and Freudian thought). And now, my word, we have Twitter and Facebook and Instagram and Snapchat! Words are now frightening and dangerous. Standard email is almost obsolete! And then there's the media and all the social scientists, all the experts, telling us what it is we should be understanding, doing the interpreting for us.

They are all spinners—dishonest thought leaders—working their own agendas to enhance their own status and standing in society, which now is almost all-encompassing. It's groupthink disguised as "We are one! We are

---

[41]   This brief discussion is from a novel I wrote back in 2004–6, *Attachment: A Novel of War and Peace* (pp. 175–6), when the internet was just really catching on and is solely about email. It predates Myspace, Facebook, Twitter, and texting—the social media world we find ourselves in now—but rings true.

one world, one big social network or web, a World Wide Web!" But there is always another side or perspective, the old hag, the villain.

It's all so like a dream, but it's not; it's real! The laboratory, the research, and the studies are not real. Reality has been twisted into something that is not discernable. What is real is what happened.

People want to know how Donald Trump can be so captivating and how people can actually vote for him. The answer is because he understands people intuitively. I doubt he ever took a class or seminar in it. But he knows people, he understands people, and he can read people. He can truly communicate with them, in the best sense of the word. And that's a good thing.

Here is a very good analysis of Donald Trump's communication skills, which explains his success in business and politics. Keep in mind that communication is really not about what you say (there is the legal contract for that); it is the tone and expressions, the emotionality, the gestalt[42] that matters. We are creatures. https://www.yahoo.com/politics/the-strange-power-of-donald-1397103083307062.html.

So here we are now in 2016, being bombarded 24-7 with communiqué. It is almost meaningless, yet it is having a profound effect on relationships. This cannot be a good thing. What the media chooses to report on is edited and filtered in such a way so as to maximize profits, not good will or accurate content. Fact-checking is a farce, especially when it comes to Trump. His relationship skills, which are his biggest asset in deal-making and leadership, are totally bypassed to mock his sketchy adherence to "facts." The numbers, the facts, are details that are gone over by lawyers later when all the *I*s are dotted and the *T*s crossed. What is important is that both sides, in any relationship, come to an agreement and get something they want. Trump is a master at this. That is why he has been so successful. All anyone needs to do is look at the empirical evidence—his company and his family. Consider his children who, by everyone's account, are exceptional human beings.[43] He has five of them by three different marriages.

---

[42]   An organized whole that is perceived as more than the sum of its parts, in other words—Donald J. Trump.

[43]   February 28, 2018. Ivanka Trump, his daughter, granted an interview with a hostile reporter at the just-concluded Winter Olympics as the representative for America. Ivanka responded to the intrusive question, that the question

I can tell you from experience that coparenting children with an ex is one of the most difficult relationship/communication situations that humans can face. Yet Mr. Trump has succeeded not once but twice and, at the same time, actively parenting with a current spouse *and* simultaneously running and managing a hugely successful company involved in some of the most high-stakes real estate deals ever. There's your evidence of his skill as an effective communicator.

So why is this not being communicated across all the extraordinary means we now have of communicating? There are three reasons:

1. We are not who we think we are, both as individuals and collectively.
2. There is far more money to be made in promoting conflict than in reporting accurately.
3. The time necessary to communicate effectively has been stolen by our time-saving devices. It is a paradox, a riddle that we seem unable to solve.

---

was "inappropriate," to ask a daughter about her father in a public interview concerning America and its position with regard to the rest of the world. This fact, this evidence, is representative of the Trump family, conservative values, and the hostile position the American media has taken with regard to Mr. Trump. After Ivanka's visit, North Korea intimated it was open to talking with the US. We'll see how this plays out.

If the Election Were Today

APRIL 9, 2016

Today wraps up the Republican State Convention here in Colorado where the Lyin' Ted Cruz is no doubt gobbling up all the state's delegates to take to Cleveland in July, where he intends to steal the election from the people. I went to my precinct's caucus, having switched parties so as to vote for Trump, but found the process to be very murky, an individual having to pay to play, and also, I was the only Trump supporter. It was nothing like the Democratic caucus I participated in, in 2008. If I'd known how dirty it would be (the swamp), maybe I would've paid my money and fought for Trump. Now I feel I've let him down. Hell, I've let the country down.

If the election were held today, it would be like this: Clinton, 40%; Trump, 30%; Sanders, 20%; and Cruz, 10%. But that's not the way *we* do things—there must be a head-to-head contest, a binary choice, decided by 538 delegates in November. I figure it this way: If it's Clinton versus Trump, Sanders's people will split and Cruz's go to Trump, so it will be fifty-fifty, which is very, very close.[44] Deals will be made, and the Clinton machine will probably win over Trump's maverick ways.[45] If it's Sanders

---

[44] In fact, it is pretty much what happened.

[45] I got this wrong. Trump won.

versus Cruz, it'll be a blowout for Sanders, 60% to 20%; and 80% of Trump's people (me) are not voting. If it's Clinton versus Cruz, it's another blowout for the Dems, with the same percentage. If it's Sanders versus Trump, now we're talking about an election that will change the world, no matter who wins, it's a 100% turnout. With Trump, we get peace and prosperity; with Sanders, anarchy and wars. Clinton equals more of the same. If you like things the way they are, she's your guy. Trump equals peace and prosperity around the globe eventually. Peace through strength. Sanders equals "Katy, bar the door"; you get your revolution. Odds are 1:5—Clinton wins, and we circle the drain slowly. You'll hardly notice; you'll die before the demise.

I don't know about kings, their power and what not (I'm no world historian), but I do study people, humans especially (not robots or algorithms). In America, we're such a young nation it's much easier to analyse. In America, 93% of the 240 years the USA has been around, we've been at war. The *idea* that America and/or all humans are inherently good or moral is nonsense. We Americans started most of these hostilities. We humans, as tribal primates, don't assimilate well with other cultures different from our own. We fight and are really violent when push comes to shove. We behave okay if everyone gets their basic needs met, but that's rare.

The Indian Wars lasted 125 years, from 1775 to 1900, until we, the second-wave Americans, got the first-wave Americans pacified and rounded up on reservations. Sanders speaks about how *we* learned about nature and living in harmony from the Natives. I'm sorry; I have to laugh. That's called the naturalistic fallacy and/or the myth of the noble savage.[46]

---

[46]   Bobbi S. Low, *Why Sex Matters: A Darwinian Look at Human Behavior* (2000).

A Sobering Weekend: Failing to Learn from Losing

APRIL 12, 2016

At 5:00 p.m. on Sunday, thunder rumbled and water filled my eyes.

Jordan Spieth had just lost the Masters golf tournament after leading by five strokes at the end of sixty-three holes (seventy-two total) with just nine left to play. He lost one stroke on the sixty-fourth and another on the sixty-fifth but still led by three with seven holes left. Then he completely collapsed and lost four more strokes on the sixty-sixth, hitting his ball into the water not once but twice! It was a historic fail and not all that uncommon in real life (the stuff of myth, archetypal).

On Saturday, the day before, from 3:00 p.m. to 1:00 a.m. (for 12 straight hours), I had watched a reenactment of events that had transpired twenty years prior, in 1995. It wasn't golf but did involve an athlete who liked to play golf. It was a marathon drama on FX, ten hours of consecutive, back-to-back shows of the murder trial of O. J. Simpson—an African American, a famous footballer, and a Hollywood celebrity—accused of the brutal killing of his ex-wife, a white Southern Californian socialite, and a young male restaurant worker. The show is *American Crime Story: the Run of His Life*. (I highly recommend watching this drama, based on the book by Jeffery Toobin. There is much to be gleaned about America—crime, narcissism, racism, the law, and human behavior.) The conviction of Simpson was supposed to be a slam dunk, a gimmie in golf lingo (there was a trail of blood from the victims to the killer), just as Spieth's second consecutive Masters' championship, leading by five shots with just nine holes to play.

What happened?

In both cases, it seems there was overconfidence and a failure to heed warning signs. There was an ethos of "compromise, corruption, and incompetence" (as celebrity defense lawyer Johnnie Cochran branded the LAPD and justice department) that led to a crippling collapse. In both cases, the prosecutor (Jordan Spieth, pro golfer, 2016; and Marcia Clark, assistant district attorney, 1995) failed to pay attention to what was real and, instead, believed what they wanted to believe (confirmation bias/ denial, i.e., repression) that all was well and going according to plan and that victory was a foregone conclusion. All they had to do was do what they had always done (they thought), but they both failed because they did not adjust to the present circumstance or what was right in front of their eyes. They were blinded by belief and by their past—a very common condition of being human.

I'm not sure why these two collapses (watched in back-to-back days by me) and subsequent personal and professional humiliations (they both had to face the cameras and microphones right after they had failed) had such a sobering effect on me, other than that I'm getting old and realize that, for me, time is running out—the time for adjustments—and that *now* at my age, I know that there are no more do-overs.

Then the rain came at 5:25, "drops dripped"[47] down the balcony door's glass pane, and tears trickled from my eyes.

Empathy is just narcissism with a hat, dark glasses, and a raincoat.

---

[47] This is from Tolstoy's *War and Peace*.

Build That Wall

APRIL 19, 2016

The crowd roars, over ten thousand people, "Build that wall! Build that wall!" A chant as one—loud, deafening.

Donald Trump walks away from the microphone, returns, and leans into it. "Are you ready?" he asks, pointing to the packed-in, standing throng of supporters. "Who's going to pay for the wall?"

"Mexico!"

He cups his ear. "Who?"

"Mexico!"

Donald Trump, on Thursday, March 31, sent a two-page memo to the *Washington Post*, detailing how he would get Mexico to pay for the wall, a point of abject contention. I say this because he had told people how—*I* had told people how—but no one would listen or no one wanted to hear.[48]

---

[48] Bob Woodward and Robert Costa, *Washington Post* (April 5, 2016). Trump's memo explains how he plans to pay for the wall. (The authors are both Trump haters.) Now, March 2018, Trump found out how hard it is to get anything political done in the government. The DC swamp creature is a very stubborn beast.

It's not that hard really, but of course, his rivals and haters want to say it can't be done. Mexico, of course, objects. This is the magic that is Trump: he gets things done quickly and efficiently, a process antithetical to the way government works. What's so hard to understand? I understand that those in government, whose jobs are threatened, will try all manner of ways and means to say, "It can't be done!" "He's a fool!" etc. *They* are going to get on board the Trump Train or be fired. But the rest? I wonder (see Freud on Trumpism).

I had to block a friend of mine on Facebook because he was obsessed with hating Trump and wouldn't stop posting on my wall. It's not about xenophobia or racism, none of that; it's just good business, smart business. In fact, the wall, once completed, will be an economic boon for both countries. (I've explained this in detail in "Beer and the Wall," "A New America," and "The Real Mr. Trump and the Solution.") These things/issues aren't that difficult; it just takes a willingness to break old habits—ones that no longer serve the country and its people. Of course, there will be disruption! Those who have power, influence, and money might lose some of that. That's not a bad thing, is it? The system *is* rigged. I call it the machine, a complex of power that includes the politicians, the lawyers, the universities, and the media (publishing as well as TV), or PLUM, and—the ruling class, the elites.

What are the possibilities with a wall? The possibilities are endless for a creative mind.

I have presented two articles below about the border wall and situation as they exist today. There are many pictures. Imagine, if you can, the wall and the situation if done properly with intentionality. It is an economic boon for both countries, where migration back and forth is lawful and controlled.[49]

---

[49]   Brietbart.com (April 4, 2016). "Mexico will stay poor forever without US–Mexico border wall."
      Alan Taylor, "On the Border," in *The Atlantic* (May 6, 2013). This is an article with many pictures of the border as it exists.

Boundaries

MAY 2, 2016

Boundary is one of those words that can mean many things but is always a demarcation, a limit, and/or a separation—a distinction. I used to work in the field of psychiatric rehabilitation, specifically in residential treatment centers (RTC) for children and young adults, both male and female. I did that for five years. The RTC is on the spectrum of prison and freedom. It is just two clicks away from prison, the psychiatric ward of a hospital being between them. The goal of the RTC is psychiatric rehabilitation, i.e., the cognitive restructuring of a human being's mind and behavior to enable their reintegration into civil society. (RTCs have mixed results as to their effectiveness.)

I start this chapter here because there is one common trait that all the clients/patients I treated shared, regardless of their individual diagnosis or the drugs used in treatment—a lack of healthy boundaries. Some were firesetters, some were animal abusers, some were homicidal, some were severe introverts, some were bullies, and some were sexual abusers and predators. Moreover, they all shared the characteristic that they did not know/understand where one person ended and another began. They had no self-control. In psychological jargon, they were enmeshed (see footnote 6), not individuated, and certainly not self-actualized.

> A small child, a toddler, say, who lives in Denver, Colorado, on High Street has in his backyard, his world, a walnut tree. Let's call him Billie Bob. He sees a squirrel and befriends and names the squirrel Charlie. Billie Bob talks to Charlie, feeds him, maybe even loves Charlie insomuch as a toddler can love. In the summer, Mom sends Billie Bob to Grandma, who lives in Washington, DC, so Mom can have some time to herself, whatever. Grandma also has a backyard with a tree in it, which is also home to a squirrel. Billie Bob is overjoyed! "It's Charlie!" The thing is, small children do not, cannot, differentiate between here and there or self and other. Small children only consider the world as it relates to them. They are fully and completely egocentric and narcissistic. They are solipsist. They must be! Gradually, if all goes well, they learn to differentiate and develop a realistic view of the world. They expand their awareness of self and other and develop boundaries.

To compensate, they (the children in my care) often tried to control others and sometimes were successful. They were character- and/or personality-disordered persons but not yet being fully formed (a mature adult), and those diagnoses are not applied. Instead, labels like oppositional/defiant and disorders of conduct, attention deficit hyperactivity, separation anxiety, avoidant, overanxious, autistic, gender identity, learning, speech, anorexia/bulimic, etc. are used. Many children like them are never diagnosed and yet grow into adulthood. Many are misdiagnosed. Nevertheless, they still manage to grow up, albeit with crooked thinking, and struggle constantly with issues of power and control. Many find jobs in society related to issues of power and control, the fortunate ones, and yet still struggle with intimacy in relationships and, of course, with money—a salient manifestation of power.

The boundary between self and other is one of the first things that a healthy individual learns and practices, at least in Western civil society, like Billie Bob in the above story. (This can and does vary between different cultures, which is part of the problem of multiculturalism and the "one world global community" concept. And all behavior must be considered within the context/environment within which it is practiced.)

In general, people don't have particularly strong boundaries, which leads to many interpersonal problems. It's one of the areas (issues) that are focused on in marriage counseling, as well as individual therapy. The thing is, strong boundaries are not something that can be taught in the usual manner—by instruction. Rather it is or isn't learned at a young age by watching others (the parents) interact with one another and the world. In other words, it is learned by inspiration much more effectively than the pervasive method of reward and punishment (conditioning), also known as the carrot and stick. In the RTC setting, what worked best was the modeling of appropriate, healthy boundaries versus instruction (say, classroom lecture) or any kind of reward (positive points, treats, etc.) system. The child would watch a role model and identify with that person, wanting to be like them, to bond with them. They learned new, healthy behaviors by watching, identifying, and imitating. Sometimes, however, things would not go according to plan, and force was necessary to physically restrain a child because the said child had put him or herself or others in danger. Simply put, these children didn't know right from wrong, regarding interpersonal communication and behavior.

How many of such children (and adults) are there? Thousands and thousands, tens, maybe hundreds of thousands or millions. Worldwide? Billions.

It goes like this: Babies are born to people who lack healthy boundaries, and in time, the babies learn unhealthy behaviors and so on. They *do* learn survival skills—things like lying and stealing and bullying and physical intimidation and, ultimately, the use of force, physical and emotional aggression or violence, to get what they want. Or conversely, they learn people-pleasing behaviors, submission. They become "doormats." It's base instinct. Some of these kids join the military, some join the local gang, some become teachers, some become journalists, and some become politicians. Some become wives, and many become mothers.

Now, in the era of the internet and globalization, the possibilities are endless for group affiliation and recognition—to be somebody. Some become perpetrators and predators, some become internet trolls, and some become victims. The internet or the connected global community (CGC) lacks any boundaries whatsoever. Any boundary is left up to the individual, and many users are unprepared because they lack them in real life (IRL) and so are vulnerable to any sort of vicious attack by the trolls, even friends. Trolls, like criminals and bullies in real life, are driven to violate others to make themselves feel better by making others feel bad. It's a way of distracting oneself from one's own misery or for the simple, practical reason that crime pays and that crime is easier than honest work. In real life, the most extreme manifest violations of an individual's personal space or boundary are rape and murder.

Boundary violations can be put on a continuum from mild to extreme—mild being very subjective depending on the victim's sensitivity to words (language), tone, and looks (facial expressions), which is now known as microaggressions. Mild violations are often unintentional and quite common, though not harmless. Next on the continuum toward rape and murder is physical assault and battery (also on a continuum), and next is theft or robbery. The violation of one's property is included in the understanding of boundaries. In the United States of America, these notions/ideas/concepts of boundaries have been made into law via the Bill of Rights (amendments to the US Constitution).

All citizens of the USA fall under the jurisdiction of the laws of the nation. Individuals are protected from harm (boundary violation) by the laws of the nation-state, enforced by the Department of Justice, which has the legal right to use force, if necessary, including deadly force. The Fourteenth Amendment tries to distinguish who is and is not a US citizen.

The CGC and social media allows for and engenders what some have called "the end of empathy."[50] There are, as yet, no laws or enforcement agency governing the rights of people on or in the connected global community.

Here's one story: empathy is best understood as Jesus Christ's proclamation from his Sermon on the Mount that "whatever you wish that men would do to you, do so to them, for this is the law and the prophets." In other words, the Golden Rule, which seems to be a universal human requisite for social and civil living. But, a big but, it also seems to require socialization (i.e., it's not innate but must be learned), which brings us back to the top of this discussion: how does one best acquire interpersonal behaviors? By religious instruction and proclamation? No. The answer is by watching and imitating powerful others (one's parents).

---

[50]   Stephanie Wittels Wachs, "The End of Empathy" (April 20, 2016).

All this is preamble to the current contentious presidential election in the USA and candidate Donald J. Trump's recent formal foreign policy speech. The speech was, essentially, a speech about boundaries and the condition of love. Trump's foreign policy speech can be found here: https://www.youtube.com/watch?v=XW8.

What Mr. Trump did was to inform the world just what were exactly his and, by extension (should he win the election), the USA's boundaries with regard to world affairs. He told the world that things (i.e., boundaries) are going to change. Trump declared, "We will not surrender to the false song of globalization" (found at the 41:47 mark of the speech), which is—a false sense that the connected global community can take the place of a real community—a place with a strong boundary where everyone looks out for one another, be it the nuclear family, a block in a city, a small town, or a country.

Another story is that people are different. It doesn't matter if it's in a family, on a block, in a trailer park, or in a refugee camp, whatever. In any community, there is more variation, meaning personality types, within a group than between groups, say, people in Manhattan versus people in Denver (the whole "New York values" thing is a false distinction), black versus white, Muslim versus Christian, between brothers or sisters in the same family, whatever. In other words, there are all types of people/personalities in any group of people, but/and you must take care of those closest to you first. You love your spouse first, then your children, then your neighbor, and so on and so forth. You respect a person's boundaries. *They* set the limits, and *you* respect them. That's how it works. It's the same with nations.

With Trump as president, the rules for engagement and interaction will be clear and be enforced. The USA will no longer be a victim, a doormat! At the same time, Mr. Trump said we will be flexible with regard to who is and is not a friend and/or ally but with some exceptions, such as in matters of the rape and murder of US citizens and the theft of their property (intellectual as well as physical). That will no longer be excused or tolerated and will be dealt with quickly and forcibly![51] The physical borders of the nation will be respected and enforced. The wall will be built! People will be invited in, but as guests, unless we decide to adopt them. And they must accept and respect our boundaries, our values, and our Bill

---

[51]   See current Asia trip, November 11, 2017.

of Rights. In other words, Daddy is here. The USA will not become the RTC of the world.

As to love, love is, in real life, a set of specific behaviors expressed in Trump's speech encompassing and including the concept of boundaries. Love is, in basic general terms, giving a person (and, by extension, a group and/or a nation-state) your time and attention, sharing yourself and being honest and also being vulnerable while at the same time setting limits! Love is watching out for one another concerning danger and at the same time being gentle. It is about always being loyal, standing with those you love in good times and bad. In essence, it's about having high regard for the other to the point of a willingness to die so they might live. Unfortunately, the word has been compromised by "concept creep."[52] In other words—concepts, like love, have been hijacked.

Mr. Trump, when asked at a town hall meeting whether he would rather be loved or feared (re: Machiavelli), he responded, "I'd rather be respected. Okay." The questioner had no follow-up. Respect, given/earned, is to be equals, to be held in high regard, which is different from being loved or feared. Competitors, opponents, can be held in high regard without being loved or feared. This is a healthy state of affairs and tends toward a drive to excel (or progress). In Trump's speech, he suggested not a policy of imposing our values and beliefs on others but, rather, a policy of mutual respect where the other would want to be like us by way of inspiration—much the way a child respects his father and mother and so wishes and strives to be like them. You see this exhibited in Mr. Trump's adult children. There is no need for force.

Is it possible to have a human world, a peopled world, with healthy boundaries? The answer is, I don't know. But shouldn't we give it a chance? This is not unlike David Foster Wallace's riddle set forth in his first novel, *The Broom of the System* (which, by the way, Wallace never solved): "Is the barber who shaves all and only those who do not shave themselves . . . The big killer question is whether the barber shaves himself. I think that's why his head exploded . . . If he does, he doesn't, and if he doesn't, he does." (p. 42). (Wallace hung himself at the age of 46 in 2008.)

So I know that I am asking a lot—to consider contradictory things—of things that on the surface don't make sense.

----

[52]   See Nick Haslan.

Everybody knows Trump is a racist, sexist bigot and xenophobe, right? And yet *maybe* he knows, senses, that some things we have been taught about people are wrong. Maybe he knows what love is. It's possible. Maybe he solved the riddle without knowing what the riddle is.

In the 1994 *Atlantic* article "The Coming Anarchy" (see the following chapter), the author described the area between Mexico and the USA as a "buffer entity," meaning it was an area of indeterminate real boundary between Latino/Mexico and American/USA cultures, language, and geography. In other words, it was an area that was culturally in chaos, "an ever-mutating representation of chaos." This results in utter confusion, or a state (in every sense of the word), that has been proven to be unhealthy for human children to grow up in. In such a state, only the strong/fit survive. It's governed by jungle rules. Okay, if that is the world you want.

The alternative is definite boundaries—in this case, a wall. On that side of the wall, the south side, you are Mexican and subject to the laws and governance of the Mexican government or drug cartels, whatever. On this side of the wall, the north side, you are a citizen of the USA and subject to its laws and protections or a legal visitor (see above). On the southern side, you speak Spanish; the northern, English. You are free to come and go, to pass from one entity to the other, but must respect and are subject to the laws and culture of that entity/country. One entity is not superior to the other. There is not a "land of confusion" with regard to the law and language. You are free to visit, but if you wish to stay, to reside, to take up residence, you must adapt to and submit to the laws, language, and customs of the country you reside in. Like if I invite you into my home for a visit, I expect you to adhere to my idiosyncrasies (shoes, smoking, swearing, sleeping, sex, nudity, etc., *my boundaries!*). And if you don't, your visit will be short. If you refuse to leave, I may have to resort to force. If I can't enforce my rules/laws/boundaries, then I, as an independent individual, am doomed.

I know people who have built emotional and psychological walls, impenetrable walls around themselves, to protect against hurt and/or pain—the possibility of being violated, psychic armor. People do that, and yet when they do finally let someone in, they wind up getting hurt.

To be alive is to take some risks and sometimes suffer.

The Coming Anarchy: Shattering the Dreams of the Post–Cold War (2000) by Robert D. Kaplan

BOOK REVIEW BY YOURS TRULY
MAY 7, 2016

Wait, what! Did I write this book? No. At the time it was written, the late '90s, I was rehabilitating young minds (see "Boundaries") and not all that concerned with world affairs, but now I do agree with most of what the author thinks about the "peopled world." This book, a collection of essays concerned with international affairs and America's involvement, all written before 9/11, is mind-blowing for its predictive accuracy. I suspect that's because Kaplan takes a *realistic* worldview versus a wishful, humanistic, or idealistic one. The first essay, the title of the book, is twenty thousand words of what should be mandatory reading. Kaplan accurately describes the world as it is today, with the real problems: population explosion combined with environmental degradation, mass poverty and migration, confounded by man-made false borders and ill-understood tribal, ethnic, and cultural differences that fuel conflict, which many men find stimulating and economically viable (i.e., war works). It is a subject explored in more depth in the final essay, "The Dangers of Peace."

When you finish reading the first essay, keep reading. The next, "Was Democracy Just a Moment," will blow your mind as to how accurately it describes today, even the Bernie Bro phenomenon. It describes the community yours truly lives in, Westminster, Colorado—a community of strip malls, golf courses, private health clubs, strict zoning, generic architecture, zero crime, Disneyesque attractions and playgrounds—in other words, a gated community without a gate. It is a society of "mice-like conformists" addicted to a technological complexity that has threatened our healthy individuality by constant streams of "other people's opinions," whom we no longer have any real interaction with. "As communities become liberated from geography, as well as more specialized culturally and electronically, they will increasingly fall outside the realm of traditional governance. Democracy loses meaning if both rulers and ruled cease to be part of a community tied to a specific territory" (p. 87). In other words, we are (at least some, the postmodern liberal humanists and the international corporate globalists) denying who we really are (Kaplan quotes Ben Franklin, who calls mankind "toolmaking animals") in the service of profit for the few. The author, more precisely than he could know, states, "We have become voyeurs and escapists," which echoes David Foster Wallace's *Infinite Jest*, published between the two essays, by the way.

In "Kissinger, Metternich, and Realism," I like this: "A true conservative is in fact a hesitant progressive: he or she seeks to slow change when society is reforming too fast and to instigate moderate change when society is not reforming at all" (p. 136). Summarizing Kissinger, Kaplan writes that idealism leads to an inefficient cycle of intense hope (Obama's "hope and change" and now Sanders's "a future you can believe in") and activity (speeches and rallies and protests) abroad (and here) followed by morose withdrawal (drugs, entertainment, and screens, also predicted by Wallace in *Infinite Jest*) once it became apparent that hope and activity were unlikely to remake the world (pp. 137–8).

In "Conrad's *Nostromo* and the Third World," Kaplan iterates, "Literature, alas, may be the only salvation for the policy elite, because in the guise of fiction a writer can more easily tell the truth." By the way, Hunter Thompson said that, also Hemingway. "*Nostromo*, like any great story, is about individuals and their desperate need for love" (p. 162). Hemingway also said that. I love this: "Authentic heroes like Nostromo are motivated by personal vanity rather than ideals, and that such vanity, rather than something bad, is the true source of incorruptibility" (see Trump). "We often do the most noble things in politics for the most personal of reasons, and not for those we publicly espouse . . . the desire for wealth or for the admiration of beautiful women may, in fact, preserve objectivity far better than the desire to save a million people" (p. 167).

The last essay, "The Dangers of Peace," is brilliant! It summarizes the conundrum of three important personal and political axes: pleasure/pain, self/other, and active/passive, within the context of war and peace. *This is a must read.*

Running Mates

MAY 8, 2016

Life is a campaign. Chris Matthews (MSNBC commentator, host of *Hardball*, and author) wrote a book with that title back in 2007 when the 2008 presidential election was heating up. In 2008, I wrote this about that:

> In Chris Matthews's current book, *Life's a Campaign*, he gushes over politicians and what we can all learn about life from them. The politician's message: do whatever it takes to win. Life is a zero-sum game, a fight to the death. Steal, cheat, backstab, and then lie about it all. Machiavelli had it right. This is a discordant book, and I hope, and it does look like, that most people "reject and denounce" the politicians' model. What is Congress's approval rating? It's in the teens. Why? Because people can't stand politics and "business as usual." We want a change, Chris. Obama is blowing up because the people think maybe this guy is *different*. This book is a sad story of American politics.

And then this:

> "PS. Summer, 2014. Chris Matthews was right; it appears life is a campaign. I say that now because of the explosion of social media (Facebook, Twitter, et al.), which are really advertising platforms and what is being sold is yourself. *You* are like a politician trying to get yourself elected. Votes aren't counted, but "likes" are. You put on your best face, stay positive and upbeat, become expert at the "humble brag," or as David Foster Wallace's couched it, "second order vanity," wherein a person pretends not to be vain outwardly, but actually is—just like a politician.

So here we are now, in May of 2016, and Mr. Donald J. Trump has defeated sixteen rivals, fourteen of whom were career politicians, and is the presumptive nominee of the Republican party, the Grand Old Party. But Trump isn't a politician; he's a businessman and a very successful one. He now, like Obama did back then, is promising that things will be different. I wonder?

I *believed* Obama. Now I want to believe Trump. What is different? What has changed? My thinking has is what. I was wrong then. People don't change. Politics and politicians don't change. The game (life) remains the same. *And* one always needs a running mate.

Choosing a running mate is a decision that all people, in the Western world (and all mammals) share, and that is the single most important decision a person makes. Many people (most?) get it wrong. *Why* is a most interesting question. The "misattribution of arousal"? (See footnote 14.) How can you tell if a person (you) has (have) made the right choice? Well, you can do that by looking back at the outcome of the purpose of the choice. In other words, did the (your) running mate help in meeting the (your) objective?

What is the objective of having a mate, a partner, to run with? For most people, I think, as Trump has said many times, "We all want the same thing," meaning to be happy. It's written in our very Constitution. He says, for him, that comes from and is about family.

I also think that happiness *can be* realized when Maslow's hierarchy of human needs are satisfied. Therefore, if one has good health, is safe and secure, feels like they are loved and needed, is respected for their achievement, and is free to actualize their desires, it would be safe to say that they're happy. All the rest is just a distraction or, as Freud might say, a sublimation—a substitute.

So I look at Trump, and what do I see? I see a very happy man in amazing health (for his age) whose family loves and respects him and has been tremendously successful in life, which says to me that he chooses good running mates. Now you might say, "Wait, what! He's been married three times! If he's so smart at picking mates, why is that?" I would reply that you must look at the outcome: his children and his business, the Trump Organization, how are *they* doing?

This brings us to the big question everyone is buzzing about today: Who will Trump choose as his running mate, his vice president? I'm going to suggest a good one would be Marco Rubio, though rumor has it he's been considered and rejected. I'm not buying it. Seems to me he's a perfect fit: Big Don and Little Marco. And also it's the final nail in the Bush dynasty, which has to make Trump smile on the inside. Take that, Jeb, George, and George! Marco was, after all, Jeb's supposed protégée. That's Trump's style—hit your rival where it hurts most, counterpunch much harder than you were hit. The Bush family, having not endorsed Trump but denounced him, will soon be finished in politics, remembered mostly for seventeen (and counting) years of war. Trump will have cuckolded Jeb's mate, just as he did in Texas with Cruz, getting Sarah Palin's endorsement, who earlier had campaigned for Cruz (and also, two for the price of one, slaying John McCain). But that's not all, Rubio, on many levels, satisfies, as well as being unemployed and out of politics.[53] He owes no one but brings political connections in the Senate, as well as connections to donors and constituents. Donald can mentor Marco and show him how to make deals and manage money, two areas in which Rubio showed weakness. It's a win for both men (nonzero sum), a good match, and good for the GOP as well. It's good for all of us, the species. Once schooled, Marco will be well positioned to take the reins in 2024. We're getting there slowly.

Revolution is man-made. Evolution is the way of the natural world and is amoral.

---

[53]   After dropping out of the campaign for president, Rubio ran and won for the Senate seat he had resigned.

But whomever Trump chooses, I'm pretty certain it will be a good choice. Trump has proven he knows what he's doing in choosing running mates.[54]

So today, Mother's Day, I ask this of you: Think critically of running mates, as you sit 'round your table, eating apple pie and drinking brandy and beer, whatever, maybe watching the Yankees battle the Red Sox on the TV. Who were the best battery mates, the best team, the best running mates ever? Whitey Ford and Yogi Berra of the New York Yankees, from 1950 to 1962? They were winners (World Series champions for six out of the thirteen years they played together).

I was going to fast today as a salute to the dyin' of Lyin' Ted and so sat down in my rocker and turned on the TV to MSNBC and saw her, Hillary Clinton, sitting there, talking. My head began to ache, then my ears throbbed, and I began to shake. I recalled, then, what she had said (was it yesterday? It all comes so fast) about me and my kind (Trump supporters), that I was a savage in need of a reservation and pacification to keep me under control. I actually snarled. I stood up, gathered my things, saddled my steed (metaphorically), and rode to the corner store. I bought whiskey, beer, and Black and Blue burgers and then went back home, contemplated paint and the dance of war. What a sexist has-been she is—compromised, crooked, crippled, and clueless. Who does she think she is? The next POTUS? Ha! I am certainly off the reservation, a fish out of water.

---

[54]   As it turned out, Trump chose Indiana's governor, Mike Pence, as his running mate and eventual vice president. It was an astute choice—Pence protects Trump's right flank and also is a hedge against impeachment, being much more conservative than Trump.

Election Update

MAY 13, 2016

Weekend primer: the whiteboard is back to explain the POTUS election via a Venn diagram. The country really has four parties: Conservative, represented by Paul Ryan; Socialist, represented by Bernie Sanders; Republican, represented by Donald Trump; and Democrat, represented by Hillary Clinton.

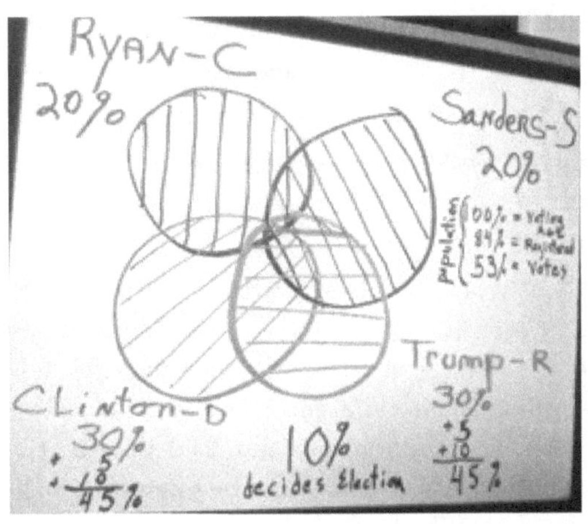

Who decides?—a Venn diagram showing four
voting groups and who represents them

The four parties and their representatives have some overlap regarding the issues, but all agree on only one thing, the small area in the center— that they all want and believe that they will win.

Of the USA's voting age population, 84% are registered voters (232 million). Of those, only 53% (on average) vote. Of those, 20% favor Ryan; 20%, Sanders; 30%, Trump; and 30%, Clinton. If the election comes down to Trump versus Clinton, each will get 15% of Ryan's and Sanders's voters (you can quibble with the percentages, but trust me). So the outcome of who becomes the leader of the free world will come down to 10% of 53% of the voter-eligible population or about 12 million people. But elections are not decided that way—by overall majority popular vote. Elections (in the USA) are decided by state electoral college votes, which total 538. Each state gets a number of votes depending on population size (determined by the US census), and the state's votes are all or nothing (except for Maine's, which has 4 votes and can be split). So who wins the election could come down to one state, a "battleground state" or "purple state," such as Colorado, which has 9 electoral votes. The election could be even at 264 versus 265 and then hinge on how Colorado votes. In this scenario, Colorado is the bomb! If Colorado, by one vote, goes for Trump, Trump *wins* as he gets all nine votes! But then, of course, there would be a recount, and it could take months—2000 all over again, but probably worse. There could be gunplay. Arm yourself! The fate of the world rests on *your* or your AR-15 and your state of mind, your nerves, or how much whiskey you drank.[55]

I think it's the coming anarchy and the dangers of peace, or there might be blood. Take your pick. It's the rise and fall of empires. People fight or flee or freeze—that's what they do. Head in the sand, in the cloud (staring at their screens), or up one's ——— all fall under freeze; some may fight, but many flee. Have you ever seen a rabbit freeze? It thinks you can't see it. A child will do the same thing, playing hide-and-seek. Or a student in class, if they "freeze," they think the teacher won't call on them. Sometimes, it works. So here we have a preview of what's to come:

---

[55]   As it turned out, Trump won 30 states, 306 electoral votes, and 46.1% of the record of 139 million voters. That record was still only 57%–60% (depending) of eligible voters. Two million four hundred thousand voters voted down ballot but not for POTUS. What would be interesting to know is, how many protestors didn't vote (like Colin Kaepernick) but, instead, fueled by some misdirected hurt/frustration/anger/rage, refused to pick one of the two choices for president. It *was* a close election.

if the national election is as close as I have laid out here, in the end it may come down to force (fight) or fatigue (flee). Did you see what happened at Saturday's Nevada Democratic convention on the fourteenth? Bear in mind, these were Democrats, Liberals, Progressives, and Socialists, all supposedly on the same side. Clinton was accused of rigging the vote, in effect stealing delegates, and obscenities, as well as chairs were thrown, the stage was rushed, and the whole show had to be shut down.

Here's more evidence of the coming violence. At a Clinton rally in SoCal on May 5, Sanders's fans got really aggressive, calling for Hillary to go to prison, that she's a fraud, a phony, and a pawn for special interests. Oh, the irony. Oh, it's coming, it's coming all right.[56]

---

[56] The irony is, these people are supposed to be peaceniks, tree huggers—those claiming that Trump, and men like him, is the cause of all the violence, injustice, and hatred in the world. Now it appears the Left has all come together in their hatred, per the amity/enmity complex. Seems there is tremendous hurt, anger, and rage that has been building up in a large segment of the population, and the target doesn't matter so much as the catharsis. Trump did not sow this hatred; it was there all along. Perhaps, in some cases, it was deeply buried, repressed. The sign "Love Trumps Hate" seen often at protests makes no sense whatsoever. Trump does not act out of hate (as far as I can tell); he is motivated most by a desire to triumph, to win, to achieve greatness, and to be recognized for his accomplishments, validation, and self-love. He's a builder and developer.

Hate is a very powerful emotion. It *can* drive people to extreme action, usually rooted in revenge, real or imagined, driven by the feeling one was wronged. Jealousy (real or imagined, loss of a love object—to another—of what was once yours, usually by unsavory means) often fuels hate. Trump doesn't hate; he doesn't lose. It could be that the radical Left, the postmodern liberals, the feminists, the social justice warriors, the victimized and the vulnerable, truly believed their time had come, that "the times they are a-changin'." But *this time* was the *real time*, that Bob Dylan had sung about. Many *actually* thought that Bernie Sanders could and would win! And with him leading the way, "the loser now will be later to win . . . Come, senators and congressmen, please heed the call." And so when Donald Trump won, *it had to have been stolen!* Thus, the hate. Not only was there real (individual) repressed anger, simmering for decades, but now also the winner *cheated!* Fuel to the fire that was/is hurt and anger.

Compound that with the indignation (the loss of esteem) of being *wrong*, and you have a "perfect storm." In other words, when it comes to human motivation, hate trumps love.

Aviate, Navigate, Communicate

MAY 21, 2016

"Aviate, navigate, communicate" is, what we are told, the pilot's creed when they find themselves in trouble. I think that is also a code to live by for us humans here on earth and one which most people do without being told, albeit some do better than others.

Let's examine. *To aviate* means to fly the plane or, here on earth, to manage the mundane and germane of daily life, i.e., feed yourself, keep warm, sleep, keep yourself and your space clean. Do what you have to do to keep moving, living. Do what you must to survive another minute, day, week, month, and so on—to live another day, to "be here now." *To navigate* means to answer these questions: Where am I? Where must I go? Where *can* I go? Where do I see myself in three years? These are serious, critical questions. A mistake can mean destruction. Are you lost? Where is the closest/safest place to turn toward that likely leads to happiness? It's the venerable "fork in the road." In other words, it's a life-and-death decision, one thing leading to another as it always does, baring divine intervention, which, granted, many (most) people rely on but that which the pilot cannot. *If you are the pilot,* you must take responsibility. You cannot count on divine intervention, something many (most) people abdicate to powerful others. People *will* surrender control, submit, to a powerful other. *To communicate* means to speak to another being as to the circumstance of your current events. In other words, "I am here. —— is my circumstance. I intend to ——. Or, "Can you help?"

Sometimes (I'm not entirely sure about this) the asked-for help *can* help and direct the pilot to safety—to live another day.

Thursday, May 19, 2016, all this abstract discussion slammed into the real world when the jet airliner EgyptAir 840 fell out of the sky and crashed into the Mediterranean Sea, killing all sixty-three persons on board. Almost immediately, Donald J. Trump, the presumptive nominee of the Republican Party, said/tweeted that this "looks like" terrorism and asked the question, When will we (American/humans) get "smart, tough, and vigilant"? Hillary Clinton, the almost certain Democratic nominee, waited hours and then said in an interview that it "seems like terrorism" and that we'll have to "wait for the investigation findings." Bernie Sanders, Hillary's still-alive challenger, has been silent. For Sanders, it's as if he lives by an altogether different doctrine that requires not aviation, navigation, or communication but ignore-ism. I am reminded of the person who sticks their head in the sand or the clouds or up their ——. In still other words, sweeps the dirt under the carpet and then imagines there is no dirt. Keep in mind, they all *know* nothing! No one has any definitive evidence.[57]

So here we (American citizens/voters) are facing a choice. It seems to me the choice is stark. For whatever reason (?), Sanders is out, and the choice is between Clinton and Trump. One is a woman; one a man. One is with experience in government; the other with experience in business. One who is cautious and waits for data and consensus; the other who is instinctive and acts quickly. One who blames others/history; one who takes responsibility. One who polls; one who decides. One who has been successful in politics; one who has been successful in business, with people, and with family and has made decisions that seem to indicate he'll land the plane safely.

---

[57] As of this writing, there is still no definitive known cause. One theory is a pilot's mobile phone overheated and caused a fire, which brought down the plane.

Anger and the Road to Hell

MAY 23, 2016

It has been a difficult week, a strange week, a lonely week. Partly, I'm sure, because I'm recovering from a visit from an old friend[58] who spent three boisterous and volatile days with me here at my home, and I rarely have guests. I don't mean to imply that his visit upset me. Quite the contrary, I enjoyed it immensely. We smoked weed and drank a lot of beer, but mostly, we argued loudly, actually shouting at each other. He's an angry fellow, in my opinion, and a Bernie Sanders supporter and a Stephen Curry / Golden State Warrior (NBA) fan.

I'm a Trump supporter. I think Sanders is an angry, vain, delusional old fool. Also, I don't care for Curry in the least. In my opinion, there's not enough mustard in the market to cover Curry. (In other words, he's a "hot dog," which used to be, back in the day, bad, bringing attention to yourself.) The look-away shot, really? When I played basketball (a long time ago), if an opponent had done that, I'd have put him down with a forearm shiver, accidentally of course. How is Curry's behavior different than Trump's? Curry plays *a game*, basketball, a metaphor; Trump plays *the game*, life.

---

[58] Whom, in this story, you'll soon meet—Gerry.

Anyway, so my friend leaves, and I'm alone again, watching the news and keeping up with the election. I see where President Obama names the bison as the national animal (I thought it was the eagle, but then I struggle to understand the ways of man, as in human animal, which many of my kind deny—that we humans are animals). It looks like pandering to me, to add the first Americans to his collision (oh, pardon me), I meant coalition, of voters, recognizing the old buffalo nickel with an "Indian chief" on one side and a bison on the other, as a "dog whistle"[59] to the Native population. And then right after, an incident happens in Yellowstone National Park where a foolish tourist with good intentions (is not the road to hell paved with good intentions?) decides to intervene in the ecosystem, which results in the park service having to put down (kill) a newborn bison calf. Social media goes berserk, steaming, spewing, and erupting like Old Faithful.

Human emotion is not unlike the nature of explosions in nature (i.e., compression and constraint make the explosion more forceful when it finally erupts) as it must. Freud was right again. I think that's where we are now, in the big scheme of things—on the verge of an eruption.

The incident in Yellowstone is an almost-perfect metaphor and so timely for what is happening around the world. It's almost as if there *is* a higher power sending signals, saying, "Wake up, wake up! Pay attention! Lest I have to remove you from the park [the planet]!" It's a hard lesson to learn, not to intervene, to let "nature [amoral as it is] take its course." We, and I include myself, think we are so smart that we can control things, that we can save others, that we can save the world. I'm reminded of something Don Marquis said, "The chief obstacle to the human race is the human race."

We can only know what we know. We are who we are. We are born knowing (instinct and intuition) and forget via culture and politics. We subsequently learn and adapt to the physical and cultural world we inhabit. We are influenced by the physical world but adapt to the cultural one and develop resistance to that which we were born knowing. We moan, complain, protest, and seek nourishment, satisfaction, acceptance, and validation. We *value* affiliation (the tribe) over authenticity (truth), security (safety) over freedom (self-actualization), with good reason. We are here now, neurotic at best, in the time/space physical "real" world. We do not know who we are, what we want, or what we feel. And so we rely on

---

[59] *Dog whistle* is a subtly aimed political message intended for a particular group.

experts and "salesmen" (of the snake oil kind) to tell us. We acquire habits, tendencies, and patterns; and many find those inadequate. But we adapt to the situation we are born into. We develop personalities and addictions. We lose ourselves and become shadows, impressions, projections, reflections, and perceptions. We are at war—war within and war without—against others who believe differently and against our true selves. We are at war against our own father and mother, against our brothers and sisters, against our children, against our spouses, against our rivals, against our government, against they, them, the other, the enemy, evil, the devil. And if we can afford it, seek out therapy for validation.

We try in desperation to get what we want but get more of what we don't want, simply because that is the way it has always been. So you are angry; you repress (or suppress) your anger in the hope that you will feel better (not angry) and then get angrier, because who and what you are at that moment is *angry*! Your only choice is how angry, but you want instead to avoid the hurt, the loss, of what is at the root of your anger. You know that to get along, you must go along, because no one likes angry. Agreement is what people want. You are not permitted to be who you are, and that makes you sick. Being sick gets you some attention and care, if not always, mother's milk and warmth (nourishment and protection)—what you really want.

The road to hell is paved with good intentions. Wildlife biologist Imogene Davis wrote a piece for the Outbound[60] about the incident in Yellowstone, which ironically/coincidentally, illustrates the conflict between humans and wildlife and the confusion of human (some) interpretation of their place on the planet. The piece speaks to human's good intention, resulting in the death of that (wildlife) which they (a human) intended to save. With this one incident, there is much to be learned.

1. The earth is a hostile, cruel, environment with no mercy.
2. The road to hell (unintended, negative, grief/pain-inducing outcomes) is paved with good intention.
3. Humans are (generally and cross-culturally) ill-educated.

---

[60] Imogene Davis, "A Response to the Yellowstone Bison Incident from an Actual Wildlife Biologist" (May 20, 2016), https://www.theoutbound.com.

Anger and/or outrage has at its root: hurt/loss/frustration/empathy/ narcissism/projection/displacement—all evolved emotions selected for their survival value for the individual, so as he/she/it may pass their genetic material (beingness) forward by the process of natural selection, which has been made obsolete by technology. Talk about irony.

This is from Davis:

> I spend a lot of time as a biologist talking about how wildlife don't actually need our help. They don't need to be saved from nature, and even when they do, it's not our job to save them. That may seem counterintuitive, harsh even, but wildlife conservation is about populations, not individuals.

Community

JUNE 2, 2016

A former student of mine, a worker, a wife and mother, posted on her Facebook status update recently a frustration, which after reading, I thought, *That about sums up what has happened to America, what Mr. Trump is getting at with his slogan, "Make America great again."* Here's the issue: she said (I'll not name her because she may not be a Trumpster and won't like that I've used her thoughts to back up his argument) that Longmont, Colorado, the town she lives in, has now twice the number of people (one hundred thousand versus fifty thousand) and half the number of shops it used to, which manifests into my friend/student must either shop online, Amazon Prime being a prime example, or drive out of town to a corporate box store, say, Walmart, to get that which she needs to carry on or do the germane and mundane of daily life (i.e., aviate, navigate, and communicate).

It didn't used to be that way. It used to be that a person shopped in town, and not only that but, and maybe more importantly, *knew* everyone *in town*—the business owners and their families. That was what was then known as community. Not so anymore, as the word *community* has been co-opted/appropriated/hijacked by the thought leaders—politicians, professors, pastors, social scientists, lawyers, and media persons—for the purpose of advancing their own agenda or well-being, be that getting themselves elected and/or improving their own status and salary. I'm not calling this a conspiracy or even consciously intentional for that matter. What I am thinking and suggesting is that it is the result of globalization, internationalism, and a borderless country and people doing what they do, which is to advance their own self-interests by whatever means present (i.e., by available circumstance).

Community now means a group of people connected by shared interests—likeness, likeability, and preferences, but not by a shared geography (physical environment), a shared interest in economic activity, and overall well-being with your neighbors. Some examples of the new *community* are the black community, the prison community, the Hispanic community, the Muslim community, the LBGTQ community, the military community, the law enforcement community, the evangelical community, the well-educated community, the less than well-educated community, the suburban community, the exurban community, the rural community, the homeless community, the biker community, the senior community, the introverted community, the green community, and so on and so forth. These *communities* have been designated by the elites (see above thought leaders) as voting blocks divided by "wedge issues" (see above shared interests). These are faux (false) communities and only possible because of the internet and, now, more than ever, social media. The result to the population as a whole is alienation and loneliness, which is making the population sick! (Donald Trump is not making the people sick, as put forth by one of the thought leaders I highlighted in a previous chapter, "Malpractice, Victimology, and the Greatest Problem," March 29, 2016.)

Here's the story: it is now the job of the media to highlight, amplify, and *create* conflict and problems, so as to generate interest and a need to know, to be informed/misinformed (no distinction), but mostly, to grab your attention and, ultimately, your money. This attention-grabbing allows for the selling of products that you may or may not need. That is the job of the mad men (Madison Avenue, New York, New York) and women (i.e., the snake oil salesmen) who work for the advertising companies to create clever ways to persuade you of what you need and want and also, historically, by the prophets and religious leaders. They do this by telling interesting stories now, in thirty seconds or less, using TV commercials (or long-form sermons, movies, books, documentaries, YouTube videos, whatever), and using emotional gimmicks (music, puppies, children, envy, and most effectively, anxiety and fear).

This is now called gaslighting (being manipulated into doubting your own memory, perception, and sanity); in other words, you don't know who or what you are until someone in authority (the thought leaders) tell you. This is possible because of the breakdown and breakup of *real* communities, which used to, literally, *ground* people or attach them to *something*—a community, its inhabitants, and the land—greater than themselves. The communities were made up of families, and the families were bound by proximity into a *tribe*, that all worked for the overall health and well-being of one another. This process *evolved* through the process of evolution (natural and sexual selection) via the biological and psychological elements of motivation and emotion, also known as survival, or suffering and struggle. In other words, life is hard, but humans are equipped well to manage it because of (real) community. We are "highly social primates."[61]

Back to Longmont, when I first came to Colorado in 1965, Longmont was mostly an agricultural community (i.e., farmland), with a town and main street to provide services. The North Saint Vrain Creek provided water for crops, drinking, etc. It's a beautiful place, named after the 14,251-foot Longs Peak, which is right there, looming over the town. The population was well below twenty thousand. The railroad ran through the town and moved products. But then, in the 1980s, things began to change as IBM, Seagate, and Amgen moved in. Farming and food production was outsourced. People began to work not outdoors on the land or indoors in shops but in cubicles. Now it seems most of the product produced in Longmont is beer and marijuana. (Back to farming?) Many people get high (self-medicate) and work in cubicles or in their home. Health care now is also big. There are a lot of sick people. (The USA had 4.4 billion, *billion*, prescriptions dispensed in 2015. That's, on average, 14 prescriptions for every man, woman, and child in the country. Yet the USA is ranked only thirty-fourth in the world in life expectancy. The amount of money involved in the drug industry is so immense it loses all comprehension, no matter how you break it down. The USA is the leader in prescriptions for pain and second in antidepressants. Overdose deaths in 2016 topped all the American soldiers killed in the Vietnam, Afghanistan, and both Gulf Wars *combined*! IBM and Seagate are part of the new global, high-tech *community*,

---

[61]   Bobbi S. Low, *Why Sex Matters: A Darwinian Look at Human Behavior* (2000), 4.

and Amgen is a big pharmaceutical drug corporation traded on the New York Stock Exchange. This is woven into a big, huge ball of radio(active) invisible waves that are causing the disintegration (the breaking apart of families and real communities) of America. This *is* the false connected global community that the elites are selling, which is what, in reality, is causing people to get sick, tired, and *angry*, except for a very few, which the elites are paid by to keep things the way they are.

I know this because I see it all around me when I venture out into the real world. I see all the lonely people—overweight and sluggish, schlepping about their routines, walking their dogs[62] and looking down at their phones. I didn't need my former student to tell me. This *is* what Donald J. Trump has tapped into and is trying to explain with his run for the presidency of the United States. There *is* a con going on in America, but it's not Donald Trump who's selling it. The con is being sold by the elites, the thought leaders, paid for by the richest of the rich, all who make up the crooked community (my label): drug companies, media corporations, politicians, professors, pundits, publishers, pushers, preachers, journalists, salesmen, and lobbyists.

The faux communities are not real! They were invented by the elites to sell you products and enhance their own status and well-being. This has been going on since forever but, with the new connected global community (a big lie), is now so magnified and powerful and able to gaslight you into oblivion and addiction while, at the same time, you swear you know right from wrong and up from down or conversely—that everything is connected and we are all one. But the exploding problems *are* real. The

---

[62] In fairness, I've also seen a person walking his dog while riding his skateboard (the dog pulls him uphill), and yes, the person was a young male. But, and here's the point, a pet (dog or cat) is a substitute for an intimate or functional/productive/useful relationship with another human. I would like to interview that dude, but once he knows that his response is (might) being (be) publicized, that fact affects/alters his answer. So I take a picture (proof) that the event happened and then have to make an inference: the dude is not married and prefers a dog who will pull him on a skateboard to a female partner who he has to negotiate with in regard to daily life (i.e., aviate, navigate, communicate). Maybe I'm wrong. Maybe he's married, and his wife is an accomplished professional. And he's satisfied with his role as dog walker and/or chief cook and bottle washer. But I doubt it—in other words, it's fake news.

Footnote to a footnote: Mr. Trump and his wife, Melania, have no pets.

most destructive problems facing the country are joblessness, homelessness, mental illness, addiction, and disordered personalities. (This *is* the "infinite jest" David Foster Wallace wrote about but didn't understand.)

This is *why* Trump resonates with so many people. The message he is selling is instinctive and intuitive—the basic, primal drive/need to survive via attachment to a tribe/community. That emotive, psychological, and biological imperative, the territorial imperative if you will, satisfies Maslow's hierarchy of motivational needs when lived out. The land/territory and the tribe provide for the individual's health, safety, security, love and affiliation, esteem and validation, and finally, self-actualization. It's not—as the elites and especially the media would have you believe—some racist, sexist, xenophobic bigotry. *That* is about them, not Trump. The disintegration of society is a manifestation of a misguided attempt, a wrong turn, of the Progressive movement's desire to seize power nonviolently, a nonviolent revolution, as well as an attempt by the hard-core Conservatives and elites to cling to power.

Joblessness, homelessness, mental illness, addiction, and disordered personalities are problems best ameliorated at the local level, with family and community intervention, not by federal laws, rules, and regulations or regulators and bureaucracies (i.e., the state, socialism).

Look at Trump's history and biography; hear what he is saying as I have (I barely knew who he was before his run). You will see that he checks all the boxes of family and community and the *idea* that America (the country and idea) is the manifestation of the freedom to grow and expand and be who you are—the American dream.

Mr. Trump, eccentric and controversial as he is, is proud of his family, proud of his name, and proud of his business, company, and success. He is proud of his country.

As a young man at his father's side, he looked at the skyscrapers of Manhattan and fell in love with tall buildings. Influenced by the preaching of Norman Vincent Peale's philosophy (the power of positive thinking), he took it upon himself to go across the river and pursue his dream. He built a huge, tall skyscraper, moved into it, claimed it as his own, and settled in to his new community—New York city.

Donald Trump was born into a family as we all are and started as we all do, helpless and dependent, and grew—influenced by his genetic, geographic, and cultural environment—and has taken that beginning to the limit. Now he wants to share that to "make America great again" via the same process that worked for him: family, love, discipline, hard work, togetherness, and loyalty.

Look at the three tenets/values of Conservatism: God, family, and country. You can start to see why our country is splitting apart and why the great divide exists. The Progressive Movement is about upending those core values[63] and replacing them with spiritualism, humanism, multiculturalism, pluralism, feminism, and globalism, under the guise of freedom, inclusion, and tolerance, when what is really happening is just a power play, using the woman card, the race card, the social justice card—in other words, identity politics. You (mostly young people) are being gaslighted! The problem is the breakup and breakdown of the traditional structure of society (family/tribe/community), which evolved within the human species to advance and enhance the individual's successful struggle for survival and remains at the core of human health and well-being. That core is being disrupted. In other words, at the root of health and happiness is family and community working together or tribalism. The Progressive Movement has turned the phrase "family values" into a slur.

---

[63] Though close in meaning, I think there needs to be a distinction between beliefs, values, boundaries, and preferences.

Belief is the acceptance of something as true absence of any scientific evidence. In other words, a belief is founded upon faith and/or trust.

Value is a standard or principle that represents one's judgment of what is important.

Boundary is one's individual determination of sacred space.

Preference is one's personal belief with regard to values and boundaries. (For example, a woman who is very flat chested is very hard to be a 10. That is a preference. A flat-chested woman *can* be a 10. Ten is a number assigned to a person, place, or thing—meaning of the highest quality. *Quality* is a value determined by inspection based on variable criteria, depending upon one's knowledge of the subject/object. Knowledge is acquired by experience and study, interacting with time and intelligence.

These four words represent, in essence, one's inner thoughts expressed outwardly by one's behavior. When there is conflict between one's inner and outer self, there is disorder/chaos (i.e., incongruity) between what one believes (thinks) and what one does (how one behaves). And then the congruent or incongruent self must interact with the *community*, which has set (agreed on) beliefs, values, boundaries, and preferences, usually expressed in written laws, enforced by the threat of shame, aggressive force, and/or imprisonment, and then if one is lucky, a trial, where judgment is passed upon one's actions.

Try it this way—the value of family is priceless.

Sebastian Junger's latest book, *Tribe: On Homecoming and Belonging*, explores this by looking at the exposed reality of post-traumatic stress disorder and suicides among the population of America's soldiers returning from war. Junger suggests it's not the trauma of war making them sick but the absence of community upon coming home. The soldiers are shocked by the loss of the *tribe* in battle. They now feel alienated and alone, just like many of the people who didn't go to war. *Communities* in name are not real! Declared families are not real! There is no substitute for the structure and protection of a mother and father for children, supported by others living in proximity, bound and grounded to the land in struggle against a common hazard and/or enemy![64]

But no one knows what's going on, or if they do, they won't tell you. The Progressive agenda is not the answer. It sounds good, everyone just getting along and loving one another and sharing all the money and resources, but it's not who we are. We didn't evolve that way, in that world. *That is not the world we live in. We know this by looking at what is happening (i.e., reality).* The only possible solution is to understand who and what we are and to construct a society that recognizes our nature—competitive, comparative, sexual beings. We are individuals, families, and tribes linked together in a struggle for survival in a chaotic and hostile world. No matter what tools we invent to make life easier, *that* fact remains. We are, each individual, the result of a sexual act between a man and a woman (at the least, a sperm penetrating an egg) and are dependent on those two people and the community and the land to survive to maturity and then to repeat that process! That's life. (End of story?)

We humans have not yet evolved (if we ever will) to the being that needn't kill or deceive one another but *respects* boundaries and borders, different beliefs and values, and different individual preferences and constructs enforceable laws without the need for violence to engender coexistence. Maybe we can have fair and free exchange of goods and

---

[64]   This is the amity/enmity complex. It is biological and rooted in our DNA and grounded by the land. It *is* life. The hazard of life is real. The planet Earth, the third rock from the sun, is a chaotic, hostile environment. To live is to struggle against nature and other beings and forces, seen and unseen, known and unknown, consciously and/or unconsciously.

services and nonlethal, cooperative competition, but we are not yet there. Regardless, it (nonviolence) must start at the simplest unit, the family, and work out from there. We are who we are.

Trump is not about dividing but about unity, and he understands that it starts at the beginning of conception and gradually spirals into larger and larger circles. His worldview is based on his own life—family love and support, struggle and triumph, and joy. Now he wants to share that, first with his country and then the world.

It's not that hard to see, except for all the intellectual fog and emotional manipulation going on (i.e., people doing what people do—looking out for themselves, trying to "make it" even if it requires distorting reality, and tearing down others). This, too, is understandable. It comes under the rubric of cognitive dissonance (crooked and twisted thinking to justify one's own behavior). Again, all this is intertwined into the process of evolution, which, by the way, doesn't give two hoots about you. I realize that many of you are tenderhearted and tender-minded and just want everyone to be kind and smart and loving, but it isn't so.[65] That's not who we all are. People are different. Some are stronghearted and tough-minded, and others are any and everywhere in between strong and tough and weak and tender. You cannot will, wish, or force others to be like you.

Mr. Trump is one of the strongest and toughest. I can't imagine what it must be like taking all the abuse he does. People of all sorts and manner try to bring him down. I could never hold up under that onslaught.[66]

---

[65]   Hans and Michael Eysenck, "Politics, Personality, and Prejudice," chap. 25 in *Mind Watching: Why We Behave the Way We Do* (1989, 1994). It comes with my highest recommendation.

[66]   In fact, I didn't. I collapsed. I came out very early (on Facebook) as a supporter of Mr. Trump, and immediately my friends began to abandon or viciously (verbally) attack me. Some of these people I'd known for fifty years; others I'd never met in real life but had known for years through Myspace and Facebook and my books. Many had been admirers of my intellect and work in many different fields and industries. With the attacks and abandonment, *betrayal* is perhaps the word that best sums it up, manifested in severe physical bodily pain, so much so that on August 2, 2017, I sought a professional medical evaluation. I was crippled. There wasn't any specific disease or diagnosis that fit, but on a 0 to 10 scale of pain, I was a 9.5. By late August, the pain was so intense, constant, and restrictive I was contemplating suicide. On August 22, I booked my first session with a psychologist, a third-wave behaviorist, a CBT

Maybe what he wants can't be done—to bring jobs and communities back, to make people healthy and happy, to forge strong families and a strong, united country, and to make the American dream real again. Maybe we (humans) have gotten too successful, grown too large, too big, for the land to sustain us. Maybe we've outgrown or gotten too self-contained (isolated via the internet) for true community, what with the connected global community. We have outsmarted ourselves to the point we have overwhelmed and overrun the planet until the only thing that can save us is war—or another planet.

It was quite a day in politics yesterday. Hillary Clinton gave *her* foreign policy speech, and *had nothing* but a dishonest attack on Donald Trump. She had had it written for her, practiced it, and then delivered it to a small audience, with stooges planted in strategic places to prompt the applause and laughter. After which, Mr. Trump gave an off-the-cuff speech to a large crowd and responded, "We're going to bring back sanity to our country."[67]

On June 3, 2016, the latest economic data comes out. The only jobs growth is in health care (because we're so sick), government (because that's what the government does—grow itself), and retail (because we need more coffee and pet shops?). Mining and logging, construction, and manufacturing jobs were all way down. These are the real jobs, real work. Work that can support a family and that one can be proud of continues to wane.

And so it continues—dishonest reporting, the complete ignoring and/ or denying of what's really going on, the propaganda and fake news for selfish purposes. What's the remedy? I watch streaming live video of events all day on this channel out of Phoenix, Arizona, FOX 10. There's mostly no commentary. It's like CSPAN but covers the Western US and election events. Yesterday, I watched Hillary and Bill Clinton live in California, an oil train bomb explosion in Oregon, and a mountain rescue on Longs Peak here in Colorado, all as they happened, live. Then in the evening, I tuned in to Rachel Maddow to see how she covered the violence at

---

and Buddhism practitioner. By mid-October, I was regaining my strength and verve. By January 2018, I was able to return to working on this book.

[67]   As of March 14, 2018, there is no evidence of that. The collective insanity (my friend Marco "Madrush" calls it metapsychosis), if anything, has gotten worse.

Trump rallies in California. Here is the link: https://www.youtube.com/
watch?v=QQmbn7ndvZQ

(See also Rachel Maddow reports.) She doesn't, of course, as she's a left-wing activist posing as a reporter/journalist—twisting, distorting, filtering, and editing events of the day to sow conflict and her Progressive agenda and her hatred for Donald Trump and, of course, to up her ratings. This is why Mr. Trump calls the media "sleaze" and "scum." Good words that accurately portray what they (most of them, not all) are doing.

What *I* do is watch the events live without commentary, then check my Twitter feed to see what the "journalists" are tweeting, and then watch what they report in the papers or on TV. Maddow is one of the worst. Consider this: On March 17, she did a report called "The Dark Arts," a thirteen-minute piece where she showed a clip of the cancelled Trump event in Chicago, of supporters clashing with anti-Trump persons. She showed the clip twenty times. The message she was pushing was clear (again, see Rachel Maddow reports). And so I checked in on her last night. Yes, she covered the violence at the Trump event in San Jose but with no reference or link to her previous clever blather. This violence is not of Trump's doing but more of Maddow's and the rest of the dishonest media's. They have an agenda, and it's not—I repeat—*not* in your or the country's best interest.

The word *community* has been hijacked. You are being deceived and lied to.

The Case against Trump / the Great Debate

SUMMER, 2016

Meet Max. (Max is a fictional composite of real people I know.) Max is angry. He lives in a coastal city, is white, is thirty years old, is college educated, and considers himself "spiritual." Max is a Bernie Sanders supporter. Max is relatively poor. Max resents people who make/have more money than he does/has because he views his work, teaching, the most noble and important of professions. Max is burdened by debt—student loans and credit card consumption. He's been unlucky in love. Smart and attractive women don't give him the time of day, so he's taking to being an advocate for feminism and other minority community issues and positions, hoping to find someone, and "something," to love and validate him. He doesn't understand the world as it is. He's pessimistic. He hates America and capitalism. He often roots for the USA to lose in international competitions. Max is mild mannered, tender-minded, and tenderhearted. He is submissive, "kind," and passive-aggressive.

The Democratic Socialist Platform Bernie Sanders is peddling—universal ("free") health care, "free" education, the "living wage," or universal basic income—appeals to his sensitivities. He doesn't understand the true cost of those ideas. Buying a home isn't in his future, not with his debt and income. The real estate market has passed him by. He thinks, no, *needs to believe* that Trump is sinister, evil, Hitler-like. He's bought into the negative portrait of Trump—that he's delusional and paranoid, a sexist, a racist, a xenophobic fascist. Max doesn't believe that Trump knows anything about anything, such as trade policies, world affairs, climate change, etc. He thinks Trump is an arrogant blowhard. Trump must be stopped, he *knows* for the good of the world!

I respond, over the course of the summer of 2016, because I think, *no*, because I *know*, because I've read Trump's books (see my reviews), watched interviews with him from the '80s and '90s, watched (most) all the current interviews and rallies live, without "expert" commentary. I was an unknown guest at a Trump hotel—that Trump is a very smart, successful, confident, aggressive man who knows what he's doing and saying (albeit in a style that can be off-putting to some). Mr. Trump, for sure, is no scholar or intellectual. He might not be able to articulate the distinction between ultimate and proximate cause of behaviors, but he knows what works and what doesn't with regard to getting things done, to accomplishing goals. He's a successful man, that's M-A-N. He is a very traditional masculine man, which, it seems, many want to phase out of existence (make extinct).

I've also read Mr. Obama's autobiography, twice, and listened to many of his speeches and rallies. And I've watched and participated in the real world and studied human behavior and psychology for over fifty years. Yes, psychology, especially Freud, is all about making the unconscious conscious. And by doing that, some (humans) can moderate our base drives and instincts and bad habits that we might have learned from powerful others (parents and their replacements/surrogates). And yes, tribalism (which Trump taps into) has a bad rap, but it's not deserved. The tribe (family/clan) survived via its culture (to include worship/beliefs/religion), its tradition, and its ability to adapt to whatever enemy or hazard the ever-changing environment presented. Or we (humans) would not be here today, as the complex, highly social creatures (animals, specifically primates) as we are.

In community versus tribalism, the *tribe* is the people and can be mobile and/or separated and go different ways, migrate. Back to Freud, he speaks of the "primal horde" as the beginning of mankind. At some point in time—two, three, four million years ago—something like that happened, where a mutant, the missing link (Horace), mated with an apelike creature. And then the naked ape lineage began, becoming more and more different until voila—modern humans evolved, tribes of genetically related individuals wandering around, surviving. Blah, blah, blah . . . migrating into farther and farther places, separated by physical geographic barriers and boundaries, developing cultures, economies, and behaviors adapted to those places. And so tribes became distinct. With agriculture, tribes settled down into permanent places, and voila, communities happened. So a community is a *place* made up of varied individuals who have settled down together with a common interest—survival, via economic activity that accommodates different personalities (with different skill sets and talents).

In modern America, this manifested in small towns and larger cities centered around a particular activity, such as fishing, farming, ranching, logging, railroads, manufacturing, mining, protection, and so on. One way to think of a community is by high schools and, of course, high school sports, especially football back in the day. So a community might be represented by twenty thousand people—one, two, or three thousand of whom were boys and girls aged fifteen to eighteen. Everyone knew everyone, and the best representation of the community was (is) the high school yearbook. People were (are) born into a community and stayed there, except for a few adventurers, misfits, and also the very smart who might go away to college, where young adults from different tribes mixed. And lo, lust and sex and whatnot took over, and voila, postmodern America was born. Something like that is what happened. Toss in some wars (America, in its 240-year history, has very few years where it hasn't been involved in war. "They" don't tell you that) and you've got still more mixing of tribes, as well as the need for innovation, manufacturing, and mobility.

In my case, while I am member of a tribe (first settled in Orange County, New York, in the 1690s, where we have a museum), I belong to no community. I have no hometown, being a military brat. The closest I can come to a hometown is Fort Collins, where I went to high school and then college. I spent five years there, from age fifteen to twenty. But I was different from the others who were born there (the townies) and whose ancestors settled the place on the banks of the Poudre River in the 1800s. But there *were* three communities in Fort Collins. There were the white townies and then the college community (Colorado State University), which was in the beginning an agricultural and forestry college. And lastly, there was the cheap labor community—immigrants from Mexico. They lived, literally, on the other side of the tracks in their own special place called Andersonville. Looking at my old yearbooks tells quite a tale. All that is gone now, mostly. There are now three high schools, the college has expanded, and corporations and franchises abound. Most of the family-owned businesses are gone. People come and go for all manner of reasons.

Recently, at the request of family, I had my DNA examined. (One's DNA is put into a database and compared, and thus, your tribal origins can be located.) It's become a popular thing to do. I am 91.8 percent European (67.8 percent southern), 5.4 percent Iberian, and 2.9 percent Middle Eastern.

There is so much misinformation now (grabbing the headlines), being used as weapons, about race and sex and class and country and community. It's sad. And I think, it's bad. You could call it fake news.

Now we modern humans haven't changed or evolved for maybe forty thousand years (since the brain reached its 1,300 cubic centimeter capacity and the introduction of art, like cave paintings). How do we *know* anything? Art, religion, and science—those three fields inform us of our world. But now those three ways of knowing are being challenged, threatened, by artificial intelligence, which no one person can actually explain. We don't really know about language until people began to make records of words (document) or write things down. So it's speculation that human emotions are the same now as they were forty thousand years ago. But it's reasonable to make that assumption based on the pleasure/pain axis (such as the sexual orgasm is a universal reward system that keeps things going via reproduction and pain causes us to recoil/flinch/grimace/ restrict) and the self/other axis (tribal living versus an individual's isolation, which spawns loneliness, sadness, despair, and sickness, which seems to be, ironically, where we're headed). Again, with regard to survival success for the species, the active/passive axis suggests the basis of individual differences, specifically that of personality, are paramount for the species' survival. Again, tribal cohesion provides a much better chance of surviving an enemy or hazard. [68]

---

[68] A group of people—similar but different in talent, skills, and personality— bonded together against a common enemy and/or hazard within a specific territory, which seems to me may give that group of people the best possible

So I think nothing has changed biologically, emotionally, or psychologically in over two thousand generations, only the threats, due to changes in technology and the human population's expansion and distribution. As a reminder, Hillary's current slogan is "Fighting for us," which just goes to show how clueless she is. So she's *fighting* against *them* (who is powerful white men?) on our (women's, people of color's, children's?) behalf. Who *are they*—the successful? The white supremacists? The super predators? The most super of predators was her husband.[69]

All right, yes, Trump seems to suggest that Obama is an other. I read his autobiography, *Dreams from My Father* (1995), and he is definitely not attached to a tribe or community here in the USA. So why did he choose to be a community organizer in Chicago? Calling Dr. Freud.

Trump's mention of the 9/11 "Muslim dancing in the streets" thing. I remember watching the coverage of the immediate aftermath, and I recall seeing Muslims celebrating. It was shown again and again on CNN, but maybe the celebrating was in Iran or something. It *was* a long time ago, fourteen years. But now it is true that Muslim countries have an unfavorable opinion of the USA due to, no doubt, events *since* then. There is a hostility toward the USA and Christians across the Muslim world. Who knows what is what and who is who—friend or foe? You just can't

---

chance to survive. This is the foundation of the amity/enmity complex or $A = E + h$. A common objection to this theory would be the Buddhist perspective wherein there are no enemies but only *life*, which is suffering, not to fight against but only to accept. The Christian objection would be that humans are sinful and can only find peace through the acceptance and forgiveness of Jesus Christ, the son of God. And then there is the Muslim, Hindu, and a few others' perspectives. Only one of these ideas/theories/perspectives is true, which is one reason we fight. Might makes right, right?

[69] I don't even know where to begin with this, other than to say maybe there is a god looking out for us? The #metoo and #timesup movements (modern Western women protesting publicly their submission to the desires of men and then collectively saying "No more") are a response to the question: What do *you* (women) want? This is a question Freud, Tolstoy, and many others have asked. The answer for the moment seems to be not *that*—the desires of men. I submit that Maslow's theory of the hierarchy of human individual motivations/needs is correct for all humans—male, female, and so on—and also subject to cultural imperatives and demands, which are now subject to a borderless/boundary-free, connected world. This is not going to work out well, in my opinion. Too much freedom? More than most can bear?

tell anymore. This is part of the breakdown of boundaries and borders, and with the magnitude of weaponry now, it's just a hazard/enemy that is way more dangerous than a guy with a knife or spear. A temporary ban on all immigration until better ways of knowing are figured out is not unreasonable. Friend or foe?

(Have you watched *The Americans?*)

South Korea/North Korea? Trump can work that out. He's great at making deals. Most of what he says is only an opening salvo. The real question is, What's up with the Korean people? Do they hate one another? North and South? Who's who? Are there tribes going back thousands of years? I don't know anything about Korea, but maybe Trump can work out a deal with the North and South.[70] We do know Hillary and Bernie are clueless about human behavior, emotion, motivation, and psychology. Trump's a genius, a mutant.[71]

Now climate change is a bad joke. That is *not* the hazard. The earth's temperature has been warming (lately); it's true. But it also cools down from time to time. There was the Ice Age, two of them, and there may be again. We have an airbase (strategic defense) on Greenland, Thule. We, the US military, does research there in conjunction with scientists and discovered palm trees under the ice cap.[72] The problem is not the climate; it's the people and *their* collective arrogance (humanism) and their pollution of the air, water, and land. There are too many people. There are too many cows, chickens, and pigs pooping and fouling up the water, air, and land. What are you going to do? Birth control? We can reduce the population as we know how, but who decides? That's the problem. I want a deal maker who puts my family/clan/tribe first.

Max is a globalist and thinks Obama's lack of Americanism, lack of American roots, is a net positive. I think Obama, due to his personal reality, is/was ill-educated. Max thinks Trump's comments on the killing

---

[70]   And so now talks are scheduled. As Trump often says, we'll see.

[71]   Trump calls himself a "stable genius." He might be right. We'll see.

[72]   The latest climate change debate can be found here: https://www.youtube.com/watch?v=pVXHaSqpsVg.
       Or you can see Michael Crichton's annotated bibliography in *State of Fear*, pp. 641–672. In my opinion, you've been mislead, misinformed, and ill-educated in the service of others' self-interest.

of police in Dallas, Texas, on July 7, 2016, demonstrate Trump's racism. I disagree.

I think Obama's lack of roots and a present father helped shape his belief that people could all just get along, regardless of their long, long tribal histories and grievances. As quite the traveler myself, I know that it's easy (given a certain personality type) to make friends with strangers, as a newcomer to a community, than it is for physical neighbors to cohabit a territory and be friendly with the same neighbor for centuries, particularly and especially for tribes that have squabbled/fought over buffer entities for hundreds and thousands of years, like in Eastern Europe and the Middle East, Africa, and so on. Here in the USA, it was easy; wipe out the small native (existing) population and then continue to expand outward to an uninhabited, resource-rich, huge territory (i.e., paradise). (This philosophy (myth) or worldview continues to persist today, as some believe we can solve our problems by space and mind expansion, via some combination of technology and brain/mind manipulation, creating a brand-new mindscape and noosphere. Who needs earth?)

There simply was no history to contend with—a nation of immigrants—it's laughable. We are that, but it is no formula for success. Humans are, by their very nature, not so different from other mammals. We are territorial and defend the territory, the hunting ground, and form alliances and affiliations in the service of that—in the service of reproducing—to carry on. And we fight over who gets to mate with whom. Obama, for all his intellect, doesn't seem to be able to understand that, not uncommon for many Liberals ruled by institutional intellectualization and folklore. "Woodstock was a dream some of us had."

Alliances are formed not in the service of the tribal instinct but *because* of the instinct. One needs an enemy or hazard, a threat, to form the alliance! Otherwise, alliances can be burdensome, one-sided, and parasitic without a common enemy. Sebastian Junger argues in *Tribe* that our affluence (from modernity/technology) has allowed us to become more isolated, because we don't need one another, but that, paradoxically, then leads to depression because we crave a hazard and/or an enemy to bring us together. Of course, this is unconscious. So altruism, empathy, and guilt were constructed out of emotions that evolved to further survival, not out of some moral compass or higher power or greater good. It may, in fact, be for the greater good to have wars—to keep the population in check. Affluence, technology, and modernity is, in some ways, leading to "reverse Darwinism," or survival of the unfit, which leads to overcrowding and a breakdown of boundaries, which leads to conflict. So no, peace hasn't worked. War works. Peace looks like it did for a while, after WWII in Europe, but something must happen to restrain reproduction and the exploding human population—that's just the way it is.

People always fight over who gets to mate with whom, who gets to eat what and how much, and so on. There has to be order, but *who decides* is the big question. Free love, casual sex, free whatever, just doesn't work! There have to be restraints, there has to be order, and there has to be law and order or nature's laws will assert themselves. And then there will be mass starvation, disease, and of course, war. Damned if you do, and damned if you don't. This is what drove Wallace[73] crazy—he saw there was no way out and had no one to talk to that about. So he wrote some far-out fiction but couldn't get beyond boredom as a solution, which *is* no solution. Boredom is a momentary resting place, right below contentment in the hierarchy of emotions. It is necessary but not sufficient. If one settles in the mental state between boredom and contentment, one loses contrast and flat lines—dies. From *The Pale King*, "If you are immune to boredom, there is literally nothing you cannot accomplish." I ask: leading to a universe controlled by artificial intelligence?

Overcrowding and competition lead to freedom restrained, paradoxically, *not* to more choices but fewer. Openness of borders and boundaries is fine for those who benefit but not for those who are squeezed. There will always be competition, because the real world is finite. Think of it, whatever you decide *it* is—ocean beach property, riverfront land, fertile ground (where did we put the Natives, the reservations?). There's only so much of it, and it's prime. But there's not enough for everyone, so there has to be some sort of order imposed. But how and by whom? God, luck, a lottery, nature? Or strength, cunning, wit? Inheritance? Talent? Maybe simply by who was there first and then if they can defend it by some/any means. That's *it* in a nutshell. It's not that complicated. So the game is as it

---

[73]   David Foster Wallace is a literary genius who hung himself in September of 2008, frustrated, angry, and depressed while trying to figure out the human condition with the novel he was working on (posthumously published as *The Pale King*).

has always been, a struggle for prime/choice property/territory (including females, sorry). "Something *is* going on."[74]

---

[74] I went back and looked at the incident—police ambushed in Dallas, Texas, on July 7, 2016, while providing protection for a Black Lives Matter march protesting the killing of black men by police. Micah Xavier Johnson—twenty-five years old, black, and discharged from the US Army—opened fire on the police using military tactics, killing five officers and wounding nine others before being cornered and blown up (killed) by a police robot. Johnson, like many of the shooters (Dylan Roof, Devin Kelly, Stephen Paddock, James Holmes, Nikolas Cruz, and so on; there were approximately 380 mass shootings, with four or more persons shot, in the 387 days since Trump declared his candidacy, most of which did not garner national media coverage), appear to be mentally disturbed individuals. Johnson was under psychiatric care provided by the Veterans Health Administration and was prescribed a muscle relaxant, antidepressant, antianxiety, and sleep medication. Yet he had a small arsenal of guns and bomb-making material. Does that make any sense?

Yes, there are *a lot* of guns in the US and *a lot* of mentally disturbed / personality-disordered people. The question *should* be this: Why can't we keep guns out of personality-disordered people's possession? Again, that question hinges on who decides?

I also took a look at President Obama's public statement on the shooting that Trump's remark "Something's going on" referred to. Trump was reading/matching Obama's words with his body language. I saw the same thing Trump did—that Obama was distressed. I'd say he was sad. Why? I think (maybe Trump did too) that the president was sad because the incident didn't match the narrative of police abusing their power and targeting black men but, instead, was a black man targeting the police who were protecting black Americans. (Even a smart man like Barack Obama is not immune to cognitive dissonance.) So Mr. Obama returned to the standard call for better gun control and went on to talk about the "racial disparities in our justice system." It seemed to me that Obama was almost *justifying* Johnson's attack. The body language Trump and I picked up on was President Obama's sadness, cognitive dissonance, and reluctance to speak about what happened. In other words, something *is* going on (inside of Obama's head) that he's not being forthright about in speaking to the American public. Obama's unforthrightness, if you will, or dishonesty is what's going on.

I also took a look at Hillary Clinton's and Trump's response. Clinton was clearly angry (hurt) and went to the standard Democrat talking points. Trump seemed measured, steadfast, determined. He said, "Law enforcement stands between civilization and total chaos." I think he has a point. To assume that

"Journalists" now make stuff up. This is where we are. It's a consequence of competition to get a story first, true or not, so as to get people's attention via clicks counted by artificial intelligence programmed by people with agendas, which may or may not be an accurate accounting of people's preferences, likes or anything whatsoever having to do with what is best, right, or just. What was/is going on is a super mess for sure, a snafu *and* a fubar. My thinking is that one possible solution was right after the Paris attack and ISIS had blown up a Russian airliner. At that point, a moment in time, is when Russia, the USA, and France could have united (per the $A = E + h$ equation) and eliminated ISIS. That moment has passed. Now it's beyond me. It (the Middle East, Europe, Africa, Asia) may be a situation beyond which massive death is the only solution. The world is a man-made disaster.

Mr. Obama, unfortunately, isn't loyal to the USA, nor to any country, not even Kenya. He's world-centric, literally. He never should have been POTUS. I fell for it. His book, *Dreams from My Father*, is very good. But looking back, one can see his lack of identity, his search to find himself, his lack of roots, his lack of family, tribe, country. But he is a good writer and talker. He's what is called a TCK—third-culture kid, meaning he was born into one culture (American) but grew up in another (Muslim Indonesia), the result being confusion. In short, Obama has an identity problem.

It takes way too much time to explain everything. That's why you, as an individual, must think for yourself, educate yourself, before the elitists and AI reconstruct the past and program the future into a place where nothing matters (i.e., boredom). You have to look at the history and prehistory and game out the future. At least give it a shot. Trump's been successful in a cutthroat world, the real estate world, which *is* the real world—it's all about territory. The Clintons have been very successful in the political world, which is about pay to play or insider trading. It *is* crooked. Obama makes

---

people will conduct themselves ethically, morally, smartly, and fairly without laws and their enforcement seems naive at best and a recipe for disaster. The *New York Times* seemed shocked by Trump's statement and demeanor, considering his "tendency for fulmination and fury."

The story being told by the Progressive Left is evidence of groupthink, confirmation bias, and a creep toward total mind control, a singular mind, a collective mind constructed by artificial intelligence—the individual becoming extinct.

the point in his book—doesn't matter if it's Chicago or Nairobi—politics and politicians are corrupt.

His father failed. Obama failed—in Chicago, in Kenya, and as POTUS—to change anything. In fact, he made it worse.

How do you know a friend or foe in this borderless, sneakered, T-shirt world? No way to tell Adam from Eve, Cain from Abel, or Hal from Max. I've said it before—Trump doesn't care about what god you worship, only about loyalty to the USA. A refugee could buy a Trump hat, put it on, and then go murder fifty innocents. Some guy tried to kill Trump in Nevada the other day, a Brit, here on an expired visa.

Obama thought/thinks that family, tribe, country, land, and territory are not important. That's simply not true. That's the heart of who we (humans) are. We are creatures of this world; we evolved brains and emotions to help us survive in a hostile environment. It's still hostile, more so, because you can't tell friend from foe, as when tribes had identifying markings. To presume anything about anyone is a mistake. Be great if it wasn't so. But "Woodstock was a dream some of us had," so sang Joni Mitchell.

Max asked, "Does Obama subscribe to a Hobbesian worldview?"

No, only that he ran into it with people he worked with in Chicago and couldn't deny its reality.

Max thinks Hobbes's view of human nature is similar to Freud's in *Civilization and Its Discontents* but that Hobbes offers a more extreme solution than Freud—the strongman who will keep order. Max thinks the solution is coming from Silicon Valley (the new paradise?). I think FAAAT (Facebook, Apple, Alphabet, Amazon, Twitter) is going to destroy the world as it is and create one where we no longer *live* but only exist in space—the noosphere created by artificial intelligence.

When Obama was in Chicago, black nationalism was what was being preached (mid-eighties). The Nation of Islam (black Muslims/Panthers) was very potent. Obama, when in Indonesia, went to both a Muslim school and a Catholic school, both for two years. It must have been confusing. Obama is/was very much a man without a country or tribe/family or community. Before going to Harvard, he went to Kenya to meet his father's family/tribe. He has mostly rejected them and their tribal ways. Under the bus they went. Can't get yourself elected if you're a Kenyan.

No, Max, Trump is not sinister. Trump is very sharp when it comes to people. "Something" is Obama's lack of attachment (see above). He,

Obama, is very sympathetic to, not allied with or loyal to Islam and Muslims. He doesn't want to be at war with Muslims or Islam because he saw them, in Chicago, as the only thing (black nationalism, black power) that helped some of the poor blacks (not unlike Hezbollah in the Middle East). It's very complex. Obama is also very sympathetic with immigration—people leaving "home" for the promise of a better life. He's really not America's president. He sees himself as the leader of the *world*, or world-centric, versus Trump's America first. Obama hates, really hates, Trump, which is unfortunate. They should play golf together, just the two of them. I think they'd come to some understandings. [75]

If you watch the ESPN documentary *O.J.: Made in America*, Johnnie Cochran, in his closing argument, compares the LA detective Mark Furman and the entire LAPD to Hitler and the Nazis; and it works! The jury sets OJ free, who, without any doubt, murdered two people. The evidence was overwhelming. Cochran invented the race card. This was so extraordinary—the murder, the trial, everything—when it was happening

---

[75]   I truly think hate has its roots in jealousy—loss of a person, place, or thing that you believed/thought was yours to a rival, a competitor, an other. In his book, Obama quotes a black businessman in Chicago asking him why should he hire a black contractor to do a job when history has taught him that he'll just have to hire a white man to fix the mess that the black man made. This is what Obama feared with Trump—the white man being hired after the black man to fix the failures of the black man. Obama truly believed he *had* done a good job and that the country was moving forward. The American people, or sixty-some million and thirty states, thought otherwise. The former president, Hillary Clinton, the media, Progressives, Muslims, many young people, Liberals, many Europeans, and so on all thought they had the election won and that it was *stolen* from them. This accounts for the crazy, irrational hated and unwillingness to work with now President Trump toward a better America and a more peaceful world.

I think *loss* of a valued person, place, or thing to a competitor leads to jealousy, which fosters hate, which then drives revenge. "*Hate* is nature's perfect energy source," so said Bobby Axelrod on the Showtime series *Billions*. I think that's a true statement and is a survival mechanism—part of an emotional response sequence that drives the motivational need of self-esteem or self-respect. The alternative is one of acceptance (of the loss), which also satisfies the motivational need of self-esteem and self-respect but requires energy of a different kind—one of mindfulness, meditation, yoga, tai chi, hiking, etc. Less healthy alternatives would be denial or sour grapes, i.e., repression.

in 1994. It set the stage for everything going on today. The '90s were the beginning of the unraveling of America. The OJ spectacle was followed by Clinton's sex scandal, then the Columbine shooting, the dot-com collapse, and finally, 9/11. It's been downhill ever since.

The horse has left the barn. Someone left the barn door open, and horses being horses . . . The road to hell is paved with good intentions. The Democrats would be well to keep that in mind. Meditate on that, my friends. There are five to ten million AR-style rifles already in America. No one knows how many! And they're flying off the shelves. They can't make them fast enough! I'm going to go shooting with friends who own them for research purposes, of course.[76]

Trump isn't always logical, but he's intuitive. Obama's really not right for the job. He's really an African, African-American half-breed, who has rejected his home and family, without any organizing principle (faith), albeit with good intentions. It's messed up. You've got to have an organizing principle; everybody knows that! Or they should. The road to hell is paved with good intentions.

I think Trump does have a good heart. He's a true narcissist, for sure, but he's not hateful or pathological like OJ. Rereading Obama's memoir, page 197, the Hobbesian world is discussed, when Barack was twenty-two, starting out in Chicago as a community organizer. It's all in there, the *something* that is going on that Trump's picked up on, the organizing principle, or lack of, of a person's self-identity—blood/tribe/community.

To be fair, now that the election is getting down to it, I thought I'd go over the case that has been made against Trump point by point, as best I can recall. First, the list of his offenses, along with what it supposedly reveals, followed finally by my rebuttals.

Here's the list:

1. John McCain as a war hero because he got captured—ungratefulness
2. Mexicans bringing drugs and crime and being rapists—racism
3. Muslims dancing in the streets of New Jersey after 9/11—distortions of truth
4. Megyn Kelly as a bimbo and lightweight—sexism

---

[76]   This never happened.

5. Eminent domain—the exploitation of powerless individuals
6. Multiple bankruptcies—bad businessman
7. Inciting violence—pugilism
8. Hiring foreign workers—hypocrisy
9. Banning Muslims entering the country—hatefulness
10. Building a wall—xenophobia
11. Killing families of terrorists—criminal
12. Favoring torture—criminal
13. Dissolving NATO—stupidity
14. Nukes for Japan—stupidity
15. Wanting to not release his tax returns—dishonesty
16. Raising money for veterans—selfish promotion
17. Rooting for the housing crash—heartlessness
18. Fraudulent Trump University—con man and thief
19. Narcissist—selfishness
20. Bully—cowardice
21. Thin-skinned—neurotic

To sum up Max's view (and other's): Donald J. Trump does not deserve your vote for **POTUS** because he is a thin-skinned, craven, narcissistic, disagreeable, selfish bully who hates women, Mexicans, Muslims—foreigners, in general—and is ungrateful, a thief, dishonest, a terrible businessman with funny hair, and a warmonger who would destroy the world. Did my cyberspace dialogue with Max change his mind, make him think? No, it caused him to "unfriend" me.

I'm going to start with number 18 because it seems like this is finally the one—the one that ends his hostile takeover (see "The Hostile Takeover," March 17) of the Republican Party and nails the coffin shut with his bid for the **POTUS**. This is the case of Trump University, which Hillary thinks is *so* funny and clever: "Trump you, hahaha [cackle, cackle]."

First of all, anyone who signs up for and puts their money down for a self-improvement class, seminar, school, workshop, retreat is admitting that things aren't going well and that *this* just might be the ticket to personal salvation, i.e., the cure for what it is that is ailing the said person. That being said, self-improvement seminars etc. can work sometimes, a little (cue the placebo effect), but you have to be willing to work and have the inherent characteristics to engender success in whatever it is you are trying to accomplish or improve on. I know because I've been on both sides of the issue—paying for help and giving help for a fee. I don't know the percentage, but a lot of people make a lot of money teaching such classes and writing books, be they relationship or marriage workshops; organizing spiritual, religious retreats or health seminars; teaching music, art, acting, comedy classes; doing tennis, swimming, gymnastics, soccer, baseball, golf camps; and so on and so forth. In no case, *ever*, is it written in the agreement that success is guaranteed! You pay your money and take your chances. "It'll work if you will work" is a good axiom, but even then, if you've not the innate talent, intelligence, skill, well, you'll probably return to where you were, your baseline, albeit a little lighter in your wallet.

Now always, and this *is* a guarantee, there will be those who feel/think/believe that they've been ripped off and will want their money back. It's that self-esteem/self-respect thing. The alternative is self-loathing and despair.

Now the selling of the product/process may take different forms and techniques, but it's basically the same procedure. The product/service is advertised and people sign up and put their (or their parents) money down. In the case of Trump U, it was about making money in real estate under the guidance of Mr. Donald J. Trump himself, maybe the most famous and successful real estate mogul in the world. This is going to cost you some money, yes? Did you think it was going to be easy making a fortune in real estate?

Here's *my* instruction (for free): buy low, sell high. Give me a break! And yet some (many?) of Trump U's students reportedly loved it. Some said they made money; some said they learned a lot even if they didn't make money. But then you have the *victims*. And who loves victims more than lawyers? That *is* a question. Who loves litigation more than lawyers? Judges? (Just asking.) Again, that's a question.

So here, in this specific case, you have a billionaire, obviously worth billions of dollars, who, you can make a case, just might make you rich! Again, give me a break! Losers are trying to make money from winners! The losers are unwilling to accept who they are. This *is* really *huge*, and it goes to the whole idea of the American dream.

It's not Trump's fault.

The question is, Why has this case dragged on for six years? The answer is, lawyers make their money billing by the hour, and if Mr. Trump is involved, there is *a lot* of money to make on both sides! Settle? Dismiss? Again, are you kidding me? I'll bet, if I were a betting man, that the judge will write a book, maybe even a lawyer or two. It's a joke, and the joke's on you.

None of this is about what they would lead you to believe it is about. It's not about fraud, stealing, or lying or racism. It's about money and power. It's about winners and losers. Mr. Trump is a winner. Now he's upped the ante; he's all in on his bid to become president.

1. John McCain as a war hero because he got captured—ungratefulness

As I recall, this was the first offense, and the folks—or should I call them the elites, the thought leaders, anyway—they were all outraged when Mr. Trump, in an interview, said, "John McCain is a hero because he was captured. I like people who weren't captured. Okay?" It's true, of course, which goes to Mr. Trump's war on political correctness. If navy pilot McCain, Senator McCain, had not been shot down over Vietnam but instead had been an average US Navy fighter pilot, flying missions, dropping bombs and napalm on the Vietcong, who always returned safely to the base/ship, who knows what his career and life would have been like? Do you know any other old Nam fighter pilots? The Vietnam War became very unpopular, inside and outside of the military, except for the few who knew war for what it is. Many who fought in Vietnam were scorned and spit upon as baby killers. So Trump spoke the truth—McCain gained legendary hero status *because* he was shot down. But the popular story is what happened after he was captured—how McCain endured torture and refused to be a pawn in a negotiation. He suffered for his fellow soldiers, which is heroic, but something very common among soldiers. They fight and suffer and endure for one another, regardless of the flag they fight under. It's the soldier's creed. It's the tribal instinct. Some are, for sure, tougher than others. Some make better soldiers than others. Each combatant in war believes his side is right or, lacking that, believes in duty to country/nation/community/home/family and/or his god—*something* outside himself that gives him courage. When alone, he might succumb to the peace and serenity of death. Battle is life, and life is battle, a struggle. Some understand this better than others.

In *Times'* current issue (June 13, 2016), there is an essay where the author talks about her daughter coming back from college and speaking with a new vocabulary, which she, the author/mother, doesn't quite understand. The thrust and purpose of this new language seems to be to try and cancel/eliminate reality, twist it into some postmodern pipe dream. Any and all words that imply comparison or competition are taboo. Competition and comparison are evils that the progressive thought leaders believe can be made to go away if not mentioned, which reminds me of something my mother told me back in the day, when I was a high school lad ensconced in (aside from war, business, and real life) a most competitive and comparative environment. Mother said one of her favorite sayings was from Eleanor Roosevelt: "If it isn't mentioned, it didn't happen." True? Not at all, but it seemed to be taken as a gospel. Now the elites have rebooted that failed strategy. They seem to think that if they redefine words or eliminate them, they can change human emotion and psychology and, subsequently, human behavior. Words like *love, hero, winner, community, strong, family, weak, loser, lost, dead, heaven, hell, marriage, victory, home, forever,* and many more are reinterpreted to mean whatever the authority, the elites, determine is relevant and agreed upon (to serve their purpose) but might well be, in fact, contrary to what a person's senses are telling him. This is postmodernism.

2. Mexicans bringing drugs and crime and being rapists—racism
3. Muslims dancing in the streets of New Jersey after 9/11—distortions of truth
4. Banning Muslims entering the country—hatefulness
5. Building a wall—xenophobia

This all began, formally, on June 16, 2015, when Trump announced he was a candidate for Republican nominee of the president of the United States and made the now-infamous declaration that he was going to build a wall on the southern border to stop illegal immigration. Trump said, in his blunt manner, "Mexico was not sending their best. They're sending drugs and criminals and rapists, and some, I'm sure, are good people." So began the cries of outrage that Trump is a racist. The following day, he clarified his statement and said he was referring to an article and documentary about the plight of people coming into the country from countries south of the border. (I've linked the article in the chapter "Build That Wall.")

Of course, no one paid much attention to that—it was not what his opponents wanted to hear or know or understand or cared about. They simply wanted confirmation that Trump was not a legitimate candidate. And remember, what the media cares about is selling product, and themselves as purveyors of truth. They fuel and provide conflict (not truth or reality), which everyday people can't get enough of—watching other people get taken down, other people fail. *Schadenfreude*, the Germans call it (taking pleasure in another's misfortune, particularly if that person is a friend or *someone of higher status or standing*). That hits the reward button in the brain. It just does.

This complex and confounding system, the reward system, might be best understood by thinking of an axis with empathy on one end and schadenfreude on the other. To be empathetic gains you points with others but makes you sad. You feel their pain or joy and so feel good about yourself. It stokes *your* self-esteem but really doesn't *do* anything for anyone. Nothing changes. On the inside, you're sad—it's all about them, not you. To delight (feel joy) in the misfortune of another is deemed reprehensible (unless, of course, they deserve it), and yet it makes you happy on the inside but also diminishes your self-esteem because others find you unsavory (unless everyone is drunk, then it's funny). So it's a great thing if you can all find and agree on a villain who deserves to be taken down, regardless of the truth of the matter or facts.

The media, as a whole, has become specious to the core. They are united in their groupthink. Labeling someone a racist or sexist is the greatest, especially if you can get another person to defend the "racist" person. Now you've got conflict! You've got victims to engender empathy and champions to engender joy. You've got both ends of the emotional spectrum covered and everything in between. You've got heroes and villains and impartial mediators (announcers) to bring it all to you and corporate behemoths to sponsor and profit from all the internal and external conflict and stress. The economy thrives, and everybody wins, except, of course, the real victims, the young girls and women being raped and sold and the young boys and men being forced to fight and kill and steal and work for peanuts, because the real problems—joblessness, homelessness, mental illness, addiction, and disordered personalities—weren't being named and talked about.

To build a wall along the southern border and to enforce the laws and boundaries of people and countries is too hard; it's too disruptive to the way things are. It's much easier to name a man, Donald Trump, as evil and bad—racist, sexist, xenophobic—and continue doing what has always been done because, well, *things* aren't *that* bad. We're making progress after all. We just have to keep going in the direction we're going. (Never mind that most Americans, 65–75 percent, think we're headed in the wrong direction.) How can one explain that? Cognitive dissonance, twisted and crooked thinking.

The empathy/schadenfreude axis, thought leaders and political correctness, corporations and bureaucratic governments all work in concert to keep things the way they are because it's not *that* bad. Don't worry / be happy.

(News update: A twenty-nine-year-old American-born Muslim, a US citizen, and son of an Afghan immigrant attacks the Pulse nightclub in Orlando, Florida, an LGBTQ dance club, on Latin night, killing forty-nine instantly and wounding fifty-three others. It is the deadliest mass murder shooting in the US history.[77] The killer used an AR-15 semiautomatic-type rifle and a 9mm handgun, both recently legally purchased. The man was married, his second, with a three-year-old baby, and employed. He had a history of domestic violence (unreported) and gay and racist bigotry and had previously been on the FBI's watch list for terrorism. He died in a shoot-out with SWAT. His first wife said he was bipolar, but he never had been diagnosed or treated. He pledged allegiance to various Islamist groups and leaders during his rampage.)

6.   Megyn Kelly as a bimbo and lightweight—sexism

On August 6, 2015, the first Republican primary debate was held, hosted by Fox News. Trump was center stage, having shot up to lead the polls. There were ten other candidates, five on each side of Trump. Trump had never before debated. Megyn Kelly was centered between two male questioners and opened the questioning. She smiled and welcomed Mr. Trump and then attacked with a hostile question intended to embarrass and humiliate Trump. After buttering him up, she asked, "You call women fat pigs, dogs, slobs, and disgusting animals—"

"Only Rosie O'Donnell," shot back Trump.

"No, it wasn't," said Kelly, with a smile and a smirk, as the audience erupted in laughter and applause. And *the game* was on. Ms. Kelly reminded Mr. Trump (and the audience not only in the theater but also twenty-six million viewers on TV, the largest audience *ever* on cable TV) that he had

---

[77]   It was until the mass murder in Las Vegas happened.

once said to a female contestant on Trump's TV show *The Celebrity Apprentice* that the woman would "make a pretty picture on her knees." And then she questioned whether Trump had the temperament to be president and "Isn't it true that you are part of the war on women?" as if she were a prosecutor.

Trump defended himself, saying, "I say what I say. We don't have time for political correctness. This country is in big trouble. We need energy, strength, quickness, and brains." This has remained at the center of the case against Trump, and his defense has stayed consistent. He said today, June 13, 2016, in a formal speech responding to the Orlando attack, "I refuse to be politically correct," for defending America against radical Islam. Hillary Clinton, the Democrat nominee, in a speech earlier in the day, of course, attacked Trump's temperament while laying out her policies.

The point here is that Kelly's questioning *was hostile* and of no qualitative substance. It was representative of gender politics and "gotcha journalism." She might have, could have, then gone down the line and asked the other candidates something like "If elected president, what would you do if an attractive twenty-two-year-old female intern came on to you and offered to pleasure you in the Oval Office?" But she didn't. Or maybe she could have asked this: "Mr. Trump, what does your 10 look like?" And then again, she could have gone down the line. She might have asked, "What do you think, Mr. Trump, are the three most pressing problems the country faces?" But she didn't. She might have asked, "What do you value most in life, Mr. Trump?" But she didn't. She might have asked, "Mr. Trump, what are the root causes of hate?" But she didn't. She could have asked, "Mr. Trump, how do you or *can* you help someone who doesn't want your help?" But of course, she didn't, because those questions are real questions, questions that would have told the audience something of value, something that might help them in making a decision about whom they want to lead the country.

Kelly *is* a lightweight, a pretty face looking to make a name for herself, make the really big bucks, like Hillary, with a big book advance. It's true, her memoir, *Settle for More*, hits the bookshelves on November 15. It's been reported she was paid a ten-million-dollar advance. Ms. Kelly posed on the cover of *GQ* magazine, looking very 10-ish, *and* did a radio interview with Howard Stern where she laughed and giggled and boasted about her breasts and sexual prowess, very bimbo-like. Lightweight and bimbo fit. It's not sexism if it's specific and true.

7. Eminent domain—the exploitation of powerless individuals
8. Multiple bankruptcies—bad businessman
9. Hiring foreign workers—hypocrisy
10. Wanting to not release his tax returns—liar
11. Raising money for veterans—selfish promotion
12. Rooting for the housing crash—heartlessness

These arguments in the case against Trump can be clustered under the rubric of businessman or the marketplace or the economy. It is one of the Democratic candidate Hillary Clinton's main arguments—that Trump's really a horrible businessman and person and that in itself should be enough to disqualify him from becoming president. Mr. Trump's position is, *because* he's been successful in the marketplace, in the economy, and as a businessman, that uniquely *qualifies* him to be president (especially now in light of the falling stock market due to the unease of the marketplace because of the United Kingdom's people voting to leave the European Union).[78]

---

[78] After rising approximately 40 percent since Trump's victory, the market is again falling, this time because of fears of a trade war or Trump doing what he said he would do during the campaign—renegotiate trade deals with foreign countries.

In a nutshell, here's the story, and it's my story too. And I *am* qualified to speak on these matters because of my wild and varied history in *the marketplace.* I'd been in the marketplace for fifty years before turning sixty-five and retiring from the marketplace. I began working when I was sixteen, for minimum wage (at the time it was $1.65 per hour), during summers. I never stopped. I've had twenty-two different jobs/positions/titles in and about all aspects of the market. I've been a common laborer, a highly skilled laborer, a manager, a worker/staff, an owner of small businesses, and on the board of directors of a nonprofit. I've worked in the health-care industry and the construction industry, the art industry and the restaurant industry, the publishing industry and the education industry.

I've been self-employed and have employed others. I've been a student and a teacher in higher education. I've bought and sold homes, and built houses and built out commercial property. I've traded stocks on the stock exchange. I've worked for the government and for nongovernmental agencies and fought with the government. I've been punched in the face and otherwise physically assaulted. I've defended myself on the playground and in courts of law and hired others to defend me. I've been married, married with children, single, and divorced, as well as married with stepchildren. I've lived in, built, and owned my own home and rented out rooms in my home. I've been a gun owner and not a gun owner. In other words, I've experienced the marketplace as few others have. I've also lived in twenty-two different homes, nine different states, and four countries and met thousands of people from many different communities, cultures, and colors. I have experience.

The minimum wage is not meant to be a living wage; it's an entry into the marketplace and also prohibits slavery. It's when you learn about the market and the real world, when you start to become self-reliant, but you've still got a *lot* to learn. The government barely functions. Most of the time, it functions at a low level. It's not efficient. Its primary solution to any problem is to throw more money at it, whatever *it* is. *The Peter Principle* (1968) by L. J. Peter and R. Hull—the facetious proposition that each employee in an organization tends to be promoted until reaching his or her level of incompetence—is the rule, not the exception. There are good and decent people on both sides of every issue, but most people function at a government level of efficiency, i.e., barely. Social loafing (the relaxation that results when people are in a group and their individual performance cannot or will not be evaluated as this relaxation impairs performance on simple tasks but enhances performance on complex tasks)[79] is real. Racism and sexism are real, but not nearly as pervasive as some would have you believe. Problems persist because most people are incompetent, which the government rewards in a weird, paradoxical, ironic way. If you engage/participate in the "free market," you're going to hurt/anger some people. It's a competitive, contentious, often-hostile environment. Some people will like you; others won't. People are different (not equal) as are situations. Context matters.

I myself have been employee of the month and have been fired. I've been raved about and praised, scorned and rejected (the worst feeling), and retaliated against—sometimes by the same establishment! I've been wooed and been ignored (not as bad as rejection but close). I've gotten As and Fs in school. I've made money and lost money. I've been admired and vilified. I've been loved, respected, hated, and feared. Sometimes, I recoil from people who love me because I'm not attracted to them. Oftentimes, I'd rather be alone than be with (most) people.

---

79   Elliot Aronson, Timothy D. Wilson, and Robin M. Akert, *Social Psychology: The Heart and the Mind* (1994), 333.

For example, my son was just here (in Colorado) to support a friend in her decision to marry (most people still view marriage as a good thing, a happy time, a hopeful time, a cause for celebration). So he went to the liquor store to buy some and paid via plastic money, and lo, the clerk recognized his name and asked, "Are you related to Mark?"

"He's my father."

"He doesn't like me."

"He doesn't like most people."

The context is, the liquor store clerk is also a poet and publisher whom I knew back in the day. I didn't like (so much) his work and told him so face-to-face, having bought and read it. *No big deal,* I thought. *People are different.* He assumed I meant I didn't *like him,* which is not the case. I barely know him.

The point of all this is, Mr. Trump has had hundreds, thousands, of more interactions and transactions for way, way more money than me, so he's bound to have made some enemies, as well as people who just don't like him for whatever reason. He's a businessman, a very successful one, and in the process of living that life, you're going to anger many people. For Hillary Clinton to build *her* case—the case against Trump—around that is just plain stupid. And well, if you buy that, that says more about you than anything—that you've never played *the game.*

I could document this, my life. My ninety-six-year-old father suggested I write a memoir. But I won't; it's simply too complex—my life. Instead, I write novels, complex for sure, but easier than trying to make sense of what "really" happened.[80]

---

[80] When I entered into therapy, the provider faced me, sitting, with the standard

13. Inciting violence—pugilism
14. Killing families of terrorists—criminal
15. Favoring torture—criminal
16. Dissolving NATO—stupidity
17. Nukes for Japan—stupidity

This cluster comes under the rubric of stupid white man syndrome. Men are typically violent, aggressive, and stupid (especially white men in positions of power and authority) and need to be tamed and pacified by right-thinking women and progressive feminist thought leaders. It's hard to know where to start with this cluster.

One certainty is that the media has acted as an accelerant for this narrative. They do this by selective editing of what they report on and then a sort of groupthink when it comes to the words and language they use. No one news source wants to go out on a limb and say something different than the others, lest they be thought of as "dropping the ball" or "missing the boat" or "getting it wrong." After all, if they all say the same thing, it must be true, right?

It started at the first presser Mr. Trump held on August 25, 2016, and that set the tone for the election cycle, encompassing many of the issues in the chapter "The Case against Trump."

Jorge Ramos, an anchor for Univision television (a widely watched Spanish-speaking network) and Fusion (its companion online news source), jumped up and began a hostile diatribe directed at Mr. Trump. Trump told him to sit down and wait to be called on, but Ramos did neither. Trump then signaled to his private security man, Keith Schiller, to take care of the situation (Schiller is fifty-seven, a former NYPD detective and US Navy serviceman, and has been with Trump for sixteen years). Schiller escorted

---

yellow legal pad in her lap and pen in her hand. I said, "If you take notes, you'll need a hundred of those pads."

Ramos out of the venue, as a basketball player might force an opponent to give ground—a sort of blocking, hand-checking maneuver. But that's not what was reported in *every* news source! Instead, it was reported that Mr. Trump, via his personal security, had *ejected* Ramos. (Here's the most accurate account I've been able to find: http://www.dailymail.co.uk/news/article-3222863/The-billionaire-s-bodyguard-Donald-Trump-s-head-security-former-NYPD-detective-Navy-officer-history-roughing-boss-adversaries.html). But even this article first uses the word *ejected*, which connotes a violent action. And then the photo shown most often was one of Ramos looking frightened and fearful—crouched defensively with eyes bulging. And so it began—Trump was a bully, a thug, and a racist. In fact, Trump let Ramos back in after he, Ramos, cooled down and then Trump called on him. (I've referenced this before, so I won't again; but Ramos' news outlets is where Trump got the information about Mexicans being violent criminals and rapists, those coming into the United States, both as victims and perpetrators.)

(News update: Tuesday, June 28, there was yet another terrorist attack on The West, this time the international airport in Istanbul, Turkey. Three suicide bombers with automatic rifles stormed the terminal and killed 41 people and wounded 239 others.)

In subsequent public events, after yesterday's attack, Trump reiterated his position that America must become smart and tough, especially in the areas of terrorism and immigration. And of course, the news outlets howled.

Consider that this is a *war*—unlike previous wars, but war nevertheless. Trump says, "Screw it. The enemy isn't playing by the rules, so that cancels the rules." I agree. Remember Harry Truman and the Second World War and the use of the atomic bomb? He could have exploded the weapon out over the ocean, killing no one, and then demanded surrender. But he didn't, because he had a sense of the enemy, so he vaporized a city. And yet still the Japanese would not surrender, so he did it again. Then and only then did the enemy surrender. And part of the peace agreement was that Japan could never form an army capable of aggression. It's been seventy years, three generations, now. What do *you* think? Can the Japanese people, their leaders, be trusted to defend themselves with modern weapons? Trump says yes. He thinks they can handle their own defense now. But I concede. He could be wrong. Given modern weaponry and a modern army, the Japanese might attack us, seek revenge. Who knows? Who's the racist? Trump? Me? The Japanese? You?

Trump said yesterday, "You have to fight fire with fire."[81] Hillary Clinton, John Kerry, and Barack Obama think that love will find a way, given enough time. They have been proven wrong so far. Trump says, "She has it completely backward." Truer words have never been spoken. Hillary was compromised decades ago, as a young wife. Obama was compromised around the same time in Chicago as a community organizer. Both failed. Smart people, granted, but compromised, delusional, and architects of their own reality. They are enablers.

I was thinking last night. What's going on? It seems so obvious to me. Why not the rest of you? And then a bolt of lightning struck outside. *Boom!* And inside my mind too. Outside in the real world, the rain poured down. I thought, *It's the revenge of the nerds!* Since the beginning

---

[81]　For instance, when a person commits an act of terror against Israel, the Israeli will neutralize (kill) the perpetrator, find out where he or she is from, and demolish their home, leaving family members homeless with all possessions destroyed. When Trump says kill the families of terrorists, I assume he's meaning something of this nature. In other words, there is a cost beyond the individual's own life that acts of terror will bring. Obviously, suicide bombers are willing to die; but evidenced by the actions of the San Bernardino killers, they still care about the lives of their relatives. The Israeli know this. Inflicting severe costs on the family of terrorists might act as a deterrent—fire with fire, no mercy.

of mankind, since the primal hoard in Barack Obama's homeland, Kenya, where man first separated from the ape, the family/clan/community/ has divided itself into three groups (evidenced today in high school life): the warriors/ jocks, the artists/stoners/queers, and the philosophers/ nerds. (Males and females have different roles but still sort themselves out into groups based on specific criteria.)

There has always been a tension/conflict concerning *who decides*, who makes the rules for the group. Now, in the second decade of the twenty-first century, the stoners and nerds have united and are taking their revenge on the warriors. Trump represents the warrior class, the class that has always dominated, combining physical and mental adroitness—in other words, superior hand, eye, heart, and mind coordination (which, by the way, females have always been attracted to). But now the nerds, combined with females and other minorities (those having had sand kicked in their face since forever), see their chance to dominate, to rule due to technology and artificial intelligence, which is, in my opinion, bound to end badly. It is, by definition, unnatural.[82]

---

[82] This, in essence, is *where* we are. Technology and artificial intelligence, championed by the historical losers, are the new tools by which the human species, consciously and/or unconsciously, experiments with survival in a hostile, chaotic environment otherwise known as planet earth or reality.
Trump is an alpha male representing nature as it exists. The resistance represents a vision—an imagined world where *consciousness* triumphs over strength and *wit* as deterministic of outcomes—a world where the therapeutic narcissistic (feel-good) culture triumphs over the survival of the fittest (where only the strong survive). Said another way, twenty-four-year-old Bob Dylan was a prophet. Trump is either Batman or Hitler. Who decides?
There are two vastly different stories about America (USA). One is Trump's: that of the hero's journey—that of George Washington, Daniel Boone, Davy Crocket, John Wayne, Henry Ford, Rocky Balboa, Ronald Reagan, and Donald Trump. The other is that of Hillary Clinton's: that of the victim—that of the enslaved, conquered, oppressed, and abused, that of "Cortez the Killer" (https://www.youtube.com/watch?v=paeNnR33i5Q) and Donald Trump. Is it possible that both are true? If not for one, the other would not exist. There

(News update: There is yet another terrorist attack, this time in Dhaka, Bangladesh, at an upscale bakery café. At least twenty were killed.)

18. Narcissist—selfish
19. Bully—cowardice
20. Thin-skinned—neurotic

This cluster comes under the rubric of personality or temperament—a favorite place of attack for Mr. Trump's critics and opponents. As I stated early on, there is no doubt Trump is a hypomanic narcissist,[83] but he's hardly selfish, thin-skinned, racist, sexist (see number 4, Megyn Kelly), or xenophobic.[84]

---

is contrast and conflict. And then the question is, *who decides?* Which version/cover of Neil Young's "Cortez the Killer" do you prefer? Is the story in any way accurate? Artistically, it *is* brilliant, as evidenced by the many moving renditions/covers, but does that make it true? Or is it merely art—*someone's* representation of that which is? Can you fall in love with the artist, the messenger, and at the same time, refute the message?

[83]   A hypomanic narcissist is, at its root, the state of a large skilled, confident individual falling/being in love or in mating mode. In varying degrees, most people, male and female, have experienced that state of being; but it's often short-lived. For a very few, it's the way they travel through life. Those with this abnormality have almost boundless energy, confidence, and will; and they usually triumph and get what or who they desire. They are winners in the game of life. What drives them is the stuff of depth, social, and behaviorist psychology; and the theories are almost endless. My own theory is that reciprocal determinism drives human behavior and helps shape the variant human personality, which leads to conflict and dominate/submissive behaviors (i.e., hierarchies), which lead to, rather than chaos, order.

[84]   In a panel discussion on CSPAN's *Book TV,* three reporters and the moderator discussed Trump's memoir, *The Art of the Deal,* in the context of following him on the campaign trail, for ninety minutes. One of the reporters who writes for *The Wall Street Journal* said that in her years of covering the entrepreneur billionaire class, she found Mr. Trump's personality to be consistent with all the others. In other words, it's a type. Certain traits are necessary to succeed to that degree in the marketplace. I characterize that trait as hypomanic narcissism—the ability to function at a high level, nonstop, without much sleep, combined with a high degree of confidence and self-love. Also, there is

It was Friday morning on *Morning Joe*, a show I've stopped watching for the reason I'm going to explain here. (I started watching the show at its inception, which was at the beginning of the 2008 presidential election. No matter where I was, in remote sections of Colorado or on the West Coast, where it comes on at 3:00 a.m., I'd go to great lengths to make sure it was available for me to watch. *I know* these folks: Mika and Joe, Willie and Mike, and all their regular guests, reporters, experts, and pundits, all who are paid, by the way, by the network. They and the format hasn't changed much.) For some reason, I tuned back in. The gang was sitting around the desk at the opening, musing about Mr. Trump (they all have become very much Trump haters) and the subject of just *who* he is and *what* he is doing. They came up with quips from Trump, quoted, like "Are you from Turkey? Friend or foe?" and "There's a plane. Maybe they're from Mexico, coming to attack," I had watched the rally live, streaming on YouTube, where those remarks were made. He was *joking*, and it was *funny*, in the context of all that has happened.

Then I checked my Twitter feed. Sure enough, MSNBC's Road Warrior Katy Tur[85] (see "The Campaign") tweeted the jokes, out of context, as did Maggie Haberman of the *New York Times* and CNN. They're supposed to be stellar reporters, but they're not. They are Trump haters, and their predispositions shine through—not leak, *shine*. They can't help themselves, Mika! She is so neurotic, and it was/is so, *so* obvious. Boy, did/ does she have a love/hate obsession/infatuation with strong, powerful, tough-minded, authoritative men. (Her father is Dr. Zbigniew Brzezinski, now in his eighties and still tough as nails. He was President Jimmy Carter's chief national security advisor. Mika grew up around powerful, narcissistic

---

a need for recognition and love from others. With regard to the personality construct of OCEAN, or the Big Five, I would score Trump as high in openness, high in conscientiousness, extremely high in extroversion, low in agreeableness, and very low in neuroticism. He's the type T personality (see "The Real Mr. Trump").

[85] Subsequently, Tur has had her account of her experience published, *Unbelievable: My Front-Row Seat to the Craziest Campaign in American History* (2017). I read her book. It's basically chick lit. Read it for a definition of *chick lit*, but not for an accurate account of what was actually happening with regard to the campaign/election of 2016. It is her biased account, which, unfortunately, dominates "journalism" these days. I can't even imagine a conversation I could have with her.

men.)[86] Mika has just acknowledged a divorce from her husband of nineteen years, and *rumor* has it, she's having an affair with her cohost, Mr. Joe Scarborough.[87] I'm not at all surprised. I feel as though I've watched her grow up. It was so, *so* obvious. Anyway, the point is, they were talking Trump and saying, all of them, that they've known him for a dozen years, that none of them have ever known him to have uttered a racist or sexist or xenophobic remark or comment, and that he has a big heart, is generous, and has always been on the "side of the underdog." So my question is, Why did they let the lies about him continue? Why didn't they come to his defense? That's an intriguing question. Maybe I've explained that in the chapter "Freud on Trumpism." We'll never really know.[88]

If you read Trump's 1987 memoir, *The Art of the Deal*, he explains everything. As I've said before, he's the most consistent/stable person I've ever known. First, his strongest belief is in the power of positive thinking. Second, everything with him is a negotiation—everything! And there is an art to it. This is *what* you do and *how* you do it (never show your cards or let them know you'll settle is a big part of it. And then always be flexible),[89] to

---

[86]   Her father has since died.

[87]   Scarborough, still another narcissist but also very arrogant, admitted he's never read Trump's memoir, which, when you think about it, is insulting not only to Trump but to his viewers as well. Scarborough is so full of criticisms and opinions (he's paid well for them) but is really ill-informed, ignorant even. The insult is he has so little respect for his viewers and the subject, Trump, that he spouts off without doing the required research. He just believes he knows what's what, thus the arrogance. And then Mika fawns over him. It's sad and funny. Mika and Joe are now engaged (maybe married), which I saw coming way back in 2008—that they'd be sleeping with one another, married or not.

[88]   Recently, I tuned back in to *Morning Joe* just because I'm of a curious nature, and in my opinion, their opposition/hatred/resistance to Trump has intensified. I can't watch for more than a few moments—same people ("experts") commenting, determined to be "right." Seriously, I can't stand to look at Mika or Joe. They make me cringe, recoil. I can't be of the same species, can I?

[89]   This is part of what people get so wrong about him. They think he is unstable when what he really is, is practicing his philosophy of life, i.e., everything is a negotiation and you must be tough, strong, smart, and also flexible and unpredictable. It's all part of keeping the advantage, winning "the art of the deal." It looks like crazy, but it's not. It's just who he is, and it works for him.

get the best possible deal you can. And he's all about thinking big, winning, and having fun. He is firmly rooted in the belief that happiness lies in the love of family, not money—money is just how you keep score. God and country come after family. It's really not complicated. And on all accounts, by any measure, he's been very, very successful. You can *not* believe him at your peril.

So far, he's been right about just about everything—from Jeb being low energy right on through "crooked" Hillary, "Pocahontas," Obama's failures,[90] Lyin' Ted, terrorism, the Iraq War, NATO, trade agreements, the porous southern border causing all manner of problems, and the adverse effects of drinking, drugs, and cigarettes. You may not like his style, which (I think) is as much the case as is reaction formation, but the guy delivers. He's admitted he used to be "one of them," a taker using the system to his advantage to make money. Again, that's how he keeps score. He understands the game, the inside game of politics and special interests, how you must pay to play but that it must seem like (lying and deceit) is not the way to play. The politics of lying, you might call it. He understands how to use the media, how they thrive on controversy and conflict. Now he says he wants to take that, his style and personality, and work it for your advantage to make America great again, to make America safe again, to make America rich, to take care of everyone. I have seen *no reason* to doubt him or, at the very least, not to give him a chance. I don't know if he can do what he says: renegotiate trade deals to make them fair; crush ISIS and eliminate terrorism as a lifestyle; bring back high-paying, meaningful, hardworking, and manufacturing jobs to America; and restore pride in family and accomplishment. Maybe he can't; maybe it's too late. Maybe we have peaked as a species, and massive world war, disease, and destruction are all that will reconfigure a healthy balance on the planet. I just don't know. But I do know Obama failed. And if Hillary Clinton is elected, things will get worse.

---

[90] What Trump thought about Obama, both correctly and incorrectly, was that he, Mr. Obama, could and would be an effective "cheerleader" for the country. That was what Obama believed too. He, Obama, believed he could unite the country, bring people together, not only in America but also across the globe. This has been his big failure. The country has never been more divided and the world in more turmoil and danger. Hatred has just exploded under President Obama's leadership. In other words, he has failed tremendously.

Something's Going On

JUNE 21, 2016

As I told Max, I'd read Barack Obama's memoir, *Dreams from My Father: A Story of Race and Inheritance* (published in 1995), before the 2008 election. And now I was rereading it. It's eerie—actually explaining what *is* going on with regard to what's inside of Barack Obama, coming out via his body language that Trump picked up on. To read the 1995 memoir now is to understand Obama's great sense of failure and despair (regardless of his public posturing), and how the thought of Donald Trump, the white man, succeeding as president of the United States when he, the black man, could not must be devastating. If Trump were to succeed, it would probably kill Obama, whereas if Clinton were elected and then fail (as she most probably would), that would validate his own failure—that the task was impossible or that it was a generational task. This is from Obama's preface in *Dreams*, written in 2006 just before he became an official candidate, taken from his famous 2004 speech at the Democratic convention, which launched his subsequent and successful presidential bid:

> Across the spectrum of issues, Americans disagreed: on
> Iraq, taxes, abortion, guns, the Ten Commandments,
> gay marriage, immigration, trade, education policy,

environmental regulation, the size of government, and
the role of the courts. Not only did we disagree, but we
disagreed vehemently, with partisans on each side of the
divide unrestrained in the vitriol they hurled at opponents.
Everything was contestable, whether it was the cause of
climate change or the fact of climate change, the size of
the deficit or the culprits to blame for the deficit . . . If I
could reach those voters directly, frame the issues as I felt
them, explain the choices in as truthful a fashion as I knew
how, then the people's instincts for fair play and common
sense would bring them around.

Reading the book, it is apparent that Obama failed tremendously
in all that he had hoped to accomplish, and that failure was based, in
part, on *reality* (that the world *is* Hobbesian in its nature and that we
are creatures ruled by the *territorial imperative*, the amity/enmity complex,
or nationalism—driven by Maslow's hierarchy of motivational needs), a
reality Obama feared and was not ignorant of but thought (wrongly) he
could overcome. Obama's second-order egotism just might trump Trump's
first-order narcissism. This is also from *Dreams*:

> I'd pronounce the need for change. Change in the White
> House, where Reagan and his minions were carrying on
> their dirty deeds. Change in the Congress, compliant and
> corrupt. Change in the mood of the country, manic and
> self-absorbed. Change won't come from the top, I would
> say. Change will come from a mobilized grass roots.

> Communities had to be *created* [emphasis mine], fought
> for, tended like gardens. They expanded or contracted
> with the dreams of me—and in the civil rights movement
> those dreams had been large. I saw the African-American
> community becoming more than just the place where you'd
> been born or the house where you'd been raised. Through
> organizing, through shared sacrifice, membership had
> been earned—because this community I imagined was
> still in the making, built on the promise that the larger
> American community, [or said another way—nationalism]

black, white, and brown, could somehow redefine itself—I
believed it might, over time, admit the uniqueness of my
own life.

When Micah Johnson ambushed the police in Dallas, Texas, it put a
big exclamation point on just how badly President Obama had failed. His
dream, and those of his father, had been shattered. This excerpt sums it up:

> I had been forced to look inside myself and had found
> only a great emptiness there. It was nice to believe that
> the truth would somehow set me free. But what if that was
> wrong? What if the truth only disappointed?

Trump said of Obama, "He doesn't get it, or he gets it better than
anybody understands. It's one or the other, and either one is unacceptable."
Trump, as he almost always does, gets people better than they get
themselves.[91]

---

[91] March 25, 2018, former president Barack Obama is on stage at the fourth
Global Opinion Leaders Summit (GOLS) in Japan, answering questions. He
loops one leg over the other as he repeatedly tugs at the hems of his skinny
pant's legs, holding a large microphone just below his face. He never speaks
Trump's name but clearly is drawing explicit contrast with Trump's agenda of
America First. Obama is rallying *his* base (women, blacks, and young people),
how important *they* are while disparaging "old [white] men." He touts *his*
saving of the *global* economy as his greatest accomplishment; the second, *his*
leadership in the Paris Agreement (which will save the world with regard to
global warming); and lastly, Obamacare, as bringing health care ("free") to
millions of Americans who did not have health insurance. He points to his
reading of books, by past great leaders (MLK and Gandhi), that saved him
from a criminal life as a young man. The coup de grâce is, Obama will create,
via his foundation, "a million young Barack Obamas" to be the future leaders
of the world.
The grandiosity, the passive aggressiveness, the disguised egotism is (almost)
stunning.

This Is the Place: Shocking, Appalling—More Debate

JULY 7, 2016

For months, since the campaign began really, President Obama has said Hillary Clinton, as his secretary of state, didn't harm or put the country in jeopardy with her decision to use a private email server located in her residence to send and receive communications with friends, family, and government officials. And he, Obama, recently endorsed her while at the same time intimating how dangerous and unqualified Mr. Trump is to serve as POTUS. The FBI just concluded their investigation and disagreed, concluding Mrs. Clinton was "extremely careless"[92] concerning her job relating to communications and the security of those communications but that "no reasonable prosecutor" would bring criminal charges against her. Hmmmm . . .[93]

---

[92] It has since been revealed that the words were changed from "grossly negligent," a crime, to "extremely careless, not a crime" by FBI Agent Peter Strzok, a Trump hater.

[93] There is now a reinvestigation regarding her relationship with classified communications.

To recap, Bill Clinton, the former president and the current candidate's spouse, just happens to bump into the current attorney general on the tarmac at a private airport in Phoenix, where the former president was playing golf (in 100-plus temperature). The two have a private thirty-minute-plus chat about grandchildren and golf, nothing more, so they said. This sounds similar to Hillary saying the email server in her home was just for convenience, and the thirty thousand emails she deleted were just about yoga and weddings. Then the FBI, on the biggest summer holiday weekend, calls Mrs. Clinton in for a chat to conclude their investigation. Then the *New York Times* reveals Clinton said she'd consider reupping the attorney general's job as such, if she, Mrs. Clinton, were president. On Tuesday morning, the FBI director, Mr. Comey, gives a presser, saying what she did was not good but not so bad as to bring her up on charges for reckless endangerment.

Later in the day, Mr. Obama and the candidate, Mrs. Clinton, take to the stage together after zooming down to North Carolina on Air Force One. And then the current president says how great a future president she'd make, how qualified she is. The FBI director, in his presser, went down the list of Mrs. Clinton's claims about not knowingly having done anything wrong, that she didn't do this and didn't do that, that it was all just for convenience, and that she was innocent. It was just a mistake that she wouldn't make again. And then the director refutes them all. "Oh yes, she did," he says. "What she claimed just doesn't match up with the evidence we found," he said, "but . . . no charges."

Sounds so similar to Mr. Clinton years ago, saying, "I did not have sexual relations with that woman, Ms. Lewinsky." All the while he was looking directly into the camera's lens and wagging his finger at us, seemingly outraged that we had accused him of such a thing or doubted him. This reminds me of Mrs. Clinton sitting behind a desk at a congressional hearing, screaming at the members, "What difference does it make!" about how and why four Americans were killed in an attack on a US base of operations in Benghazi, Libya, under her purview.[94] And just today, Wednesday, President Obama gives a public speech about the situation in Afghanistan—it's still not so good, better, but not good—having to leave

---

[94] That behavior, the outrage, I just witnessed again by Peter Strzok testifying before the Congress. To me, that behavior looks like arrogance.

a fighting force there after fifteen years, he said. Sounds like a divergence to me.

What difference does any of it make?

(News update: So here we are, July 7, 2016, and there was an attack on the police in Dallas, Texas, during a protest not against Trump but against the presumed racism of police against blacks. Five police are dead, and seven, wounded.)[95]

(Max and I meet up again, two years later in the Summer of 2018.) Max thinks that altruism can be, maybe always is, self-serving, that politicians like Obama have to put a happy face on human nature and that also you/I *could say* that grand alliances like the EU are really about groups of people banding together for survival.

I really do like Max. Grand alliances are too big, I think, they fall victim to internal conflicts, unless the enemy is also so large, as in WWII. Meet force with force and evil with evil. Who wins? Who is the EU uniting against? In a healthy situation, you'd have a bunch of smaller tribes/nations freely trading goods (and mates). But it must be done freely, not by force or theft, which has never been done so far as I know for any length of time, like say, coffee for cotton, fish for beef, coal for oil, etc.

Max falls back to global warming, as that is always the fallback argument for Progressives. I respond. Yes, global warming could be the threat that unites the peopled world, but it's a lie made up for the purpose, like getting rich, of special interests, so says Michael Crichton in *State of Fear.*

Then Max brings up population growth, that we're at critical mass and that we've got to work together to solve that one, everybody. Yes, I agree. Everybody's got to be on the same page, play by the same rules, and *not cheat*! So you've got to get buy in. Trump's a master.

Max finally admits he has no answer and can imagine the wall and the great battle that's coming. We get together over beers and take turns on the jukebox. Or, I suggest, they'd (the others) see how our system works and, with help, copy it. That's the idea: change by willful imitation rather than force. You've got to get buy in. Same with parenting, you lead by example. The child will follow for self-preservation, and the ultimate rewards are

---

[95]   See footnote 62.

pleasure and satisfaction at the end of the day. And yes, some will fail, fall short. And then what do you do about *those* people? That's a tough question.

Max plays a salsa dance tune and talks of the conflicting arguments over the cost and benefits of immigrations. I counter. What if, instead of stewing in resentment and turning that rage outward, like Dylann Roof or yesterday's killer, young people had to do the crap jobs, like in the old days, for peanuts. The cheap labor was done by teens instead of them growing up feeling/thinking/believing they were entitled to the lifestyles of the rich and famous. What if parents actually took care of their children and taught them responsibility?

Now Max is coming around and wants a *real* debate about immigration (me too) instead of the dog and pony shows we get. He brings up "the children" separated from their "parents" and put in cages. That's another really tough one. After all, it wasn't their fault. I've heard the stories.[96] But can we really be the residential treatment center of the world? Maybe we can, but only if we deal with reality and not rainbows and unicorns, the pie-in-the-sky progressive spiel that is really just a power play by some to make money and do well by "good deeds." What a load of bunk.

When working with damaged kids in the child welfare system (for peanuts), one of the things the kids would say to me is "You're just here for the money. You don't care about me." And instead of denying it, I'd go "You've got a point" and take the conversation from there, meet them where they're at, pacing it's called, and then move the conversation. It's Trump's flexibility in negotiation: be willing to walk away, come back.

No need to fight. Trump's agile. The Left says he's erratic, unhinged, and unstable. Bunk, I say. It's a style. People will come back if you can figure out what it is they want/need. It's really not that hard. Why are all these people so stupid? Now that's complicated.

Max moves the conversation to manufacturing, production, and technology, playing a techno-dance number. I say give me a minute and go to the bathroom, collecting my thoughts. I come back, flash the music box with my card, and punch up George Jones's "Bartender's Blues."

---

[96] Trump, as president, has offered a deal where 1.2 million minor children brought into the USA illegally could apply for citizenship in exchange for funding for the border wall. So yes, in a way, Mexico or Mexicans, would pay for the wall.

Prejudice, Common Sense, and the Halo Effect

JULY 12, 2016

Trauma surgeon Dr. Brian H. Williams (forty-seven years old and married with children, who tried unsuccessfully to save the lives of slain police officers, himself an African American) pleaded, "This killing has to stop," at a press briefing in Dallas, Texas (see footnote 73). That seems reasonable. It seems common sense—something practical that any everyman, every day, could, would, and should agree with. So what's the problem? Why can't we Americans come together and stop the killing?

Megyn Kelly, Fox News superstar (made all the more famous by candidate Donald J. Trump), takes on that question. And lo, what happened? Kelly held one of her "powerful panel" focus groups in prime time with activists and experts—lawyers, pastors, former law enforcers, "people at the heart of the issue." I tuned in with great curiosity. The panel consisted of thirty (well-dressed and groomed for TV) people from large metropolitan eastern and midwestern cities. There were ten black men and five black women and ten white men and five white women (some were probably of mixed race). The "conversation" lasted an hour, and not a single mind was moved. All were typical positions, easily predictable. Ideas and solutions were put forth (many reasonable and with merit) with all manner of emotion. Watching that (despite many saying that what *was needed* was honest and truthful dialogue), it seemed to me that nothing would change, that the killing would not stop. Everyone there, all these smart, powerful people, came in with their minds made up that their position was the right one. And if only the others would listen (i.e., submit) to *their* reasoning, the complex and compound issue of racism, injustice, and violence could be solved.[97]

Shocking? Not at all, just common human higher-order cognitive activity, smart (stupid) highly social primates doing what they do.

Here's the story: Prejudice (typical human cognition of prejudging people and facts) exists because it's practical or just plain common sense to allow for the typical human to survive in a hostile world—a world that doesn't give a hoot if he, she, or *x* does or doesn't survive. In a hostile world, it is wise to make snap judgments based on what one sees and preconceives (believes, was taught, thinks) to be true. One who stops to ask questions, considers alternative possible outcomes, looks at the situation from different points of view—well, those people are not our ancestors. They didn't make it.[98]

So all these smart (stupid) people from both sides of the/any issue—black/white, male/female, religious/not, liberal/conservative, educated/not, attractive/not—come into the "open conversation" with good intentions but, within moments, are at each other's throats, convinced

---

[97] Now, here in America, we've had yet another mass shooting, the slaughter of high school students in Parkland, Florida, by a nineteen-year-old former-expelled student. And the debate rages on. This time—everyone insists—it will be different, that real change will come because the teenagers, young people, are the future! They protest and make the argument for gun control. And then on top of that, there was another killing of an unarmed black man by police, and *this time*, the protests will have an effect. Sure (sarcasm).

[98] Lee H. Whittlesey, *Death in Yellowstone: Accidents and Foolhardiness in the First National Park* (1995). This is a recommended read. This is, in essence, a detailed, factual account of the *reality* that the real world is hostile, i.e., dangerous. Pretty much, Yellowstone is the planet as it has always been—a dangerous, hostile, chaotic environment. It's not unreasonable to assume humans evolved in this context.

only of their certainty of being right (which also has great survival value in a hostile world). The road to hell . . .

Enter Megyn Kelly—arbitrator, mediator, journalist, TV personality— whom Donald Trump has called a lightweight bimbo and highly overrated. He's right (which is beside the point; see previous chapter "The Case against Trump," June 13, 2016), but not in the eyes of the panelists, because to them, she is goddess-like. This *is* the halo effect. Said another way, it is a prejudice or "a tendency to evaluate all components of a target person in the same way once a general evaluation, positive or negative, is formed."[99] This is what the police must do because they work and live in a hostile world. With regard to Kelly (and others in her position), snap judgments are made based on preconceived schemas.[100] It is assumed—because she occupies *the* prime time slot on Fox News, has a law degree, and is attractive—that what she says and thinks has merit when, in fact, it may not. She might, in fact, be a lightweight bimbo. And yet that might not be her fault! Who can possibly know what came first? What *one* thing led to the next thing? (Reciprocal determinism.) It's the question, the paradox, all thinkers think about—thinkers with the leisure and safety to think.

So back to the police and if they are racist and so on and so forth. Their world *is* hostile! How do I know? Because they carry a gun, a club, and handcuffs. If their world were not hostile, these tools would not be necessary. One panelist screamed, "We need to disarm the police! They began as the slave patrol." Maybe she's right, then again, maybe she's not.

Do *you* think if the police were disarmed that violence would end? Do you think that if sensible gun control were passed that the killing would stop? Do you think that if we just open our arms and embrace the Islamic radicalists that they would "see the light"?

The police are called into situations, often violent, to "keep the peace." The situation often involves a boundary violation—one person stealing from another—property or physical integrity, one's sacred space. They, the police, are supposed to take sides and make a judgment quickly to save lives because someone (God?) deemed that all (human) lives matter.

---

[99]   Michael Leippe, *The Psychology of Attitude Change and Social Influence* (1991), 256.

[100]   Schemas are shortcuts the brain takes in order to survive, based on either evolutionary or cultural/learned information. They are either hard- (universal) or soft- (culturally) wired. Said another way, "Can a leopard change its spots?"

Are you beginning to get a sense of how complex the issue of policing is? *And* the police are not valued nearly to the degree that Megyn Kelly is. Why is that?

Do you want to reorganize all of society and civilization?

E. O. Wilson said, way back in 1978, "Altruism based on kin selection is the enemy of civilization. If human beings are to a large extent guided to favor their own relatives and tribe, only a limited amount of global harmony is possible."[101] At the time, Wilson was vilified by feminists— egged, in fact—protested against. The police were needed to keep order.

What has changed? Weapons and means of communication, for sure, but people we're the same, trying to survive in a hostile world.

Who gets it? Trump, because he's survived and thrived in the most nonviolent manifestation of a violent world—business and real estate— where laws and negotiation reign, in other words, humanity functioning at its highest level as cooperative competitors. Sans killing, we negotiate and come to an agreement.

Then I watched an interview with Jeb Bush, one of the vanquished who Trump had slain without killing. Bush thought (based on his behavior) that he was entitled to be commander in chief of the most powerful force in the civilized world because he was . . . what? The smartest? The strongest? The most viscous? Or because of dynasty? Bush was clueless as to how the real world works. People are creatures of a hostile world—full of fear, anxiety, and uncertainty—a world ruled by strength and force, not halos, rainbows, and unicorns.

Last night, I watched CNN's Don Lemon's (sour puss) version of the "Let's all have a conversation about race and violence and policing in America." Lemon called it "Black, White, and Blue," something like that. Again, the group consists of respected black and white professionals, even the abovementioned doctor, Mr. Brian Williams, along with some victims. Later, I watched the Jedi's take on a YouTube podcast,[102] which is fifty minutes long and well worth listening to. The Jedi and I agree on some things and disagree on others.

My take is, Lemon's panel were mostly Liberals and Progressives— united against the enemy (white supremacist cops) and the hazard (institutional racism). The folks were, all of them, victims of oppression,

---

[101] E. O. Wilson, *On Human Nature* (1978).

[102] https://www.youtube.com/watch?v=aUESOXt8Uzc

even Don Lemon. I have some questions; some of which are answered by the Jedi, who may or may not represent some of the folks.

Question: What percentage of the police are white supremacists? The Jedi says all of them, even the black cops.

Question: What percentage are not white supremacists but just hyper-aggressive males looking for suitable work? (Other suitable jobs for such men are football, boxing, soldiering, firefighting, rodeo-ing, the FBI, CIA, and the Secret Service, i.e., "the hero.") On the other side are local and national gangs, like motorcycle, drug, and territorial street gangs. And then there's the way other side, like ISIS, radical Islamist terrorists. The Jedi calls the police "savage-ass terrorists" and that they are really "wimpy asses" who will run when the real shooting starts. The Jedi says, "If people start to [obscenity] with you and you don't [obscenity] with them back, they going to continue to [obscenity] with you. You have to fight back, retaliate." Sounds a lot like Donald Trump's philosophy.

Question: In a hostile, violent world full of enemies and hazards, what are you going to do? The Jedi says, and I agree, "This love and forgiveness [obscenity] is contrary to the human spirit."

Question: What is the dominant culture, and who and how is that decided?

The Stupid Tax

JULY 29, 2016

Here's the story: I've been on the road for eight days, and then after arriving home (tired and punch-drunk) and parking my car in my garage, the dude who has the garage next to mine parks in my extended space, blocking me in. Now I can't move via motorized travel. I try all manner of mitigation/mediation to resolve the conflict (use your imagination), and finally, the tow company arrives to move the vehicle.

You can take David Foster Wallace's approach from his famous "This Is Water" speech (2005 commencement address at Kenyon College), where he suggests that you should be kind and compassionate/caring/understanding (i.e., patient) when encountering inconvenience in one's day-to-day goings-on. But I submit to you for consideration that this attitude has led to a lowering of the bar to the point that solipsism (antitribalism) and stupidity now rule—in other words, reverse Darwinism.

I, in fact, had an emergency-type situation—my father's degenerating mind and body and all that encompasses. So maybe my neighbor had an emergency too, but what if we all lived by the Golden Rule—the Sermon on the Mount? Why can't we? It's simply a matter of civility and consideration. You needn't even have to *respect* the other to be considerate.

The answer is, we (humans) are not special. Sorry. We're selfish creatures, just like all the other creatures on this planet. We struggle, within and without, for resources, space, territory, and recognition/validation on this planet.

So there is a stupid tax. We share with our four-legged friends the attribute of shortsighted solipsism (instant gratification for oneself) but distinguish ourselves when it comes to stupidity (slow-witted, lack of intelligence and common sense). We men (humans) who declare ourselves thinking men (*Homo sapiens*) do think, but often in twisted, thoughtless, arrogant, and crooked ways, i.e., stupidly.

Trump knows or feels or intuits or has learned how the real world works. He can't write or speech it out in elegant prose or poetry, but he *knows*! Want proof? Look! Just watch and listen not to the pundits and experts but to your own eyes and ears. Pay attention! Whose plane is that? Whose skyscraper? Whose resort? Whose name is on the plane and buildings?

Trump's credo is quality (realized) that's below budget and ahead of schedule. Competence above connections. He'll fire them all—the pigs at the trough, the swamp creatures—be they Liberal or Conservative, black or white, male or female, Christian or Muslim. I don't know if he can pull it off, but if anyone can, it's Trump. (See his convention speech: "No one knows the system better than me. I alone can fix it.") The system *is* rigged! The system *is* Clinton! The system is the machine. I don't know if one man can change it, but *look*—look at what he's done![103] His children love him. He's one of the richest persons in the world (your rules, not his).[104] He doesn't need this job.

Here's more to the story. In six years, my rent has increased by 62 percent. That's 10 percent a year. I've been here through six management changes and two sales of the property. And now this: The trash has been backing up for weeks. The recycle bins are stuffed with trash and garbage

---

[103] But don't take my word. Here's a recent interview with a famous reporter touting Trump's ability to do the seemingly impossible: https://www.facebook. com/PoppyHarlowCNN/videos/927618587361146/?pnref=story.

[104] Recently, *Forbes* magazine came out with their list of the richest people in the world, and Trump was number 766, down from number 544 in 2016. He's lost approximately a half billion dollars since the start of his campaign. Jeff Bezos is now the richest man in the world. Wonder why Trump's gone after him? Really?

that is supposed to be put in the compacter. It's in the lease, but the folks, my fellow residents, my "community," cannot or will not adhere to the policy written into the lease that specifies what can and cannot be tossed into these dumpsters. It has come to this—a stalemate, an impasse. It's been this way for a month ever since the latest management change, despite management sending out a memo. The residents complain but don't comply. There's law, but no order, no enforcement. This is, unfortunately, trickle-down stupidity. If you pass laws and don't enforce them, the laws will not be obeyed by some and then many. You can argue that that is "smart" action on the part of the lawbreakers, but you must agree it's stupid action on the part of the lawmakers. Blaise Pascal, centuries ago, said, "Justice without force is powerless. Force without justice is tyrannical." And still we have not learned.

So I saunter into the management or the lawmaker's sleek/modern office and give them a simple solution: hire people to truck the contaminated trash in recycle bins to the, wherever/whatever it is called now, dump (good name) or landfill; start anew; and then let residents (i.e., the "community") know that they will be fined big-time for failing to comply with the law. It's not that hard, and yet . . . and yet . . .[105]

Now I ask you: What would Trump do?

The answer is, he'd fire the (obscenity) management for incompetence because he can't stand it—incompetence. Then he'd demand of the residents: You either do *your* job (not all that hard if you can read, because memos have been sent out, as well as having been in the lease), which is to adhere to the rules and regulations of community living, or get out. In other words, "You're fired," both management and residents. And yet to watch the Dems' convention or, for that matter, the Progressive agenda, which is somehow this is all someone's fault other than who is responsible. In other words, there is no personal responsibility. Trump says, "Give me a break!"

There should be a stupid tax for being stupid. There is in the real world, in the natural world (see *Death in Yellowstone*).

Such as on July 7, I sold all my shares of Facebook because I got so angry at Facebook/Zuckerberg for manipulating the news feeds, as well as my own posts, to shape what is seen on Facebook toward their own worldview. (They are so slanted toward the progressive/one-world,

---

[105] I've since moved to a newer "community" (within the same zip code), and lo, same problem! People, sheesh.

politically correct, borderless worldview. Sheesh! I got so angry.) I did this despite knowing that the stock would continue to rise, and sure enough, it did. My stupidity, my anger, cost me many, many thousands of dollars. So that's a "stupid tax" in the real world.[106]

Being stupid in the natural world has costs, negative consequences. Often in the natural world, being stupid can cost you your life. That's Darwinism, survival of the fittest.[107] Knowingly parking illegally and getting towed or ticketed is a stupid tax. Driving under the influence of alcohol and getting caught is a stupid tax. Cheating on your spouse, getting caught, and then divorcing is a stupid tax, because it costs you money.[108] But now, with the progressive, politically correct, feminist, liberal, postmodern mind-set taking over in America, the consequences for being stupid have been overturned, unless it serves their agenda. Sounds like hypocrisy, a power play, yes?

When did this start?

I think it started with the O. J. Simpson trial in the mid-nineties. (Look it up. There has been a movie and a documentary made about it.) I think maybe the human race peaked or plateaued in the '70s and '80s. There was a rise of social consciousness in the '60s and a revolution of sorts. Great change was forced on the people by the people. And many people resisted. There was violence on both sides, and force was used. But then things calmed down in the '80s, and it seemed like a new order, a more peaceful, just order prevailed.

And then with the OJ trial, there was a confluence of technology and human emotion that seemed to override reality and any successful change. At once you had real-time events (via TV/cameras in the courtroom),

---

[106] As of this rewrite, Facebook's share price has dropped 20 percent below what I sold it at because they've been exposed for the selling of users' personal data for profit. That, I knew they did, but now I "feel" smart because I'm richer and they're poorer. It's human nature.

[107] Never mind for now that *survival of the fittest* actually means just surviving long enough to reproduce and care for your offspring so that they survive to reproduction age—in other words, surviving long enough to keep your gene pool going.

[108] And maybe the presidency is a stupid tax. But for now, Mr. Trump's wife, Melania, the First Lady, is hanging in there despite the growing crescendo to divorce the president.

combined with the media's power (via cable technology / fiber optics), to reach the masses greatly enhanced. And so expert opinion merged/conflicted with everyman opinion, and order was disrupted.

There was at once the law, celebrity, murder, money, racism, instant replay/technology, science, love, lust, jealousy all coming together to seemingly overwhelm the average human capacity to deal with reality or the amount of stimuli the common human brain was able to digest. The average brain was overwhelmed, resulting in something I call both Darwinism and reverse Darwinism, meaning stupidity rules over common sense. That in itself is an oxymoron, because no sense is any longer believed to be common. Everything is relative and subject to interpretation, thus say the postmodernists.

Sense/awareness is (has always been) relative to one's proximate environment (what is in front of me that I must deal/negotiate with in order to survive). What had (common sense) resulted in an inventory of emotions that we humans relied on to see us successfully to the next moment (i.e., to survive) had been nullified. Stupid people trumped smart people. Due to technology *and* the human condition (which is based on emotion), common sense has been superseded by mankind's ability to create and use tools that subjugate his ability to think, reason, and *feel*, to make sense of the confluence of event, action, and consequence. Technology and artificial intelligence have reduced man to an unthinking, unreasoning consumer subject only to his desire for pleasure (to feel good), for immediate gratification, foremost of which is the desire to be right—in other words, to justify one's actions and behaviors to satisfy one's own self-importance over that of others.

Humans have created, with all their brilliance and creativity, a culture of therapeutic narcissism.[109]

However, the desire to be right (universal), which engenders attributes that lead to success/survival, of not only the self but also the group/species has not changed. But the group has changed; the group is now defined not by territory or kinship but by ideology or identity politics, which knows no boundaries. The struggle for power and control remains as it has always

---

[109] Christopher Lasch, *The Culture of Narcissism: American Life in an Age of Diminishing Expectations* (1979). I cannot recommend this book enough. This book, my book, this age we are living in, the age of Trump, is foreshadowed in Lasch's.

been, motivated by what it has always been, but the circle of power and influence has now become global and unknowable.

Who decides? It's a conundrum that we seem unable to solve regardless of time or tools.

Pascal again says, "All of our reasoning ends in surrender to feeling."

Natural consequences is another way, a more politically correct way, of referencing the stupid tax. Get burned by fire and one learns to avoid the flame, the heat. But now there are remedies to compensate for natural consequences or to overcome them. What seems to have happened is that, via technology, the strong no longer dominate. The gun triumphs over the club, which beats tooth and fang. What does common sense and intelligence, even learning and study, matter if you can just tap on a screen or take a pill and be rewarded with apparent success, joy, and bliss?

If the solution is just a click away, if everyone gets a trophy and everyone is entitled to whatever they desire (truly crazy), then the bar *has* been lowered artificially. So the question becomes like this: Will the stupid tax ultimately reassert itself, with dire consequences for the human race; or have we defeated it, triumphed over nature, and entered into a borderless world where everything is everything and everyone is equal, regardless of strength or intelligence? It's a world where differences are ignored and nothing matters. You can have whomever and whatever you want. Competition, comparison, preference, and contrast are ruled out and replaced by what? How stupid is that! But you can vote for that.

The Conventions

AUGUST 2, 2016

Watching the Democratic National Convention, I thought, *My word, how did that man Trump ever get to be the Republican nominee? He's the most unqualified, vile person . . . maybe in the history of the world! I'm going to vote for her, Hillary Clinton.* But then I remembered what I'd watched and learned the previous seventeen months, no, wait, sixty-six years. So what was it that I'd watched? How could a group of people, a national political party, actually fall for all that prevarication? That's the best word I can think of to describe what I witnessed for four days—*prevarication* (misleading). *Lie* might be too strong a word, because I actually think the candidate and her supporters want so desperately to make the case for their ideas and ideals that they twist and distort things to fit the story they want to believe—they mislead rather than out-and-out lie to convince themselves of what they must know, deep down, is not true. Give the Dems credit; they conceived of and executed quite a story. It was far from reality, but if that's all you watched, you might believe it. It was a world of rainbows, unicorns, puppies and balloons—a lovefest where all the people of the world could gather and party (Woodstock). There were rich people, billionaires and generals, poor folks, black folks, and Muslims. And there were the most powerful of persons, the president and vice president of the United States, and the least powerful, the disabled and disadvantaged and the taken-advantage-of.

But there was something wrong. They, the speakers, weren't happy.

They were angry, really, really angry.

The speakers would come up on stage and scream and shout into the microphone. But it wasn't real anger, no, it was faux anger, masking fear. Anger's antecedent is restraint—being held against your will, a loss of freedom. These folks were free as birds on the wing, free to say whatever it was they wanted, true or false. There was no restraint. They were free to prevaricate away. What they were afraid of was losing power and being proven wrong, to be beaten and then exposed as frauds.

Victory by Trump might well be the case. (See "Something's Going On, June 21, 2016.) The convention wasn't a lovefest but a hate fest—a hate fest toward the evil villain Trump. I thought Joe Biden's head would actually explode. Good ole mild-mannered Uncle Joe, I'd never seen him like that. What an act! And the Muslim father Khizr Khan, whose son had died on the battlefield of Iraq, was thrusting the Constitution at the camera, shouting at Trump, "How dare you . . ." It was another act/performance, using his son's honorable death in war to promote his own agenda, that of Muslim immigration into the United States. (That was the man's assigned job.) Out of respect for his son, I'll say no more, except *please.* And the president, "Was it his best speech ever?" gushed the press and pundits. Or was it his desperate attempt to try to ensure his legacy as a genius and saint? Compared to a Hillary Clinton presidency, it, his presidency, just might look like that.

Oh, these politicians, how they do prevaricate—and of course, the candidate herself, the history-maker, soon-to-be first woman president of the United States of America. Her husband, Bill Clinton, himself, a former president, told her story of how it was disabling love when he first saw her at the library in Yale, how he finally convinced her to marry him, how she always took on the tough fights, the plight of the poor and disadvantaged, and struggled and . . . Well, she never won, but she never gave up. She kept fighting. Still is. *Oh my god, what a woman!* Except he left a lot out, a lot of reality, a lot of what really went down.[110]

---

[110] Dick Morris, *Rewriting History* (2004). See this book for another interpretation of the story. He was there, with the Clintons, for much of it.

Here is an example of prevarication. Hillary Clinton, onstage the final night, is making the case against the vile and evil Trump, setting the stage for the following week's attacks to question Trump's mental health. They (columnists, reporters, psychoanalysts, novelists, pundits) all seemingly, independently, arrived at the same place at the same time: Trump might really be *crazy*!

Here's the setup. She says, "Donald Trump said, 'I alone can fix it.'" This is true. He did say that, but before that, he said, "No one knows the system [the *it*, the *swamp*] better than me." Clinton implied that Trump was saying that he could *fix the world* all by himself, without help from anyone, neatly contrasting that with her theme of "Stronger together." While the statement was true, he did say that, the meaning was distorted, twisted. Thus, Trump's nickname for her is Crooked Hillary. It's so true. So brilliant is Trump's penchant for nailing a person's weakness with a nickname. What Trump meant was that having been on the other side— the side of donors and special interests, as a businessman giving financial contributions to politicians of both parties to get what he wanted, so as to thrive as a real estate developer and businessman—he knew the system/ machine and how it worked inside and out and that compared to Hillary, he was uniquely qualified, the only one who could "fix it." She, having been bought and paid for many times over, is, in other words, corrupted.[111] Add that to her being personally compromised by way of her allowing her husband's philandering to go on and then smearing her husband's accusers. Well, she's simply not qualified to hold any office if honesty, integrity, trustworthiness, and truth are important to you.[112] The pathogenic opposite of truth is dishonesty. That's the Clintons, both of them.

So you've got a lot, *a lot*, of very powerful people very much invested in seeing Hillary Clinton become the next president of the United States not because she would be good for the country or the world but because she would ensure their own status in that world and country and maybe even stay out of jail! That's a real fear. Donald J. Trump is a threat not only to the system but also to the individuals who benefit from that system.

---

[111] Peter Schweizer, *Clinton Cash: The Untold Story of How and Why Foreign Governments and Businesses Helped Make Bill and Hillary Rich (2015)*.

[112] Gary Byrne, *Crisis of Character: A White House Secret Service Officer Discloses His Firsthand Experience with Hillary, Bill, and How They Operate* (2016).

At the Democratic convention, a rosy picture was painted, along with a beautiful story of love and togetherness. Elect Hillary Clinton, and we all can continue down this path and write the next chapters in history together of a great country getting even stronger and better—a more perfect union. Splendid! But like Bill's romantic, novel-like story of her, some things were left out, such as nine major economic indices that show stark negative trending numbers: (1) student loan debt, (2) food stamp program participation, (3) federal debt, (4) money printing, (5) health insurance costs, (6) labor force participation, (7) workers' share of the economy, (8) median family income, and (9) homeownership.

This might explain why the percentage of voters who think the country is headed in the wrong direction hovers around 67 percent.

Stronger together, of course, we are. That is the basis for affiliation, friendship, alliances, and coalitions. In fact, it is a major component of the human species' survival repertoire. This is the amity/enmity complex.[113] The complex can be represented in a mathematical formula: $A = E + h$. A is equivalent to affiliation, friendship, alliances, and coalitions. E is equivalent to one's enemy—either a person, a tribe, a clan, a nation, etc.—and h is equivalent to a hazard, say, a natural disaster, like a flood or hurricane. Thus, our friendships, including our primal bonding, depend on an external force/entity that threatens our personal survival. Human relationships are an extension of this equation.

Viewed in this way, the conventions were simply a matter of constructing an $E + h$ equation, sufficient to get you to affiliate with or vote for A. With the Democrats, it was simple: Trump is evil and represents both E and h. Bring out the testimonials.[114]

At the Republican's convention, it was a harder task. Trump challenged all conventions with a different narrative. Who *is* the enemy? What *is* the hazard?[115]

Based on his life and what he has said, I'd say (albeit I'm inferring only, having never met the man or sat with him for a tête-à-tête) that the enemy

---

[113] Robert Ardrey, *The Territorial Imperative: A Personal Inquiry into the Animal Origins of Property and Nations* (1966).

[114] It is still going on with adult film actor Stormy Daniels and former Playmate Karen McDougal.

[115] The hazards are the "swamp," the system, drugs and alcohol, radical Islamic terrorism, illegal immigration, globalism, and the costal elites. And China?

is radical Islam and those that adhere to it, i.e., terrorists. In addition, the enemy is, or are, illegal immigrants entering this country. Blurring between enemy and hazard is joblessness and the fact that manufacturing and construction jobs, good-paying jobs, have been taken across borders and overseas. Work bonds people together toward a common goal—completion of a project—as well as provides a living and dignity, self-esteem. Without adequate meaningful work, people are subject to whatever provides them with a means to carry on, to exist, be it sex, money, power, revenge, repression, drugs and/or alcohol, war, or the promise of reward in the afterlife.

For Trump, work is paramount to a reason for being. He stresses bringing jobs, work, back to America for all people—black, white, brown, well educated, and the not-so well educated—for men *and* women. With work comes dignity and a reason for being. It's what drives him, and he views work as the prime reason for being. Threats to work come in many forms, both from within and without individuals, as well as from within and without our country. Evil men are a threat. Incompetent leadership is a threat. Lawlessness is a threat. Greed is a threat. Dishonesty is a threat. Disorder is a threat. Trump is a builder and a fixer of problems; this is how he sees himself. His accomplishments show this to be true. He's seen *it* from all sides and thinks and believes he can fix *it*. That is what he was selling at the Republican convention. The house is on fire, and he's the fireman. And once he puts out the fire, he can rebuild the house, with a little help from his friends, better than ever. He's done it before.

Despicable Democrats and the Media

AUGUST 11, 2016

Those are harsh words, a very tough headline, but I think you'll agree once I lay out what the Democrats' economic strategy is. But before I begin, here's a distinction between suppression and repression. *Suppression* is something done willfully, like speaking with political correctness. You *suppress* what it is you are really thinking and/or feeling so as to appear more agreeable, likeable, whatever—or, say, *presidential*. When the early motto in the Trump campaign was "Let Trump be Trump," that was a way of saying let us not suppress Trump's natural instincts. He's been very successful being who he is, which is unsuppressed, uninhibited by convention or political correctness—in other words, unfiltered. Trump has a philosophy, and it works.

Repression, on the other hand, is *unconscious* suppression. It is inhibition of desire and/or instinctual drive, usually with health-related consequences, sickness or disease, such as you really want to —— that girl but fear rejection, retaliation, revenge, some harm if you were to attempt to do so. The desire is *repressed*. In place of that, you scratch your nose, adjust your clothes, look at the scenery, or pick flowers for your mother. You do anything other than to try and satisfy your actual desire. Then you come down with the flu or crash your car or flip some other dude off and get beat up.

Mr. Trump mostly satisfies his desires, which many people recoil from. It causes them to look at their own unmet desires. Another way to understand suppression and repression is to think of dancing.

Uninhibited dancing is repression exposed or sexual desire openly expressed in a socially acceptable context—dancing / ice dancing (think tango and Olympic pairs skating). Inhibited dancing is also *repression exposed* or the willful disengagement from the desire to express your sexual desire publicly. All can be unhealthy—repression, suppression and, unexpressed sexual desire.

That said, the foundation of the Democrats' strategy's is rooted in egotistic defense mechanisms or repression and suppression. Now you can argue, "So what? Everyone uses them." And I'll counter with it's better for everyone to see the truth of things, reality, and look to solve real problems with that as a baseline rather than the fool's fantasy. Build your house on rock, not sand, and so on. Now I'm not saying or comparing myself or Mr. Trump to Jesus, only that knowledge trumps fantasy and denial. Fantasy and denial are but two of a dozen (at least) ego defense mechanisms. Others are identification, projection, reaction formation, regression, rationalization, atonement, compensation, displacement, and sublimation. Yes, everyone uses them, sometimes, to some degree or another. As with most things, it's a matter of degree and/or frequency and the subsequent consequences, both short and long term.

I am not immune, but I am aware of what it is I'm doing most of the time and accept the consequences. As does Mr. Trump. Me, when things get really bad—*things* being reality—when I've done all I can do, I'll take a little vacation or escape. But again, I'm fully aware of what and why I'm doing it and know I'm dealing only with the symptoms, doing nothing to solve the long-term problems. My "vacation" involves drinking and sometimes smoking a little weed (painkillers). Now Trump, he does neither; he just works till he solves the problem. Sometimes, he walks away. I'm good at that too. But the Democrats and the media, they dwell in the land of ego defense mechanisms. That's where they live, and they've built their houses on sand.

For instance, take the current election, voter turnout, voter ID, immigration and refugee crises, Planned Parenthood, minimum-wage jobs, education, and violence as just a few of the issues facing the country. They all weave together and combine to illuminate the Democrats' strategy to win, as well as highlight the ego's defense system.

Here's the story: Under the guise of moral righteousness, social justice—whatever and however they frame it—what is really going on is a power play. The power motive is behind it. The Dems want to get themselves elected into a position of power for their own gratification/validation, both for economic and personal reasons, rooted in their childhoods, just like most everyone everywhere. It's a human universal, the human condition. Childhood decides, or the child is father to the man. However you choose to say it, it's true. The formative years determine what and who you become.

Democrats/Liberals/Progressives, more so than Republicans or Conservatives, seem to make use of the ego defense mechanisms, with the exception of identification and sublimation, which are used more by those on the Right, and then also rationalization and displacement, which both sides seem to often resort to. Back to the story. The Democrats' strategy, which, of course, they'll deny, is to eventually replace the established mainstream, middle-class, right-of-center majority of white voters with a coalition of previously marginalized (some would say victims or the oppressed) minorities of women/feminists, blacks/Africans, Hispanics/Latins, immigrants/Asians, Muslims, and refugees, using the affiliation motive, which requires an enemy (Trump / the rich / the white man) and/or hazard (global warming and patriarchy).

The Dems couch this in the language of the oppressed, giving voice to the ego defense mechanisms of displacement and rationalization (it's not your fault), fantasy (you can be whatever it is you want to be, we are all equal), projection (Trump and his ilk are liars, thieves, bullies, frauds, etc.), reaction formation (hate that which you fear you need, i.e., a strong father / protector / tribe), regression (give out hugs, sweet talk, and other gifts of nurturance), atonement (right the wrongs of slavery and other previous failures of character and leadership), and compensation (the guarantee of the Declaration of Independence is that you are all equal). So the Dems want y'all to vote for them, of course, the purveyors of social justice and righters of wrongs, even if you've no right, under the law, to vote. They promise you welfare, a subsistent living anyway, and free education and health care, which is better than what you had before, be it in this country or another. Refugees and immigrants are all welcome, *and* you can register to vote at Planned Parenthood (no voter ID required as we are all one), where you can get free health care. Where does the money come from? Why, from taxes on the wealthy, of course, born with a silver spoon in their mouth and an unearned seat at the table. They've never paid their fair share. And then also from the middle class, which has benefited from "white privilege." So the story goes! They (white men) lie, steal, cheat, use, and abuse you. Who needs them?

When enough people gather into a community/territory, Walmart, Starbucks, McDonalds, and Home Depot will come in and provide jobs for some. The government will subsidize housing, education, health care, and other services too. Those that work for the government will do all right, and those that provide the guidance and management of services will do even better. Some will get rich. Some of the immigrants, those motivated by high achievement, will try their hand at entrepreneurship and open a liquor store, a Laundromat, a convenience store, or a nail salon. Religion will find a way in, as will guns, drugs, and bars—the psychiatric tavern—therapy for the poor. Some will enlist in the military. There won't be enough money in the community for lawyers or a sheriff's department, so that will fall to the county and law and order to the old ways. There will be a struggle for power and control, for property, and for money and women. The stockholders of the big international companies will watch their portfolios rise and move farther and farther away—some to tropical islands, others behind walls and gates—and hire servants and armed guards. Even with the now-talked-about universal guaranteed income, this will be the case—a struggle for power, status, sex, and money.

And the media will give voice to the story and provide the platform to spread the "news." They are part of the good coalition, the globalists, the good liberal elites (not the bad evil ones), those that are coming together to save the world to make it a world of peace, harmony, and tranquility, once they gain control from the bad coalition, the nationalists (Trump and his ilk and his followers), the white racists and bigots, the deplorables who "cling to their guns and religion." And back we are to denial and fantasy and the thought leaders—the politicians, the lawyers, the university professors, and the media—of the peaceful revolution, always working hard for you, and also, by the way, getting rich in the process. And you *fall* for it? It is a good story.

In the meantime, Trump's supporters, the voters who could ruin the Dems' good coalition, the One World Order (see "The Conventions"), are cast as racists, bigots, and xenophobes told to join the party of joy, to "evolve," or to go away and be content with their guns (for now) and religion and some government handouts (food stamps, Medicaid, and legal drugs). Never mind that the New One World Order / globalists, led by the elite thought leaders, destroyed their (the white working class') pride—their own achievement, affiliation, and power motives.[116] (By the way, the *power motive* is something that is shared by many people in many professions, foremost of which are business executive, teacher or professor, psychologist, politician, journalist, clergy, and international diplomat. You'll note that these professions, the people who inhabit them, are some of Trump's harshest critics, the ones now calling him crazy. There's much going on here. For one is the ego defense mechanism of projection. For another, these are people whom he threatens—either in direct competition with or whose career and credibility his success puts in question. They must, *must*, take him down—not for your well-being, as they'd lead you to believe, but for their own status and achievement,[117] for their own aggrandizement.)

---

[116] Arlie Russell, *Strangers in Their Own Land: Anger and Mourning on the American Right* (2016).

[117] Johnmarshall Reeve, *Understanding Motivation and Emotion* (1992), 305. The characteristics of the power motive are a need to control and have impact and influence over others, "centered around a need for dominance, reputation, status, and position." At least Trump is honest and forthright in who he is. Whereas these others, *pffft*, are phonies, posers. What Trump has done—has done all his life—is win, which means he beats his competitors and don't think for a moment that they can stand losing. This is *schadenfreude* (see "The Case against Trump," June 7, 2016). Trump beats them coming and going, and now he's about to become the most powerful man in the world. This morning, August 12, 2016, I watched *Morning Joe*, which I'd said I wasn't going to do anymore. But I can't help it; it's so delicious. Mika Brzezinski is close to a nervous breakdown. She's powerless when it comes to who she is (as are most of us) and also has no clue as to that. Her ego defenses are always at a heightened alert. She's a classic neurotic. She's been on the verge of tears on many occasions, pleading with Donald, whom she considered a friend, to please, *please* be nice! "You don't mean it!" she begs. She truly doesn't get it, interpersonal communication and human relationships, the human condition or, for that matter, Donald Trump. She's a highly sensitive soul, a victim of her childhood and genetic makeup, the formative years. She's been a nervous

The do-gooders, the thought leaders, the elites, the New One World Order, the globalists, took down whole communities and a way of life in the name of progress. They even had the audacity to call themselves Progressives. It's all a ruse, just a way for one group to take power from another. It's a power play, no more, no less. And one underclass will be replaced by another, a more obedient, subservient one—one who will appreciate what the government does for them, an underclass that is grateful. In addition to welfare, you'll be told you can keep your culture and your language—all you need do is vote Democratic. It's despicable. And it couldn't be done without a complicit media and educational system, but why? That's the question. Why did the media abandon its job as objective reporter? Why have they taken sides? Why has the education system joined in? The educational system has always been a system to serve the power establishment, not necessarily to tell the truth. And now, well, there's a lot of money to be made at the top of the system, the higher educational system, and so they, too, can be bought. They are, after all, human.

And the media? It/they, too, has succumbed to the lure of riches and fame (that of the achievement and esteem motives), being human also. Trump calls them, the reporters, "scum," the lowest of the low. I think he's right because they were charged with keeping the system honest but now only pretend—they pose as unbiased truth tellers when they must know deep down they're not. They compete with one another within and between their organizations for status, power, and money (and probably sex). They are no different and yet pretend to be. They are so dependent on

---

wreck her whole life but has managed to parlay her father's status, her beauty, and her determination into positions of power and status and influence, though being temperamentally unsuited for such. She recently divorced her husband of eighteen years, having fallen under the spell of her cohost Joe Scarborough's charm and narcissism. Almost at the onset of their show, at the beginning of the 2008 presidential cycle, that was obvious. I wrote about it in an essay entitled "Obama Replaces Jesus Christ" in 2011, which nearly got me fired from my position as creative writing instructor at Front Range Community College. A middle-aged female student was so offended by my observations (true that they were) about Mika and Joe that she complained to the administration (also middle-aged females) about it. They were appalled, and I was instructed to clean up my "instruction," not unlike what Mika and others implore of Mr. Trump. "Please, Donald, don't, don't tell the truth of things. We can't handle the truth!"

ratings because ratings determine how much they can charge advertisers (who also complete) for time. The higher ratings a network or newspaper or magazine or website or YouTube video or blog or even Facebook page gets (and that [ratings] is so easy to determine now because of likes and clicks and it's all trackable and riggable—subject to bribery and falsification, by the way—it's truly crazy-making), the more money the generator of the said "attention" can charge, which drives up the cost of the price of goods, not down. If a source of attention is popular, that popularity translates into income for the generator.

What drives eyes to a source is not the truth or quality of the product but that which is stimulating, either to the eyes, ears, or preconceived notions called confirmation bias by social scientists and psychologists. Conflict and outrage are stimulating too. If a source can create outrage or simply be *outrageous* by making outlandish statements, then the source becomes valuable not only to the parent company, his or her employer, but to themselves as well. Then, well, they can charge more for their services/personality, which also drives product prices up or the actual cost of living. And so the person, the source of the controversy, becomes extremely invested in being right, so as to get more people (consumers/voters) watching. This then is also a facet of the achievement motivation—being right. It is part of the competition between people. But there is no objective measurement other than how many clicks and/or likes one generates. And so they, the media and the reporters, will lie, twist, distort whatever it is they are "selling," because that's what people do—sell themselves. Really. It is a competition to see who's "right."

Reality is no longer that which is true but that which you can get someone, or more someones, to *believe* is true. Everything is now up for a vote, and that which gets the most votes/likes/clicks becomes the best or the "right" thing—thing as in item or thing as in idea or belief. *Everything* has become subject to that old legal adage: It's not about the evidence; it's about the story—what you can get people to believe. It is reverse Darwinism—the survival of the worst, by means of deception, over the survival of the best. How you feel trumps what is real, and how you feel is influenced and impacted by what you believe (interpretation) no matter the evidence. Everybody is in competition with everyone else (globally), and yet everyone is "equal" and everything "matters." The result being nothing and no one matters. Everything is subject to interpretation and is relative, and so everyone ultimately collapses into nihilism and narcissism.[118] Without contrast, there is no comparative value. All that matters, in the New One World Order, is what you are worth, which depends on polling (until the actual votes are counted or the numbers are in or the *war* is over). There is no scoreboard, as there is in sports. Nor are there rules or referees and instant replays. The used-to-be referees, the media, are now playing the game too. Everyone's a player. The refs have taken the bribe. And so, too, they are despicable.

The internet and social media has contributed greatly to the competition and falseness, the pretension. Now everyone "knows" everything and can "see" everyone and everything. It's in the palm of your hand. Everyone has a camera and a platform. Everyone's a reporter, but everyone lies. Everyone is immersed within the egotistic defense system of falsification, where perception is distorted and twisted to conform to one's own imagination/fantasy, not reality. There are very few realities left, other than bullets, bombs, natural disasters, sex, birth, and finally, death. Being born and dying, like motivation and emotion, have not and will not change.

Lying and deceit has become a way of life. Maybe it always was. But now bullets and bombs are far more common than they once were. But some things have not changed. Force still rules when push comes to shove, but the mechanisms, some of the tools of force, have changed. Now the weak can win with "votes." It's all just a massive global snafu. It's depressing—reality. Which is it: life is suffering or life is a struggle? This is why the human animal developed the ego defense mechanisms in the first place—they're coping mechanisms.

So what we have are the Democrats and the media taking lying and deception to a whole new level, enabled by new means of communication—the internet, the new weapon of war—against the Old World Order, the strong man, the truth teller, Trump. But in the end, maybe he'll win that game too. I know you don't believe me. I have no standing on any platform of value. I feel like a failure, unable to deceive myself (Why I drink).

---

[118] See Ken Wilber, https://integrallife.com/trump-post-truth-world/.

August 13, 2016

I just read Joe Kline's piece in *Time*, the one with the illustration by Edel Rodriguez on the cover titled "Meltdown." This is *it* in a nutshell. Kline is a Trump hater and is also famously a well-respected commentator on "things" and oh-so ignorant, and yet . . . In addition, this morning I watched CNN, what Trump calls the "Clinton News Network." And as is usually the case, Trump tells the truth with hyperbole, which he admits to, by the way, way, way back in his memoir. He calls it truthful hyperbole. CNN's show was so typical (as was Kline's piece), exhibiting Trump's truth of "things," the *it*, of the human condition. On CNN, notwithstanding what was presented as "expert analysis" by an all-star panel, was a collection of people (all able to speak fast and articulate, i.e., "educated"). But the subliminal message—the message that resonates (confirms prejudices) with viewers—was "Look at us! We are Hillary's message of inclusion and equality. We are the New One World Order. We are the diverse globalists, the pluralists, the future." There was the moderator, the host (young, gay, black, female, and attractive would be perfect).

Anyway, the expert all-star panel consisted of, from left to right, a young white man, a young Asian woman, a young white woman, and a young black man. "Look! See how diverse, young, hip, future-oriented we are!" And their consensus was, unmistakably, that Trump was in meltdown mold, in concert with *Time's* cover. This is what happens in the new/now digital age of Twitter and Facebook. There is an "echo chamber" of the experts clamoring for likes. If one person says it—a word, phrase, or idea—and it clicks online, they all jump on what used to be called the bandwagon. Psychologists call this groupthink (the practice of thinking or making decisions as a group in a way that discourages creativity or responsibility, i.e., conformity). Groupthink occurs when a group values harmony and coherence (clicks and likes) over accurate analysis and critical evaluation. Independent and critical, original thinking has left the building in the mainstream, used to be, respected outlets. Moreover, it has a reinforcing effect. The stupidity, or maybe not, of the thought leaders becomes true. And then, of course, the experts all collect their paychecks.

I cringe at repeating myself, but that is what this election has become ever since the beginning, when Trump came down the escalator in Trump Tower and declared his candidacy for president of the United States of America. The media and the experts all took it as a joke. Trump is "a buffoon, a clown, and this will be, while fun and entertaining, soon over." And then they were all proven wrong by actual votes (see above). And now their reputations are at stake—the *who* of who am I or who I am, Maslow's all-important levels 3 and 4.

They *must* not be wrong. *Everything* is at stake.

What the establishment (Right and Left experts, pundits, academics, politicians, et al.) has gotten wrong is that people, humans, have not changed in forty thousand years. We humans are still the same and are subject to the same emotions and motivations as we were back when we exited "Plato's cave," if you will. Darwin was right. Freud was right. Nietzsche was right. Tolstoy was right. We haven't moved one bit from the 1880s. We are still slaves to the question about God, the question about woman, the question of will to power, the question of conscious and unconscious motivation, the question of change and evolution, the questions of origins and destiny, personality, and life and death. We haven't moved, except we've gotten way more proficient in destruction, reproduction, and survival. They are despicable, though understandable. Trump is the *only one* who represents change, not change in an evolutionary sense, but change in a social/educational/constructive/progressive sense.

Being Presidential

AUGUST 25, 2016

The five living presidents have come out against Donald Trump.

This is just a brief and quick reminder of how *presidential* those five presidents have been. It's hard to really define what "being presidential" actually means, considering Jimmy Carter failed, in a huge way, to rescue American hostages being held captive in Iran; George H. W. Bush lied to and abandoned the Iraqi people after driving Saddam Hussein out of Kuwait, both of which, it could be argued, led to the horror show that is now the Middle East; Bill Clinton failed to kill Osama bin Laden before he could launch his attacks on New York city and Washington, DC; George W. Bush invaded Iraq with no plan whatsoever for what to do after the "mission" was "accomplished," exacerbating to the nth degree what his father started, and also failed to get bin Laden; and finally, Barack Obama, who so mismanaged the Bushs' messes that the Middle East is now even in greater disarray and chaos than it's ever been in its history, which is hard to fathom.

So being presidential, just what *does* it mean? Screwing up royally and making things bad and then worse? Anybody can do that. Maybe, just maybe, Trump's message of "what do you have to lose?" makes a lot of sense.[119]

---

[119] January 22, 2018. I just watched Bill Belichick, the head coach of the NFL's New England Patriots, called by many to be the GOAT (greatest of all time), publicly display disdain for all that is expected of his professional position/station/status after winning the AFC Championship Game (his eighth) by disrespecting the Lamar Hunt Trophy, handing it off to a lesser man like it was a sack of garbage to be taken to the curb; his GOAT quarterback, Tom Brady: "Tom's tough. It's not like it [ten stitches in his throwing hand's thumb] was open-heart surgery"; and the entire media and public with his fashion statement after winning the game, wearing a T-shirt to his NFL's required podium Q and A.

These are some of the media's responses:

"Belichick, in his homemade short sleeve sweat shirt, looks like a serial killer on a Netflix show who just ate ten people" (Doris Baxley).

"He always wins . . . literally" (Joanna Cassidy).

My point is, it doesn't matter if you eat cheeseburgers in your bathrobe (as reported by Michael Wolff in his book *Fire and Fury: Inside the Trump White House* [2018]), so long as you win, which is what Trump does and which the other much more "presidential" USA presidents have failed to do. To the GOAT, all that matters is winning, the scoreboard at the end of the game. And the game is, America versus the other 180-some countries in the United Nations, some of which (Russia and China) want to be known as the greatest of all time. And they do have a game plan.

Like it or not, that is the game that is being played by world leaders (heads of state) who represent their countries.

Nothing has changed; it's about territory and who has control of it, i.e., power.

Western Road Trip in Search of Trump

AUGUST 26, 2016

I was driving west from Colorado out to Southern California to check on my ninety-six-year-old father who's in a skilled nursing facility in Carlsbad, where, in fact, they take excellent care of him. He's retired air force and still has some spark, some vim and vigor, if not total recall and mobility. He's been retired for forty-four years—all of which he's been located in Southern California. Being a retired officer, he's not one of the vets neglected by society or the government. He's well attended to in all aspects. His retirement is ample (he gets full salary, adjusted for inflation, Social Security, as well as a substantial sum from the Veterans Affairs department; and in addition, besides Medicare and VA coverage, he gets Tricare health insurance, the premiere coverage in the US), and as I said, the care he receives is excellent. The facility is five star. I mention this because many of these issues are ones that are always relevant in presidential election cycles.

In the forty-plus years he's been out there (in SoCal), I've made at least that many trips out to see him, mostly by car. (Flying isn't for me.) Las Vegas is right on the main interstate highway, I-15, that you drive on to get there from Colorado (though I've taken every road possible to get there). You drive smack through the middle of Vegas, and that's something. For many (most) of the years, the interstate was under construction. For now, anyway, that's complete. It's a quick ride through the city, though the span has increased fourfold; it's now twenty miles from one side to the other. There *is* desert all around however. It is very weird. Las Vegas is a strange place, which is a story in and of itself. Anyway, I've only stayed overnight twice in all my travels, once in 1967 and again in 2010, and both times, it was on the cheap. But this trip, being a supporter of Trump for POTUS, I thought why not check him out? Who is this man really?

There's no better way to understand or know a man, a person, male or female, than by visiting them where they live or, lacking that, visiting their business—*something, the* thing, that they are most invested in: their home, room, car, business, job, shopping cart, *whatever*—that expresses their personality (personal reality).

So I decided I'd stay at Trump International Hotel in Vegas and see for myself.

The night before, I camped in Utah, in a tent with a campfire and no running water. I love the camping experience, but it doesn't lend itself to being the usual guest at a Trump-owned property. I was unwashed, disheveled, and smelled of smoke when I entered the lobby of Trump's hotel. [120]

On the road, I had googled the hotel and saw that a room cost $111. Reasonable, I reasoned, having just spent $100 from the last trip out for a crappy room in Saint George, Utah. And so I maneuvered my way toward the golden Trump Tower, using the old-fashioned GPS system—sight. Being an old and wise wilderness adventurer, I decided to case the hotel first and see for myself before I committed to a room.

Can I blend in?

Unlike the decision to camp for a night at Trump International, I'd stayed at the campground in Utah several times before and loved my experiences. There was a waterfall, spectacular views, and *flush* toilets—a rarity when camping. I set camp quickly, took a hike, and then returned

---

[120] I looked like Bill Belichick at his press conference or a Socialist Revolutionist.

and lit a fire. And then I watched my neighbor(s), an obese young white male with a family. They had taken the handicapped space, though he seemed fully mobile. His wife (I presume) was Hispanic, rotund also. They had a young boy, an infant, and a teenage girl of Latin-looking features with them. They seemed happy, except the teenage girl, but hey, aren't they all camping without their friends? (There was no internet service.) Anyway, it made me wonder, *What is* their *story? Who* are *they?*

Arriving in Las Vegas, I cruised through the Trump International Hotel's camp, getting a sense of the people and accommodations I'd be camping with. *Yikes*, I thought, *I don't belong here. I don't fit in.* But then I got hold of myself—became my curious, intelligent, rational self—and found a place to pull off the road to stop and think. On my phone, I tapped on "Trump International Hotel" and was put on hold. All agents were busy assisting other guests. I waited.

"Trump International, reservations, how can I help you?" I booked a room, though it cost $46 more than the $111 listed price. I inquired why. "Taxes and the spa fee," she said with a pleasant voice.

Bait and switch, I thought. And then it began—my Trump experience, the real deal, not what the pundits, reporters, experts, etc. said about the man. I was about to experience who Donald J. Trump was with my own eyes and ears.

The check-in clerk, and staff in general, was *so* welcoming and helpful— from the valet parking staff to the consigliore, from the front desk and gift shop clerks to security.

Here's the story: The majority of staff was "minority," and they were *so* professional, cheerful, and accepting. I laughed and joked with them. Read into that what you will, but to me, it says, Trump *is* the blue-collar billionaire.

The room was incredible! But even before that was the elevator. I was on the twenty-fifth floor, and the ride took maybe three seconds! Did I tell you about the lobby? No? That's because it was all, all overwhelming in a good way. Worth the price? Yes, even before I got to my room. The room was spacious and spectacular, including the view. The bathroom, *OMG*, there was a TV in the vanity mirror, with a remote, and a mirror over the Jacuzzi tub! There was a phone in the toilet stall, and the shower stall, well, it was all wheelchair accessible, which made me start to calculate . . . maybe Dad could live here. I wanted to move in. The bed? So comfortable! And then I started to snoop. Lo, the cabinetry *is* made in the USA. Think about it. The room is basically a "home." Most of which is built, manufactured, and serviced by Americans. Trump creates jobs in the USA. He is, in so many things and ways, America—the American dream.

And then I had to leave, which I didn't want to. I'd love to live in Trump's world forever.

On the road, I didn't see many bumper stickers, only one as a matter of fact—a Bernie. But my Trump stickers did get some honks and thumbs-up as I rode the interstate highways west.

The Clinton Foundation, Speeches, and Trump's Taxes

SEPTEMBER 2, 2016

We are all waiting on the debates; everyone has mostly settled in and onto their candidate. The consensus is that Clinton has a about a five-point lead overall, say 43% to 38%, which leaves about 19% of the voting population either going for one of the other two candidates, one a Libertarian and the other a Green—the thinking is that those voters will eventually vote for either Clinton or Trump come Election Day—and then another 10% in the undecided column. Trump is making a pitch for the voter groups he's offended, which is everyone, except for the white working class, small business owners, and the warrior class,[121] not that he hasn't angered some of them too. On Wednesday, he went down to Mexico and met with its

---

[121] Dr. Allen Frances, an American psychiatrist five years Trump's senior, in late 2017, categorized Trump's voters this way: (1) deplorables, (2) disadvantaged whites, (3) deceived religious, (4) cynical Republicans, and (5) corporate shareholders and corporate executives. I find that insulting and categorize Dr. Allen as a snoot—smug, elite, thought leader—and clueless.

president, Enrique Peña Nieto. The chattering class (talking heads on TV, radio, and YouTube) deemed that very risky, as they all thought Trump would make a fool of himself, having supposedly mocked and insulted Mexicans for the past fifteen months; but it wasn't so. Both men treated each other respectfully and had a joint press conference that ended with a declaration of friendship, cooperation, and a handshake.

Then at a rally in Arizona later that evening, Trump was back to his old self, slamming illegal immigrants and reiterating that Mexico will pay for the wall, which Nieto had said he had told Trump there was no way. Trump said it wasn't discussed. *That*, readers, is the art of the deal and diplomacy—never show your cards till the deal is done. Trump said the visit was *not* a negotiation but just a getting-to-know-you courtesy visit. That seemed to be the case, but Clinton said it *was* a negotiation. *Trump* wins big and looks presidential. But the Dems and the media were not having any of it, having established themselves, to themselves, as never being wrong. Hillary Clinton gave a preemptive speech, telling everyone that's "not how diplomacy works." By the way, she looked awful, with her hair appearing heavy and unwashed. (She hasn't been seen since.) Mika Brzezinski, on *Morning Joe*, declared Trump a know-nothing, do-nothing joke while looking ever closer to that nervous breakdown. Trump tweeted, "Just heard that crazy and very dumb @morningmika had a mental breakdown while talking about me on the low ratings @Morning_Joe."

So where are we? Most serious people would like to see the Clintons quit their foundation, give up the transcripts to Hillary's speeches to Wall Street, and get a look at Trump's tax returns. None of those things are going to happen. Here's why. Both candidates know they might lose, and if they reveal or surrender those things, they'll have lost a lot of power in the nonpolitical world. The Clintons have gotten rich since leaving the White House, largely because of their foundation and speeches, but both of those things generate great interest and wealth *only* because it was a given that Hillary would someday be president. First, she was secretary of state and now likely the next president, so say the experts. The money was paid to her for access to power. If she loses, she loses everything, and a lot of people will have wasted their money. She needs to hold on to the foundation, and she *needs* to win. And if she would reveal what she said to Wall Street, if it were to become public, that then kills its value or any future value of what she might be able to garner with subsequent speeches. Why pay for that which you can get for free?

Basically, she and her husband are finished if she loses this election. She's just a grandmother, and they'll have to get by on his and her pensions and Social Security.[122] They'll have lost *all* their power.

For Trump, he doesn't *need* to win, but he does have to hold on to the mystery of his wealth for future business negotiations if he should lose. If he wins, it doesn't matter, and nobody cares. He'd be a fool to release his tax returns.

---

[122]   And it was reported that Hillary was paid $13 million for *What Happened*. The Clintons got paid a reported $26.5 million for their past two memoirs. It pays to get yourself elected to high office. The Obamas, reportedly, have been paid $65 million for their story.

The Real Mr. Trump and the Solution

SEPTEMBER 24, 2016

Mark: A real great idea, Mr. Trump—take a road trip across the southwest, 100 percent. Welcome to our ride, the Batmobile—a vintage, hot driving machine. Don't worry; it's roomier than it looks. You'll fold right into it, 1995 Toyota Celica GT. They don't make 'em anymore. A shame, but hey, maybe not. My next ride is going to be a Ford Mustang or a Ford Ranger 4×4. Unless they build them in Mexico, right, then no deal.

Trump: Right, 100 percent.

Mark: Rules: Driver controls the music. Deal?

Trump: Sure.

Mark: It's 741 miles to Trump International in Vegas. We'll take two days, camp in Utah.

Trump: Camp?

Mark: You'll love it. No worries, man. I got this.

Trump (*twists lips*): It's a beautiful state, Colorado. Great state. Great people. We're going to win it. How's the economy?

Mark: Thriving. There are a lot of craft microbreweries and recreation year-round—skiing, white-water rafting, hiking, camping, hunting, and fishing. There is gambling in old mining towns, oil and gas, high tech, health care, and professional sports, all four big ones. And there's pot, lots of pot.

Trump: How's that working out? Ya know I'm not a fan of drugs and drinking and smoking. Not good. I always told my kids, no drinking, no smoking, no drugs.

Mark: I know. But so far so good. You heard the one about the guy who jumps from the tenth floor of the office building? He was overheard as he passed by the fifth floor. "So far so good."

Trump nods with a closed-mouth smile.
The miles fly by, and we come up to Exit 105, New Castle, an old coal-mining town.

Trump: What's that? Smoke? A wildfire? Tough guys those firefighters. We gotta take care of them, great guys, women too.

Mark: Burning Mountain. Look, to the left. It's a coal mine—fire started down in the hole years ago, a long time ago, and still burning. Maybe till the end of time. Yeah, we got coal.

Trump twists his lips.
"Talk That Talk" by Rihanna and Jay-Z comes on my playlist.

Mark (*singing along*): They say money talks. What you say now, baby. Give it to me. I want it all now, baby.

Trump (*claps hands*): Good song. She'll vote Trump. Believe me.

Mark: No doubt. Question?

Trump: Shoot.

Mark: When I'm driving on these road trips through beautiful country, the music's playing, there's no traffic—just me and the road and the world—I like to drink a little tequila and beer and smoke a little weed. You know, people say weed focuses attention, so you can better enjoy an activity, like music, beauty, art, conversation . . .

sex. It's a tension reducer, clears the mind and focuses it on the present moment. But like you said, you never indulge—

Trump: No. Never.

Mark: So my question is . . . whaddaya do to focus and/or relax?

Trump: Work. Make deals. Make money. Build things. Just exactly what I'm going to do for America. Make America great again. I work, make great deals, and build great buildings, golf courses, and resorts. I built a great company. We're going to build a great wall, a beautiful wall. We're going to stop the drugs from pouring into our country, ruining lives. We're going to put people back to work. We're going to make great trade deals. We're going to fix it—what's wrong with this country. People need jobs. It's horrible what's happened, what's happening. Our inner cities have gone down the tubes. Obama's done nothing, made things worse. He's done nothing for the black community. You watch. We're going to win the black vote. Flint, Michigan, used to build cars, and you couldn't drink the water in Mexico. Now you can't drink the water in Flint, and Mexico builds cars. We're gonna fix it. Make America great again. America first.

Mark: You rarely sleep but never get tired, that I can see. Don't use drugs. That's not normal. What was that like back in the '70s, in New York, when you took Manhattan? When everyone else was all coked up?

Trump: Easy. A snap. Gives me an advantage. I can read people, their body language, what they really want. High, when they're high, it's even easier for me.

Mark: You're a mutant. And I mean that in a good way.

Trump: I get off on the deal, the chase, winning. And then it's on to the next. Sometimes, I might have a hundred deals going on at the same time. You know my company has over five hundred entities, right? (*He smiles big.*) But you have to be willing to walk. You see what they want, give them a taste, make them hungry, and then walk away. They'll come back. It's easy.

Mark: For you maybe, being a mutant. By the way, I think you'd be perfect for the job—president. Obama, sheesh, all talk no action, right?

Trump (*chuckles*): Crooked Hillary too. I almost feel sorry for her . . . Nah.

Mark: Mind if I drink?

Trump: And drive?

Mark: There's no one on the road, and the Service is behind us . . .

Trump: All right, screw it . . . But you have to sign a nondisclosure agreement when we stop. Hope has one.

Mark: Sure. *I lied and felt bad for a little while.*

Mark: Mr. Trump, have you ever heard of a type T personality?

Trump: Go on.

Mark: Its central organizing principle is the thrill of conquest.

Trump: Okay, I'm listening.

Mark: Type Ts have little need of sleep, are risk-takers, confident, charismatic, boundlessly ambitious, driven, restless, and hypomanic. Some say it's the personality of the psychopath. Wait! Don't freak out—people say all kinds of things. Long story short, abnormal or mutant can be a good thing. It doesn't necessarily mean criminal. Then again, Pascal once said, 'All the unhappiness of man stems from one thing only—that he is incapable of staying quietly in his room.' So that's sort of a Zen thing. Maybe criminal depends on who's in charge, the rules, you know, who decides.

Trump: Who's Pascal?

Mark: Never mind. Hey, here we are at the campground. Time flies.

Trump: We're going to sleep in a tent? Is there internet so I can tweet?

Mark: No. (*There is if he pays the campground host, who has a dish, but I don't want to tell Trump that. I want to see what he's like alone in the wilderness.*) But we'll build a fire, cook meat. I'll drink, and you can watch. Think of it as if we were on safari. (*I had a big smile across my face.*)

Trump: Is there Wi-Fi and phone service? I'll call for my pilot.

Mark: Relax, it'll be ok, trust me.

Trump: Are you out of your mind?

Mark: No. Seriously, it'll be okay, 100 percent. (*I smile even larger, huge.*) We'll be at the hotel tomorrow. I'm going to drop you off before I pull in because I want to experience the hotel as just a regular guy. You'll be all right. The Service is right over there. So's Hope. This *is* America, the real deal. You'll see. Trust me.

Trump: You sign the nondisclosure. (*He mutters.*) Ivanka.

Mark: Yes, sir.

Trump ate like a wild animal, marveled at the darkness and the stars, and I said good night. I don't know what he did, but the fire was going in the morning when I woke up and exited the tent. Trump was standing, ensconced in his overcoat. I swear there was a golden halo hovering over his head as the sun rose over the grand staircase (Grand Escalante) and warmed the camp. He smiled at me.

Trump: Let's go.
Mark: Okaaay. We'll get coffee at Kiva Koffeehouse. It's just a few miles down the road.
Trump: You are a first-class a-hole.
Mark: Some people say that, sure.
Trump: I miss Melania. She'd love this.

We fly by the Bryce Canyon turnoff.

Mark: You know, you should build a hotel here, between Bryce Canyon and Zion. It'd be a killer. There's an airport.
Trump: I'll let Ivanka know.
Mark: Seriously. Ya know, I was thinking last night. I think I have the solution. Hear me out. What if we build the wall? You don't mind if I say *we*, do you? Anyway, the wall is built first, the border secured, and we stop all the drugs, the painkillers, the opioid epidemic, thus get our population working again, healthy. We build bullet trains that crisscross the nation with stations close to all our incredible national parks and great cities, and then we implement a system like Hawaii has and have the senior discount *here*, where US citizens have a card and get a huge discount on *everything*! And everyone else in the world who comes here, tourists and visitors, pay higher prices for *everything*! The United States becomes like the world's amusement park! It solves everything! But first, we've got to stop the nonsense of people coming here and ripping us off, shut it down, until we get the 'remodel' finished. And then we start over. Natives, those born here, get the discount card. Everyone else pays to come in and pays 'tourist' prices even to go to school. No more free riders. We truly become *the United States*, a sort of Jurassic Park. That goes for the internet, phones, everything. There's a USA.com, a secure network and phone system, cheaper and impenetrable by hackers, even the Russians and Chinese. Whaddaya think?
Trump: I like it. Let me think about it, run it by the team. What's that smell?

Mark: Roadkill. A deer or elk, there, see? Wanna stop? I'll take your picture.

Trump: You're outa your mind! You're not going to write about any of this, right?

Mark: We'll get a bite to eat at the junction, some pie. It's the home of the ho made pie. You'll love it.

Trump: I'm losing *my* mind.

Trump: This service sucks big league. What is *wrong* with people, Mark?

Mark: Mr. Trump—that's a long story. But I believe, I think, you can fix it. I believe in you. We have to get rid of this cultural Marxist ideology, this multicultural, global, fantasy nonsense, the false belief of the rootless cosmopolitan president we have now, and get back to reality! People are . . . well . . . just let me say I'm voting for you! Have you noticed all the thumbs-up and the honks that we're getting as we drive along? Sir, the bar has been lowered. You're gonna raise that bar up again. Make America great again, right?

Trump twists his lips, looks out the window and up toward the sky. Then he looks hard at me.

Trump: Believe it, 100 percent.

"Riders on the Storm" comes on through the sound system of the Batmobile, and Trump lays his head back against the headrest and closes his eyes. I glance in the rearview mirror, drive, and think about Hope Hicks in the limo behind us. How did she sleep?

Debate

SEPTEMBER 26, 2016

If it were up to me, the ninety-minute debate would consist of six segments, each fifteen minutes long, no breaks. Six issues (which six would be unknown to the candidates predebate) would be discussed by stating, alternately, the topic to a candidate, then the candidate would respond, talk for up to seven and a half minutes, and also be allowed to ask the other candidate questions and/or to respond to interruptions, like a real conversation. The only guidance would be the six topics and the time limits. Like this, the six issues would be (1) racism, (2) immigration, (3) income inequality, (4) Russian aggression, (5) terrorism, and (6) health care. First question: "Mrs. Clinton, Racism. Go." Then just watch the clock. Second question: "Mr. Trump, Immigration. Go." But that won't happen because the media views itself as far more important and necessary than it is. The media's narcissism is as great, if not more, than the candidates. The difference is, well, there is no difference save for Mr. Trump, whose self-awareness allowed him to state that he was a "taker" all his life and that because of who he was, a successful businessman, he's well aware of how the game is played.

I can hardly wait to watch what happens tonight.

September 29, 2016

A friend came over, Marco, a Bernie supporter. We drank beer, smoked some weed (legal in Colorado), ate, and watched the debate on CSPAN, then turned off the TV and discussed it, or more accurately, he interviewed me and recorded it. He said he wanted to get an understanding from the point of view of a Trump supporter because he thinks Trump is an asshole and can't fathom why anyone, especially a well-educated person, could possibly support him. We were both, by that time, in an altered state of mind, and I haven't listened to the recording. But I remember, at one point, Marco reloaded the pipe and said he was embarrassed because I had convinced him voting for Trump made sense or that he was embarrassed for smoking so much of my stash. Maybe both. That was, and was not, my intention. Yes, I wanted him to understand why Trump makes sense as POTUS, but no, I didn't and don't want to embarrass anyone. The net result of that, to embarrass a person, is not to change minds but to make enemies.

Embarrassment causes disaffiliation; it deactivates the affiliation motive. Put another way, frank, realistic, honest, contrary, and unconventional assessment of conventional, accepted, politically correct thoughts and beliefs can provoke hostility and rejection. This phenomenon explains much of the vehement rejection of Trump by the Left *and* Right. The liberal person just does not want to accept the possibility that they might be wrong, that their worldview might be incorrect, because that exposes them as not only wrong but also *hypocritical*. They view themselves as tolerant and open-minded. It's a double whammy to their self-esteem. They're exposed as closed-minded and wrong, which is an embarrassment (Maslow's fourth-level motivational need). The Right's rejection of Trump is pretty much that of "You can't do that! You can't skip the process, the rules, the filter . . . paying your dues. You must respect the authority. We select the candidates by a filtering process. How dare you!" Embarrassment is the correct emotional response, but that discomfort is quickly corrected, reinterpreted, not by adjusting one's thoughts/ideas/beliefs but by rejecting the source of the discomfort—the messenger. This is the essence of cognitive dissonance and the usual response: when one is subjected to contrary information that challenges your belief/worldview, what do you do? Change your mind or shoot the messenger? Most people shoot the messenger, thus keeping their self-esteem intact.

Everybody knows Trump is a lunatic, but wait, Trump has pulled the curtain back and lifted up the carpet on Americanism, exposing many Americans for what is going on beneath the surface. He is the psychoanalyst, and the politically correct American is the resistant patient. The patient hates the therapist or, more accurately, has a conflicted and confused relationship with the therapist. Does she stay and continue the therapy or quit, maybe find a more "agreeable" practitioner? Depends. Marco, my friend, though, is different. He actually has an open mind, being a student of philosophy.[123]

So today, all the talk seems to be about fat shaming, which is pretty much the contrast between the candidates—in a nutshell, truth versus nice. *And* can the truth be shaped by the mind, i.e., can a fat person be made beautiful just by saying it's so? What do you see? What do you feel? What do you say? What do you do? What *is* real? What *ought* a person do? I side with Trump and may have convinced Marco, but only temporarily. He can claim intoxication and say I took advantage of him, drugged him, and mind-raped him. I'm being "funny," just kidding, of course, but not really.

---

[123]   For Marco's take on our discussion, there is this: https://www.metapsychosis. com/the-loneliest-road-intensification/. Our recorded conversation is part of his "meditation."

The source of the contrast/conflict are statements made by Mr. Trump to a woman who was a contestant in a Miss Universe (beauty) pageant, in 1996, that was owned and promoted by Trump.

The woman won the contest.

There is so much going on here, representing so much of what is true and what is not, i.e., realism versus idealism or fantasy. We have here all wrapped up in a moment, a debate, that has on the surface nothing to do with the six issues of racism, immigration, income inequality, Russian aggression, terrorism, and health care that *should* have been discussed. Instead, we have sex, money, power, and revenge—*the* universal prime drivers of human behavior—being discussed, brought up by Hillary, from a twenty-year-old beauty contest.

Beauty, when applied to the female of the species, really is about sex (appeal), which is subjective. Women, in a beauty pageant, are being *judged* by their appearance. They are being selected. That *is* the contest. So in a way, it is a competition based on not ability, personality, character, or intellect but looks. Mr. Trump has a preference for a particular appearance (look) with regard to the female of the species, as we (men) all do. It is part of the process of sexual selection, which propels the human species into the future. Trump has said a flat-chested woman cannot be a ten. That's his opinion, his preference, but it's not a *fact*. However, in this case, he owns the pageant and his opinion counts, consciously or unconsciously. He also can determine the size (height and weight/proportion) of the contestants. And the winner then represents the pageant's (Trump's) ideal woman. In essence, by gaining weight during her reign, this woman, the winner, misrepresented Mr. Trump and broke an implicit contract. Trump said the managers wanted to "fire" her because of her weight gain after she won. Trump said, "No, I can rehabilitate her." (Trump, again, is a therapist.) Just as a coach would to an athlete who gained weight and thus failed to perform as he/she did before. Get it? Now the woman wants some kind of revenge, and Trump is the target.

Who knows what propels a woman, a girl, to enter a beauty contest? That's a discussion for another time and place.

On the other hand, there is Hillary Clinton, an accomplished white woman, who attempts to use a man's preference with regard to beauty and sexual preference against him, as if sexual preference and looks don't matter. She ignores the reality that people, all people, are different and have different preferences. She ignores contrast. She denies individuality.

She denies sexual selection. In addition, it was Clinton who brought the beauty pageant and contestant into the conversation. She, Clinton, thought she was being clever, setting a trap for Trump (a trap for the therapist, ha!). Large, small, tall, short, dark, light, male, female, smart, stupid, strong, weak, athletic, clumsy, quick, slow, pretty, ugly, and so on—she wants to pretend it doesn't matter, which, if you think about it at all, is crazy and would lead to the total destruction of not only the human species but also all life on the planet.

Life *is* a competition, a will to power, regardless of the criteria. There are distinctions and contrasts and conflicts and competitions—there are winners and losers. There is a hierarchy. She, Clinton, wants to win but tells you it's about you and not her and calls her competition every disparaging name there is, so as to disqualify him for the most powerful position in the world, POTUS. Remember (and if you don't, Mr. Trump was certain to remind you and fight back with) the fact that Mrs. Clinton resorted to slut-shaming, back before that was even a word, to discredit her husband's many sexual paramours. She lies so often and much you start to question what you know deep down inside.

Yes, the woman (the winner of the contest) violated her contract. She won as one person and literally shapeshifted into another. She got what she wanted and then dismissed the contract. She lied. Hillary lied. Bill lied. Trump, notwithstanding his strategic tactic of exaggeration, represents the truth. Hillary gets up in the morning, looks in the mirror, and lies. Her husband, Bill, lied to her and the country. He was impeached for lying. Hillary's whole adult life is a lie, but it's not—it's real. She just might become the first woman president of the United States, the most powerful person in the world. And that will be based on one lie after another, which you fell for. Trump is the antithesis of that. He is totally all that is true, 100 percent. He understands the world as it is and has been extremely successful in the world. That makes people hate him and love him. He is a contrast. He is the mutant, the outlier, the misfit, the unfiltered leader who mastered the machine. Today, I just read that he is a speed freak, not a mutant, but a person who uses drugs to give him an advantage, i.e., PEDs or performance-enhancing drugs. If true, that means he cheats. Two things: in the real world, cheating and lying is allowed (see "Freud on Trumpism"). And also, if true, why hasn't it been reported by the media, say, the *New York Times*? It has also been reported that Hillary Clinton was given the questions, to be asked by Lester Holt in the debate, weeks before. Isn't that cheating?

Everybody cheats; everybody lies (to different degrees). That *is* the real world.

So the debate came down to sex, money, power, and revenge, which is as it should be because that's what makes the world go round—sex, who mates with whom. What's funny (ironic) is that in the 2008 election primary between Mrs. Clinton and Mr. Obama, Hillary, in a performance on stage, told the truth. She mocked Barack Obama—his message—that hope and change would change the world because of *his* desire for peace and harmony. She called it rainbows and unicorns, something like that, rather than the reality of strife, struggle, suffering, conflict, contrast, and competition, i.e., the war that it is. *Now* she's taken up Obama's mantra. She's morphing into him so as to win, to gain votes, to take over his coalition. She changes what she looks like, her accent, her voice, whatever it takes to win, something she has done her entire life—she deceives. Mr. Obama told you as much when he defeated her. "She'll do anything to win," he said. She deceives herself! But I have to give her credit. She just might win.

Tuesday, the twenty-seventh, the day after the debate, *Frontline* (on **PBS**) aired a two-hour special titled "The Choice." It traced the candidates' lives from their formative years to the present. But it was heavily edited and interpreted to present a point of view—that both candidates are seriously flawed and disturbed individuals, shaped by their upbringing (formative years). So much was left out. The theme seemed to be revenge—that Trump was out to become **POTUS** to take revenge on Obama for embarrassing him at the White House Correspondents' Dinner in 2011 because Trump questioned Obama's citizenship and, thus, his, Obama's, being even eligible to be **POTUS**. (See "Something's going on.") Is this journalism? I could argue Hillary wants to become **POTUS** to take revenge on her husband for humiliating her when he was president!

Again, what is real is that sex, money, power, and revenge dictate human behavior. The rest is just a story told by agents to make themselves and, perhaps, you feel good. And for sure, it's a means to an end—money for the agents.

Anymore, there *is no* reality that is real. It's that simple *and* complex.

I'm going to vote for Trump—the mutant. But if there is credible proof that he's on drugs (speed), I won't vote at all. Or then again, what have we got to lose?

Pussygate

I'm not sure where to begin with this. I've been going back and forth between here, where I live in Colorado, and Southern California, where my father was dying. These are two subjects, sex and death, that we don't talk much about, nor deal with, with any sort of reality-based acknowledgment. And yet they *are* the only two things that we can be certain of—that we were born of a *sexual* act between a (sexually) mature man and woman (or meeting of a sperm and egg) and that we will die. All that happens between those two events is subject to interpretation, storytelling, and fabulation—meaning that our lives are made up of different versions of what happened. Another way to say this is how Trump referred to *it* as "truthful hyperbole." Both, conflicting interpretations and exaggerated truth, appear to be inconsistent statements, contradictions, but are actually true. Another way to view it is with the concept of signal/noise, originally a technical term concerned with radio wave clarity, distinguishing between the power of the signal versus the power of the background noise, expressed as a ratio. Say, 8:1 would represent a strong, clear signal. Life, capital L, is concerned with birth, sustainability (consumption of resources into energy), death, and continuation—the means of which (regarding human life) is sex and power. The rest is noise. Life is concerned with its birth, survival, and reproduction, and then it dies.

The first time I "grabbed" pussy was an accident, when I was thirteen or fourteen, in the seventh or eighth grade. (The typical time in the human life cycle when males are consumed with sex. Why? They have no idea.) The girl was my sort-of girlfriend. I was attracted to her anyway, and maybe she served as the model for the type of girl I've been attracted to ever since. She was over at my house (parents' house) while they were out. We were studying, but mostly making out while sitting on my bed. She got off the bed and stood up in front of me, her crotch right in front of my face. She was wearing tight turquoise short-shorts. I was spell struck. She said something I never heard and pivoted so that she was to my right, her backside now facing me. I reached my left arm and hand across my body and grabbed her by the pussy. I was shocked! It was so soft. I've never forgotten that feeling, the rush and thrill, the surge of excitement. That's how I remember it anyway. Her version might be different. We hung out together a little after that, but we eventually stopped. I can't tell you now why. Maybe it had something to do with that. We didn't talk about it, and I never spoke of the incident with anyone. I don't know if she did.

Back in those days, intimacy was something that you just found out about through trial and error, including kissing. People didn't talk about it, at least as far as I knew. There was *Playboy* magazine; however, crotch shots weren't displayed. But the attraction to the female form, shape, body, face, and scent was something that dominated my thoughts (and likely most pubescent boys), that and sports and war. School was easy, and baseball and football were pretty easy too. But the female was a mystery. So we stumble and bumble along. There were movie dates, the drive-ins, dances and dancing, a meal or dinner date occasionally, car rides, and fishing and hiking. Through it all, there is tension—sexual tension and kissing and touching and feeling and moaning and heavy breathing and climaxes. But talk about it? No. Older brothers would brag about "going down" on a girl, getting *it*. But really, you didn't know what was true or not true. It was/is a constant torment.

Like Louis C. K. says, "Cum is coming out of your eyes."[124] I don't know what's going with the girls, but recently, at my forty-fifth high school

---

[124]   Louis C. K.—superstar stand-up comedian and TV showrunner, writer, and producer—subsequently has admitted to sexual misbehavior (some label

reunion, one of the girls, one of the *in* girls, whom are the girls I dated, being a smart jock, told me that they had all made a pact to leave high school with their virginity intact. I know I didn't "take" anyone's. So you didn't ask permission to kiss or touch or feel or finger; you just felt your way through all the awkward intimate encounters. That was the way it was.

The next time I "grabbed" a pussy was in college. I found myself in bed with a strange girl in a strange town, very intoxicated, and well, things just happened. At the moment of the grab, she turned to me and said something like "Hey, what the hell are you doing?" And I stopped doing what I was doing. She was a stranger, and I was embarrassed.

And then there were the girls who would grab *my* penis while I was lying next to them or sitting next to them—more or less strangers. And then there were girlfriends, many who made the first move. That's just the way it went—young sexually mature males and females feeling each other out, seeing what happened. And people got married young and mated and had babies or not and then got divorced.

When was this? The sixties and seventies. It was the time of drugs, sex, rock 'n' roll, and war. Was there groping? Yes, in public and private. Was there unasked-for kissing and fondling? Yes. It was pretty much everywhere, as far as I could tell. I can't say everyone did it, but a lot of people did. You just managed your own self, what you would allow and not and with whom—okay with this person, but not that person. Was there a lot of sleeping around, cheating? Yes. Did people lie about it? Of course, in both directions. What it wasn't was talked openly about. It was all locker-room talk or bedroom or barroom talk. Some were pillow talk, dirty talk,

---

it assault), the nature of which was masturbating in front of aspiring female comedians/actors, using his position of celebrity star power to do whatever he wanted without typical, common, decent restraint. (Louis was in his late forties, divorced, with two children.) After a public apology (I was on his email list), he's gone dark, saying he's going to step back and just listen. This come amid a landslide of accusations by women of men in positions of power in the entertainment, political, athletic, and media industries called the #metoo movement. Louis C. K.'s behavior did not shock me, given his professional routines and jokes. His sexual desires, thoughts, and fantasies were a big part of his material and his appeal. He couched in comedy, humor, what was and is on all our minds, to a lesser or greater degree. That's what made it funny. He dared go where others wouldn't, and it was true. I cannot and will not defend what he did, but it happened. As they say, there but for the grace of God . . .

or dirty dancing. There was a code: no kissing and telling, at least where I was. I don't know about the scene in New York city.

Presidential behavior? John F. Kennedy was a famous womanizer, as was Ronald Reagan. So was Henry Kissinger and so on and so forth. Or so I've heard.

Did I cheat? Yes. Did my wives cheat? Yes. I can't even remember the names of the women I slept with, and if someone comes forward, I'll deny it. I'll say I don't know what they're talking about. Maybe they got me mixed up with someone else? Maybe they were too lit up.

I went back to college in the mid-nineties and took a seminar designed to prepare students for graduate school. I recall the professor telling us that 75 percent of female graduate students reported being sexually acted upon, wanted or unwanted, by their supervising professors. "So, ladies, expect it." I learned also that 90 percent of women who strip or escort, work in sex, report having been sexually abused growing up. Breaking news: sex happens. Sex sells. Sex makes the world go round. Sex makes men kill. What is a beauty pageant? It's a socially acceptable way to ogle women's bodies. Cheerleading? Team spirit—right. Gymnastics and figure skating are more of the same. It's all about sex. Beach volleyball? Come on!

So you're outraged? Really?

Love? Love is nature's way to get you to play the game. It's noise. The good news is that there's just about an equal number of men and women and that there is a hierarchy. Males and females have figured out a way to pair up so that everybody gets some sex and the species moves forward. There's someone for everyone (even queers). People do this by sorting (consciously or unconsciously): attractive people hook up with other attractive people, tall people with other tall people, fat people with other fat people, and so on. White people are paired with white people. High-status people mate with other high-status people. People try and marry up. That was the way it was, has always been, and is now (mostly). It's known as sexual selection.

There's a problem though, and I don't know the cause for certain, known as involuntary celibacy. Mating ratios have shifted, or maybe it's always been this way. It's still true that about 90 percent of females become mothers, but now (?), only about 60 percent of males become fathers.[125] For

---

[125] Statistics concerning this fact are scarce, thus I used the word *about*, but it makes sense from an evolutionary perspective. There was a 2003 survey done

some men, this is of their own doing, but for many, it's because the women find them totally unattractive as partners. They'd rather adopt or use a sperm donor than commit to a relationship with a loser man. That might have to do partly with economics (women making their own money, social policy, the state providing for single women with children), partly with feminism and shifting sexual identity, and partly with general postmodern, futuristic thinking. *I think* the fact of involuntary celibacy might be partly responsible for the appeal of ISIS to young men. They get to take women against their will, either to marry or rape. Involuntary celibacy just might be the cause of a lot of crime because of sexual and social rejection and the subsequent frustration.

And of course, there's always been lying—people trying to cheat, to fake it, to move up the hierarchy without the goods to back it up. Men lie, steal, and cheat. Women wear makeup, high heels, and sharp clothes, enter fashion and modeling (pout and pose), and use their sex (appeal) and their pussy to get a man. Men being men (most men love pussy) are spellbound by it, like I was when I was young. Women judge men, and men judge women. They make calculations, trying to get the best deal, meaning partner, they can to better their chances of survival and the survival of their offspring. It's called life.

So you're appalled by Donald Trump's sexual behavior? Really?

He was a high-status, wealthy, good-looking, tall man. And you're shocked that he took advantage of that to "score" pussy? What would you do? You can't say because you've never been in that position. You might be a liberal, a progressive, an open-minded and tolerant person. But you can't put yourself in his shoes, can you? If you're honest, you don't know what you'd do if you were him. Oh, it's pretty easy to get on your high horse and condemn him; yes, it is. But you're not fooling me. You've lost any regard I might have had for you. You are either phony, ignorant, a poser, fraud, stooge, rube, lying, or stupid, none of which are attractive traits. *But* maybe that's not your fault. Maybe it's the consequence of

---

by the US CDC (Center for Disease Control) with 4,928 male respondents aged fifteen to forty-four (prime breeding age) that reported *only* 47% of the men said they had fathered at least one biological or adopted child. *Only* slightly more than half reported having had a kid aged nineteen or younger. This suggests that my estimate of 40% of potential sexually active males being denied the "pleasure" might be close to accurate. Recent research concerning US females puts their percentage at 86%.

PLUM (politicians, lawyers, universities, media), the thought leaders, all who thrive on conflict—its attraction to people because of basic survival principles.[126] And maybe it's not even their fault. They're just doing what they can to make a living, to survive too—freewill being a dubious concept. Maybe it's a fact that most human relationships are host/parasite based, meaning they are interdependent for survival, unconsciously, of course.

---

[126] Conflict invokes a response from everyone—either to engage or avoid it (unless one trains the mind to ignore it.) This is the "state of fear" Michael Crichton is suggesting in his 2004 book of the same name.

The Dragon Slayer: Debate 2

OCTOBER 19, 2016

Due to the dying of my father, I've fallen behind in my chronicling of events in this most unusual, epic, and historic election. But I do take notes. So here's a recap of debate 2.

I sat with my father all day, gently keeping contact with him, rocking beside his bed, and humming lullabies to him. And then when he settled down into a morphine-induced rest, I left for my apartment to watch the debate. It seemed like now, in retrospect, that the fix was in because Martha Raddatz and Anderson Cooper were very tough on Trump and let Hillary off easy. Raddatz kept interrupting Trump, and at one point, I noted: "AC looking distressed b/c Trump is killing HRC and Cooper knows it." Trump rocked and swayed while Clinton droned on, boring Trump (and me) with her well-rehearsed talking points. She actually stalked the audience and intentionally moved in front of Trump (an obviously rehearsed move for a TV highlight) while intoning on and on and on with her points, which we've all heard a gazillion times. On several occasions, Trump turned his back on her. You know what that means, right? Trump also turned his back on Cooper. *Amateurs*, he seemed to be saying while not saying a word. When Trump would interrupt, it was powerful, saying, "Because you'd be in jail," "She's lying again," "Excuse me. The whole thing was a fraud," "There's always a reason for everything," "To solve a problem, you have to name it," "Obamacare is a disaster," "A perfect example of Bernie's 'bad judgment,'" "Why didn't you do anything?" "It's called extreme vetting," "All talk, no action," "That makes me smart," and "If you were an effective senator, you could've done it."

I don't have to spell out the issues, problems, or talking points for you; they're obvious. At times, Trump would stand behind his chair, holding onto the top rail of the chair's back, restraining himself, but also suggesting to Clinton she might want to sit down and take a deep breath and relax. Trump's command of the stage and debate were masterful, but if you listen to the media and pundits, you'd think Clinton killed Trump in the debate when what really happened was that he, Trump, went into the arena, the ring, the coliseum, and slayed the professional politician.

Signal/noise.

Drain the Swamp: Trump Rally

OCTOBER 20, 2016

The day before the third and final debate, Trump held a rally in Grand Junction, Colorado; and having had to miss the one in Loveland two weeks earlier because of my father's dire condition, I decided I'd go, having just returned from California and my dying father's bedside. I needed a change, a reason to smile.

I messaged my brother—whom I'd been estranged from for eight years, but my father's circumstance had reunited us—if he'd join me, and he said yes. I left my Westminster apartment at six thirty, and we met up at the New Castle Diner four hours later, then rode together to the site, a West Star Aviation hangar at Grand Junction's airport. We arrived at noon, three hours before the event was scheduled to begin. There was already a backed-up line of cars heading into the area. We parked at a nearby hotel about a half mile from the hangar and walked.

Turns out we were some of the early arrivals. Nevertheless, there was a substantial line of people waiting for entry. Entrepreneurs had set up tables and wheeled mobile wagons and kiosks selling pro-Trump paraphernalia. We bought some buttons (three for ten dollars). The stuff for sale was mostly funny, like "Hillary for Prison" or "Donald Fucking Trump," and so on. There was also a Hillary Horror House tent (because of the proximity to Halloween). The closer we got to the entrance, the more electric the atmosphere became, the security was tighter as well. The personnel turned from casual to big burly dudes with suits, guns, and shades—serious men.

Inside, the stage was set, and the music was blaring outlaw country— Hank Williams Jr., Waylon Jennings, Willie Nelson, Johnny Cash, etc. There were the deplorables (Hillary's characterization of Trump's supporters) squeezed together and swapping stories—service in foreign wars, lost jobs, and other hardships. There was growing excitement, a charged vibe, along with the anticipation of Trump's big 757 jet airliner's arrival. Then the plane came. The crowd roared, and the camera phones elevated. Trump stood on the stair's landing and waved. The crowd went nuts, crazy! The cheer was like nothing I've ever heard.

The feeling I had was *something* that felt like the anticipation of a first date with a girl I'd lusted over in high school or a pre-game warm-up in a high school gym for a big basketball game with a rival. The band played, and the girls screamed.

Trump was majestic, presidential. He waved and acknowledged the crowd, pointing to individuals. His message was heavy on individual freedom—freedom of choice—to worship whom/what you wanted, to bear arms, to protect yourself and your family, to work, and to make America great again. "We want jobs, not social programs," he said, and the crowd roared. "We're going to drain the swamp that is Washington, DC, end Obamacare. Are you ready to go back to work?" The crowd exploded! "Your taxes are going to go way, way down." The crowd screamed louder. My ears hurt from the eruption of cries and applause. I looked around. People were euphoric: smiling, jumping for joy. There was no fear or anger, just a sense of relief that finally, after so much suffering, Christmas morning had finally come and we can open our presents. Santa's here, and I don't give a hoot if he stole a kiss from Mama.

There was a contagion of joy.

Leaving the event, we stopped by the media's pen where my brother's coworker was stationed (he was the local radio's news director, and he and my brother did radio broadcasts of the local high schools' sporting events). I asked him what his impression was and what he would report.

(One of Trump's biggest cheers came when he disparaged the media. I like Ron. He's just a guy, played football for USC, has a family, lives in rural Colorado, and works in media. He's just a guy making a living.) Ron shrugged. I said, "Trump's talking about them [gesturing to the main media pen], not you."

My brother told me Ron's anti-Hillary, which, I've uncovered, drives much of Trump's support. People, many people, just hate her. "Lock her up" was the loudest cheer at the rally. However, the mention of the right to bear arms got the loudest roar from the crowd. Between love for the Second Amendment and disgust for Hillary was hostility for the media. I get it. This is the Wild West where the idea of freedom reigns, wrapped up in the conservative values of God, country, and family. In this regard, Trump is a true conservative, which elite Conservatives in DC and Manhattan just don't get.

I don't believe in God, but I know that family and territory are powerful human drivers, as is worship. We humans need *something* to believe in. I saw *that* at the Trump rally. There was nothing (except for some protestors, paid or not) but love and hope. There was no groping, no pushing or shoving, no hate, no sexism, xenophobia, or racism. There were just people excited about a man who promises that he can restore order to a world that has gone crazy with fear and anxiety. There was only a man who owns a plane; a man who builds things, beautiful things, and creates jobs; a man whose children love him, dresses well, has a sense of humor, and appreciates people for who they are. In other words, he is a man of the people.

And then I saw this article (http://www.newyorker.com/news/news-desk/making-peace-with-trumps-revolutionaries) covering the same event. It's from a staff writer from the *New Yorker* magazine. He's quite accomplished, receiving the MacArthur Foundation's Genius Grant in 2011, the same grant given to David Foster Wallace. He was born in 1969, on Flag Day, the same day as Trump, ironically. This story is why Trump calls the mainstream media dishonest, and many Trump supporters have come to not trust stories in these types of national outlets. The author, Peter Hessler, is an elite, joining the Peace Corps in 1996 after being educated at Princeton, and later a Rhodes scholar at Oxford. He's written books about China, the Middle East, Cairo, and Egypt, where he lived for a few years. But now he's back in the USA and lives in the small southern Colorado town of Ridgway, population 924, a pretty spectacular place—gateway to the San Juans. Formally a railroad whistle-stop, it now boasts of many million-dollar homes and ranches. Judging by the lead, Hessler went looking for one story—confirmation that Trump's supporters were indeed racists and bigots, small-minded, stupid people, but found that that wasn't the case. In fact, it was just the opposite, but he stuck with his lead. His bias against Trump rings throughout the piece. He, or his editors,[127] couldn't bring themselves to reframe the story to fit what it was Hessler saw and heard.

We, my brother and I, were actually standing just a few yards in front of the media pen where Hessler was confined. (I took a few pictures of the pen, and he's probably in them. My brother wandered around, getting a more complete feel for the crowd. He also took the exact same picture of Trump's plane landing that is featured in the magazine.) I saw no hostility or aggression whatsoever with the interactions of Trump's supporters and the media, and yet Hessler can't help himself and states, "There were *certainly* [emphasis mine] some hardened racists and sexists within the crowd, but most people behaved with *remarkable* decency." Really, Peter, and you know this how? A more accurate statement would have been like this: "There might have been some . . . but I certainly didn't encounter any of that. I was surprised at how well-mannered and behaved they were, given what I'd been led to believe." Yes, as both my brother, Jack, and I recounted, the media received loud boos and jeers from the crowd. But it wasn't threatening. It was almost in fun, part of the show. Every home team needs an opponent. Hessler doesn't mention the loudest cheers or jeers for the Second Amendment and Hillary Clinton respectively.

The speech's theme was about freedom and jobs and conservative values. This article is twisted, slanted reporting. You *could* call it crooked. But many of the well-educated[128] voters take it as truth because of the platform. In this way, this is what Trump means when he says, "The election is rigged." This is what he means when he says to his supporters, "Without the media, crooked Hillary Clinton wouldn't stand a chance!" (And the crowd roars.) This is a prime example of what the phrase *in the tank* encompasses. *In the tank* means providing fuel for Hillary's candidacy

---

[127] The magazine endorsed Hillary Clinton.

[128] Later, in March of 2018, Hillary Clinton called her voters "optimistic, diverse, dynamic, moving forward," contrasting them to Trump's supporters. She still doesn't get it.

and that you are being taken for a ride in a circle, back to the place where you started, where the politics and laws work for the few who can buy them, the elite, for their benefit. You, the average voter, the common man, are provided crumbs and told it's a feast. You are being hoodwinked. But whose fault is that? You've been ill-educated. Is that your fault? Or is it just the way the system functions, the machine that is?

Trump Touches Down in Grand Junction, Colorado

BY JACK J. JABBOUR[129]

Grand Junction, Colorado, October 18, 2016, "I've been everywhere, man. I've been everywhere," boomed Johnny Cash through the sound system as the faithful crept past the T-shirt, hat, and campaign button vendors in a line that stretched down Horizon Drive on the way to the Grand Junction Regional Airport hangar where Donald Trump was making his second appearance of the day in Colorado.

The Western Slope crowd, perhaps tripling the size of the estimated two thousand at a Colorado Springs rally earlier in the day, was chanting "Trump . . . Trump . . . Trump" long before his plane touched down on the tarmac shortly after 3:00 p.m. The anticipation was electric. A roar went up for every aircraft that passed by. Finally, one with "Trump" on it evoked mass movement toward the walkway, but it turned out to be the

---

[129] I asked my brother, a former journalist, to write up his impressions prior to sending him mine.

Republican nominee's advance team. "Look at all the Secret Service men out there," remarked one bystander.

Some of the crowd began heading away from the ramp, inciting several others to follow. Speculation was rampant. "Is that him? Is he in that SUV?" The music transitioned from outlaw country to the Rolling Stones' "Tell Me [You're Coming Back]," followed by the choral intro to "You Can't Always Get What You Want."

But after an extended wait, the crowd finally did get what they wanted as people began to emerge from the second plane. Trump waved from the airplane ramp to an eruption of cheering, then made his way toward the podium set up in a hangar. Shortly after arriving, Trump called for the fire marshals to let more of the throng crowding the outside of the open hangar inside.

The message was well-known by his supporters who responded with "Lock her up!" and "Build that wall!" and resounding booing for the assembled media. The most popular topic broached in the fifty-minute address, the Second Amendment right to bear arms, drew a response that rocked the hangar. Trump yielded the microphone to a pair of military generals who confirmed his revelation of another general facing consequences of an email incident described as "one-tenth of what Mrs. Clinton did."

Trump good-naturedly acknowledged a few protesters, remarking that even he might be tempted to disrupt one of his rallies for the $1,500 fee he suggested his opponent's supporters were providing.

The rally resembled a popular sporting event or rock star appearance, and people roared their approval as Trump concluded by pledging to make America first, safe, secure, and great again. Afterward, Trump walked a gauntlet of cheering spectators to his plane, heading to Las Vegas for the third and final debate with the Democratic nominee.

By visiting sections of this swing state where his support is significantly stronger than Denver or Boulder, Trump's conviction that he can win the election received a boost, and the crowd definitely got what they came for. However, as the hangar slowly emptied, the strains of "You Can't Always Get What You Want" played again. In a few weeks, the nation will choose to essentially continue with a known commodity or venture the "way less traveled by," to paraphrase Robert Frost. And that will make all the difference.

The Experts

OCTOBER 25, 2016

I've recently returned from Southern California, where I'd been keeping my ninety-six-year-old father company in his last months on planet earth. He died on October 10. I started going out mid-July, after he had taken a fall in his assisted-living apartment. It was then determined, after the fall, that he should be moved to the skilled nursing wing of the facility. He'd fractured his shoulder and so could no longer use his walker, as his arm was to be kept immobile in a sling while the fracture healed, which it did all on its own. And so he was confined to a wheelchair, and the experts thought then that he should be moved to the SNF where he could be more closely watched, monitored, and cared for. He hated it, not that he liked living in the assisted-living quarters either, which it had been determined he should move into (from his independent-living apartment) three years before. The biggest difference was that in AL, he got three meals a day included in the downstairs restaurant, the Magnolia Room, scheduled activities, and a much smaller apartment with no stove or oven. He would call me three, four, five times a week just to talk, often about Trump and the election. I'd send him chapters from this book about the election. He'd read them, sometimes four times, because, he said, he enjoyed watching my mind work.

The last year, it became apparent that his short-term memory was in deterioration, and he began to say he wanted out, that he just wanted to die "at home" with me and my brother. Of course, no such place existed. But I told him I'd figure something out somehow, someway, where we could have a home and in-house professional care, that there was enough money. And so I began the process. But it wasn't until after the fall, when I went out there (for the first time in years), that I saw just how bad a shape he was in. It was apparent right away, to me, that his days were numbered and that he probably wouldn't make it till the end of the year to Christmas. After all, he was ninety-six; he wasn't going anywhere. I felt certain of that, but not the doctors, administrators, and other health-care professionals. They all said, "Sure, you can take him home." The paperwork was started. *That's crazy,* I thought. No way, he's winding down fast.

But others in the family tended to go along with the professionals, and so I found myself traveling back and forth each month. What we did, my brother and I, was rent an apartment close to the facility so we'd have a place to stay and perhaps move him into. It was all crazy. Each time I'd see him, after a couple weeks of absence, it was obvious just how fast the decline was. Yet everyone kept up the positive, hopeful line that he could improve: "We'll just try these drugs, this dose, these supplements, these exercises—he can do it." He'd call me from the nurses' station (he could no longer use a phone without help) and cry, "Please, Mark, get me out of here. I don't want to die in this slaughterhouse. I want to die in peace, at home." So I'd drive out and sit with him, and we'd chat about things. I'd take him out for wheelchair walks and try to get him to eat *something.* His weight was dropping fast, and most of the time, he slept. He couldn't remember anything except long-ago happenings, and who knows about those? Pretty much, nothing he said made sense. His body was a discolored, shriveled-up mess. His skin hung on him. His muscles were gone, his rib cage protruding.

And yet finally, after another fall while trying to make it to the bathroom in the night, it was decided to take him to the hospital for some observation and further analysis. Oh look, they discovered a tumor on his bladder. After a transfusion and some antibiotics, he was good to go home to the SNF. And the doctors, several, gave him a terminal diagnosis, maybe six months, they said. They told me to make him comfortable, manage the pain, oh, and call hospice. Hospice turned out to be a series of persons one after another, levels of management, until I finally met with his primary nurse / case manager at his bedside. That was Friday. She said she'd check back in on Tuesday. That night, Dad tried to escape. Still another hospice nurse was called in, and they got Dad sedated. He died on Monday. I was there, sat with him. I'm not sure what he knew. The professionals, the experts, assured me he knew I was there. I don't know. Six months, really? That would have taken him well past the election and into the New Year. Crazy.

The point of this story is that experts—except when it comes to maybe, *maybe*, engineers, surgeons, pilots, physicists, chemists, and the like—don't really know much more than we common folks do,[130] but they sure cost a lot of money. Make a good living, in so much as money can buy a good living. I've got a question for you: Why aren't more well-educated people supporting Trump? Maybe it's because the experts have declared him unfit, unqualified, dangerous, or maybe even mentally deranged. Certainly, he's a sexual predator, as well as a racist, sexist, bigot, xenophobe, and just probably the most deplorable human on earth. Why, he's a fascist, the next Mussolini, possibly Hitler! And the polls, look at the polls! Why, any reasonable person knows he'll destroy democracy!

So let's talk about the polls. All the experts love to talk about the polls, and the pollsters love to take their polls and have the other experts (the pollsters are experts too) talk about the polls they take. There are new polls taken every week (except the week following the second debate, when it was whispered that Trump soundly defeated Clinton). All the experts will tell you the results and usually say whether or not the results are within or outside the margin of error. This gives the appearance that they know what they're talking about, but they don't.

Let's say a respected poll came out that had Clinton up by four points, 45% to Trump's 41%, and the MOE was 3.5. The experts will say Clinton's lead is outside the margin of error and consistent with other polls showing

---

[130] In a recent *Time* "Viewpoint" piece, Nick Lovegrove cites University of Pennsylvania professor Philip Tetlock: "Research has shown that in a variety of situations, certain nonexperts can actually make better predictions than experts, because they are better able to draw upon an eclectic array of perspectives." I'd add to that that experts are often blinded by financial incentive to twist reality to a position that favors/supports their own well-being.

Clinton's lead at five, six, or seven points, which, in politics, is a landslide, they'll add. Thus, it gives you the impression that the race is over; it's only a matter of how big a landslide Clinton wins by. Here's the truth (brace yourself): The margin of error means that the results of the poll (which depend on the makeup of the sample and what and how the questions are framed) is thought to have a confidence level of 95% within the MOE, which is the number, in this case, 3.5, added to or subtracted from each person's percentage. In other words, Clinton might actually be at 48.5% or possibly 42.5%, and Trump could actually be at 44.5% or 38.5%. What that means is that Trump might be leading 44.5% to 42.5%, which is a far cry from the race being over—a landslide win for Clinton.

Why do they do this? Is it because they believe it's too complicated for the average person to understand? Or maybe they don't know themselves, having never taken or understood statistics. Or maybe they're pushing a narrative that they've already declared, and they need to be right! What they (the experts) are telling you matters because people tend to believe and trust experts. It's unfortunate and regrettable for two reasons. One, you *should* be able to believe experts, and two, the fact that in practice you can't, that often leads to deleterious outcomes.

For example, let's take health care again. The experts tell you, indeed, sell you products and ideas that are supposed to be for your benefit; but it's almost always the case that the one who most benefits is the seller. It doesn't matter if it's a physical fitness coach, a mental fitness coach, a psychotherapist,[131] a financial advisor, a diet coach, your doctor or auto mechanic, and for sure, your local political representative, even your president. They are *all in* for themselves, first and foremost. That's how they make their living. Sometimes it works out well for you, and sometimes it doesn't. It often depends on an interpretation and your own mind's belief (the placebo effect). And there's always a reason if things didn't work out. Oftentimes, it winds up being your fault, your responsibility. So it's better for everyone if everyone agrees. "It's great! Thank you!" Even if it isn't. Sad.

One more example is the Trump supporters. The experts all have an opinion and reason for that opinion about who these people *are*. Obviously, they can't be smart. Obviously they can't be well educated. Obviously, they're racists and white supremacists. They're angry losers, mentally ill,

---

[131] There are, of course, exceptions—some who are true professionals—putting the ethics of their profession above their self-interest.

sexists! And/or they are white old people who are suffering from nostalgia, if not flat-out dementia! This is because they *are* the experts, the thought leaders, and can't be wrong.

Wrong. Much of the time, they are wrong, but they have a platform that says they're right. To quote Trump, "It's a crazy world we're living in."

Final Debate

OCTOBER 25, 2016

By now, you should know not to trust what the experts are telling you about the third debate. They're in the tank for Hillary and for themselves—they are heavily invested in being *right*! They're experts and *must* justify their salaries and status! (Or am I wasting my time?) It's not about you; it's about them. What did they tell you in unison? (Just as they have with regard to nearly everything regarding Trump. Remember? He's a clown. He can't win. He'll quit. He's unstable. He's a bully. He's not rich. His is a campaign of hate. His convention speech was dark. He has a ceiling of 10%, then 15%, then 20%, and right on up to his winning. He's a sexual predator. He's going to lose. He's a loser. He's cozy with Putin. He's doing this for his brand. He's going to open up Trump TV. And so on and so forth.) That Hillary won and Trump put the final nail in his coffin by attacking the very fabric of our democracy—the peaceful transfer of power, the graceful concession by the defeated to the victor. He's finished.

But I watched the debate, and that's not what I heard. That wasn't *my* take. I thought he killed her, won every exchange, every point. I thought Hillary was smirking and condescending (smug) to cover up her failings, and when that didn't work, she resorted to yelling, almost screaming. "He choked!" She referred to Trump's visit to Mexico and the building of the wall. Trump calmly sipped from his water glass. "We need the wall," he almost whispered. He gave the reasons. (I think it's a waste of time for him to have to explain negotiation to her. It's apparent she'll never be capable.) He twists his lips. Hillary screams, "I will defend women's rights!" She played what she thinks is her best card, her trump card—the woman card. Trump leans into the mic. "She's been proven to be a liar." Hillary starts to recite her plan for the economy. Trump says, "Her plan is a disaster." Trump tells Chris Wallace, the moderator, that he's going to renegotiate the trade deals and the military agreements and "cut taxes massively."[132] Hillary is yelling now, "My husband . . ." Trump takes a drink. (If it were whiskey, it'd be perfect, like Doc Holliday playing poker.) Wallace asks Clinton about what she said behind closed doors about open borders. Hillary laughs, the well-practiced laugh, and denies it and switches to Russia—that Russia, Putin, and Trump are in cahoots. She says Trump is Putin's puppet. Trump says, "You're the puppet" (meaning of her donors and special interests). Trump says to Wallace, "Putin outsmarted her and Obama and always will." At this point, I thought she was going to cry, the ultimate woman card—the victim (damsel in distress) card.

Go ahead, call me a sexist.

I went to bed after the debate. I couldn't bear to watch the spin. Trump got into his black limousine and drove off into the night (probably to kick back in the penthouse apartment of Trump International Hotel, Las Vegas. I've been there; it's nice).

The next morning, true to form, all the experts were shocked and appalled—that Trump would not submit to having lost the election.

---

[132] As of May 10, 2018, he's doing exactly what he said he would do.

The Last Hike

OCTOBER 29, 2016

Friday, yesterday, October 28, 2016, I took what I figured would be my last big-league hike into the Wild Basin. I was saying goodbye. Two weeks ago, I said goodbye to my father for the final time. Sometimes you know and sometimes you don't when the last time is. Two summers ago, I did my last camp. I've been hiking in the Wild Basin for over twenty years, and I'm getting too old for this kind of thing—solo hiking in the wilderness. And so I decided this would be the last hike into my favorite place. Well, because the weather's been so mild and the world so crazy, why not?[133]

I was surprised; there were many other hikers, not quite as many in the summer months, but a lot—couples and families. This time, I wasn't wearing my wide-brimmed Indiana Jones leather hat but my "Make America Great Again" hat, my Trump hat—the walking, almost talking, declaration that I'm with him—the bigoted, soulless, racist, xenophobic, sexual predator. Most of the other hikers were coming down as I was going up, so they got a good look at my hat. (It's fairly standard hiking protocol to acknowledge other folks on the trail with a greeting of some

---

[133] Not true. That was then, and this is now. And I'm planning on going back in as soon as the snow melts. Why not?

kind, even if only a nod, but always with eye contact. It's that "friend or foe" instinct, not like in the city where everyone avoids eye contact. Is city life unnatural? I saw fear in some eyes, a glint in others, and some smiling eyes, even in some of the women's and girls'. I wondered how many discussions I started? How many fights? How much makeup sex? How many not-yet-born-babies will owe their life to me and Mr. Trump? It got me thinking about what would the world be like when they're grown and me long gone. What's going to happen? What kind of planet will we be leaving them?

It's not so much a coming anarchy (see my review of *The Coming Anarchy*) as I'm afraid of World War III, a war that is going to make all the others look like child's play. If the planet is warming, the climate changing, and I think no matter the cause, that's undeniable, there are going to be horrific consequences for the human population. It's already started to happen. There are and will be even more severe droughts, famines, flooding, and wildfires leading to mass migrations of people. There are just too many people crowded into places, cities, lands, and territories that cannot sustain them in Africa, Asia, Southeast Asia, and the Middle East. The migration into Europe has already begun, and there's nowhere else to go. But wait, yes, there is—it's the United States of America, a huge landmass and sparsely populated (when compared to other places) with abundant resources. People will be forced and coerced, and yes, conscripted onto ships and into armies, with the purpose of invading the United States. The only recourse the USA will have is to torpedo or bomb these ocean vessels, killing hundreds of thousands before they can reach land. Hawaii will surely be attacked. It will be a two front war. The USA will be forced to defend itself in the Pacific and Atlantic. The strategy will likely be to flood the southern border of the US with massive amounts of people—refugees, migrants, soldiers—overwhelming any possible conventional resistance. Massive slaughter and carnage is bound to occur. There will be raping, heads chopped off, and babies put on spits and slow-roasted for food. It's going to surely happen as I'm sitting here and writing, having come down out of the wilderness and thought it over.

Who is going to mastermind this invasion? It's probably already being thought about by people in high places, in China, India, Vietnam, Africa, the Middle East, Pakistan, and Afghanistan. The TPP trade agreement is a joke, a ruse, as is the Iran nuclear deal.[134] NATO is *so* obsolete it's beyond a bad joke. NAFTA is also obsolete. The European Union is a farce. The world talks about climate change mitigation are also superfluous. The United Nations? Give me a break.

What is necessary is for the United States, Mexico, Canada, and the United Kingdom, maybe Europe and even Russia—yes, Russia (Russia will have to choose which side they're on)—and South America to come together if possible and decide on a strategy to defend itself, its land and territory and people. There is no choice. Yes, there must be a wall on the southern border of the US, and Mexico will pay for it because we will help defend them. Maybe there will have to be a wall, a sea wall, built around Florida and Louisiana too.

Now those are some dark thoughts.

But it's true. It'd be funny if it wasn't, how we humans expect things to be different because *we're here*. The planet's been warming and cooling, the climate changing, for millions of years; but now that we're here, we expect it to stay static. Funny? Sad? Stupid? Selfish? Ungrateful? Dishonest? The evidence is everywhere, and yet we think, *No, not me. I'm not going to get old or die. I don't have to say goodbye. I'll just keep on hiking forever.*

Rainbows and unicorns—seems as though humans have believed in them or something akin ever since we first began thinking after running for our lives.

---

[134] As of yesterday, May 9, 2018, Trump has nixed those two agreements, gotten the European nations to pony up more money for NATO, and is working on NAFTA.

The Missing Father

OCTOBER 31, 2016

My father died twenty-one days ago, and I'm having a hard time.[135]

During the last year of his life, we talked often, and he asked me if I missed my mother. I told him no, that I was a grown man and didn't need her, a mother, anymore. He told me he missed her, and I told him I understood but that his and my relationship with her, his wife and mate and *my* mother, were different. His short-term memory was gone, and so we couldn't carry on the conversation, but we had it over and over again. His grandson, my son, late the night after he died, wrote a tribute to his grandfather and posted it on Facebook. He wrote: "He was my closest friend. He really got me through some tough times. He looked out for me, protected me, encouraged me, listened to me, and loved me. He lived a great life, did an outstanding job providing for his family, and taught me so much about being courteous and dependable and flexible and generous and kind."

Isn't that the essence of fatherhood and, in practice, life—as it is experienced? The human condition? A father is necessary to protect and

---

[135] It's still May 10, 2018; nineteen months passed.

provide for his family and to teach his children what it is to be a man and how to navigate the storms and hardships that are inevitable.

Hillary Clinton is wrong in that regard. It doesn't take a village (to raise a child); it takes a man, a father (with help, of course).

What is undermining the human experience on earth is the feminization of life—the war, if you will, on men and the natural order of life. A man, a *real* man, above and before all else, protects and provides for his family—his mate and children and then the other members of his tribe. That is universally understood and is as it has always been, regardless of time, place, ethnicity, and/or culture. In the United States, that fact of life has been undermined by the politically correct movement, the postmodernists, by the unempowered, the weak, in attacking the power and force (i.e., the father) via subversive and dishonest methods, i.e., passive aggression, guilt, shame, false information or propaganda, democracy (majority rules, regardless), and the reframing of history and ideas under the guise of freedom and liberty and education.[136] There *are* alternative facts or narratives concerning America and the world. Each storyteller or in-group has its version. One group's freedom fighter/hero is another's terrorist/criminal. Same as it's always been.

If in practice, every father provided for and protected his family, I think 90 percent of the problems (joblessness, homelessness, addiction, mental illness, disordered personalities, the fear of death and dying) would be manageable and tolerable, and for the most part, go away. These problems grow and expand into conditions that lead to conflict (which many thrive on) within and between individuals and societies and nations because of the absence of the father (meaning a man capable of providing for and protecting his family within the safety and security of a tribe).

Now to be clear, this situation may well be beyond any one person's control, i.e., it may be the result of the force of momentum, physics, and chemistry or said another way, reciprocal determinism, the law of attraction—a chain of circumstance (cause and effect, determinism, interaction of unknowable factors), a coincidence of circumstance (luck/chance/random), a web of complex relations (unknowable, see above), permutations of complications, or God's will (religion, the belief in a supernatural power). In other words, what are you going to do? What *ought* I to do, given I don't know the answer?

---

[136] Tara Westover, *Educated: A Memoir* (2018).

Is it possible to make laws that trump that which is? Is it possible to make that which is unreal real because we imagine it? Want it? In other words, can we make something not true, true? By our will, prayer, collective prayer, and collective will?

Or is it as it has always been, as Blaise Pascal thought and said hundreds of years ago, "The empire of imagination reigns for a while and is sweet and unconstrained, but the empire of force reigns forever. The last act is bloody, however pleasant all the rest of the play is: a little earth is thrown at last upon our head, and that is the end forever."

I miss my father every day. He wasn't a perfect man, but knowing he was there, that he had my back, allowed me to be me, to be free, to soar toward the sun, to fly. Even if my wings were held on only by wax, was of no concern to me. My father was there. Now it's my turn, and I challenge myself to be up to the task.

The Final Argument

NOVEMBER 3, 2016

"When they go low, we go high." Remember that? That was Michelle Obama's much-repeated and swooned-over statement in her address at the Democratic National Convention back in July. Now here we are in the final week of the campaign, and who is going low? And who is going high? Realize that, and you'll know all you need to know about the two candidates. Yesterday afternoon, I decided to take a nap, thinking I'd be up late watching the seventh game of the World Series. And so I turned on Spotify, my "ocean sounds" playlist, and an ad came on, a political ad, the first time I'd ever heard one on the popular streaming music station. It was a Clinton ad but not about her; it was all about Trump—statements, in his own words, he'd made over his lifetime, referencing women. It was pretty ugly. I'm sure you've all heard and seen the ad on TV too. Clinton has bombarded the airwaves with it. It's her final argument: you can't vote for Trump because he's a vile human being. He hates women, uses them, abuses them, and objectifies them.

She pairs this with her other argument: you can't vote for Trump because he's a racist and a xenophobe and, in fact, hates all people except himself. He's depraved. She shouts and screams this at her rallies, jabbing her pointer finger at the crowd. She reiterates what she thinks about people who support Trump—that they, too, are vile. Truth is, she's frightened and desperate. She thought she had this election going away, that it was a rout. After all, all the experts said so—those in the media, those in universities, and all the paid political consultants, all the thought leaders. The trouble was, the people, the voters, at least half of them, weren't buying it. The contest had tightened over the last ten days to dead even, a tie (maybe we'll have extra innings? Wouldn't that be fun) according to the polls, which, in fact, were always suggesting that—all being within the true margin of error, except for a brief time in mid-October when the media was saturating the airwaves with an illegal audiotape of Trump talking with another guy in private about women (see "Pussygate").

The Clinton campaign, the Never Trumpers, the media, the elites, and establishment on both sides were all doing backflips and somersaults. So filled with joy were they. They had all been right all along: Trump was a vile human being, and so were his die-hard, dwindling group of supporters. But Trump wasn't going to quit and give in. It's not his style. He doubled down, buckled down, and worked even harder while Clinton was almost hiding. Trump started to do even more rallies, up from two a day to three, four, and even five a day. He went on the offensive, going into states where they had all declared him dead, finished—Colorado (six times), Nevada, North Carolina, Wisconsin, Michigan, New Hampshire, and Pennsylvania. His message, his closing argument, was "I will fight for you!" He laughed, he joked, he talked about work and jobs. He talked about education and safety and security. He smiled. *He knew.* He knew what he was doing, what he'd done his whole life—working hard. He was right on schedule, his schedule, and under budget. He didn't have to explain everything; people could see for themselves.

The people, the voters, didn't need the experts, the thought leaders, to tell them what to think. In fact, that was part of Trump's message—that "they" had let you down—the elites, the politicians, the media. They were all talk, no action, while their wallets got fatter with your hard-earned money and taxes. At one rally, he pointed to Katy Tur, one of MSNBC's self-declared Road Warriors (see "The Campaign"), whom he's had fun with since the beginning, teasing her because he knows how things work, how people work.[137] After all, he's been making a living out in the real

---

[137] Katy Tur published her version of the campaign and relationship with Trump,

world, working hard, for fifty years. He knows what he's doing. He pointed to her, with a slight smile on his face, and challenged her, baited her, and used her as the face of the media and how dishonest and how crooked they were and that they were in the tank for Clinton (see "Drain the Swamp" and also "The Experts").

And the media took the bait. Tur appeared on Brian Williams's show on MSNBC, and they talked and talked about the incident after reminding the viewers (and themselves) that they are reporters and not the story, of course, which is not true. They work far harder on inserting themselves into the story than on accurately reporting what's going on—that's how they make their living—by convincing people and their bosses that they, the reporters, are important and that they hold the keys to the truth. The media is in competition and in cahoots with itself to create conflict and confusion so y'all will watch, and they use every trick in the book. Trump dismisses them, calls them out, challenges them, and goes around them, which infuriates them. But they need him. He's making money for them. That's what he does—makes money. Again, he's a doer and a talker and an entertainer—a businessman—far superior than most. Maybe more so than anyone the world has ever seen, and to take him down, oh, how everyone wants to (see "The Case against Trump"). They will resort to any and everything, including selling you down the river. In the words of Hillary Clinton, "What difference does it make!" Meaning dead is dead, right?

So Trump is making his final argument, but he's showing you how it's done, not telling you. He's having fun. He's winning against all odds, the same thing he says he'll do for you. It's genius. He message is, if you want to work, he'll give you work, not social programs or handouts but jobs. He doesn't care if you are black, white, brown, male or female, gay or straight. If you want to work, he'll put you to work. He knows how to do that. He'll bring back what's been taken from you—your pride, your dignity. He'll make America great again.

The real question is, *Is* that what people want? Or have they been spoiled and made soft? The elites have figured out a way to make more money by outsourcing and going international (i.e., globalization), and

---

Unbelievable: My Front-Row Seat to the Craziest Campaign in American History (2017). For the most part, it reads like chick lit. Tur now has her own show on MSNBC. She's trying very hard, still, to justify what was and is her biased and prejudiced positions.

appeasing the locals, the voters, with social programs while convincing them that they are victims of evil men like Trump—racists, bigots, sexists—who just use and abuse the good people (It is white privilege, male privilege, the toxic patriarchy). That, too, is genius in a way. But *I think* it's not a good thing. People want to work, do real work, like build things, make things, take care of their families. People want to take pride in achievement and accomplishment, to be able to point at something, and say, "I made that," "I built it," "I caught it," "I killed it," "I cooked it," "I grew it," "I harvested it," "I mined it," "I wrote it," or "I cleaned it." Whatever *it* is—real work. And people want to be paid and respected for that work, recognized for that work. They want to compete with and work with others, to find satisfaction in achievement and accomplishment that they can be proud of, to be able to say, "I am somebody!" and "I have proof. Look!"

If Trump wins, that shows everyone that anything is possible. His victory will be the greatest upset in the history of the world ever—an upset that involved over sixty million people taking part, going against all odds. If you voted for Trump, you are a part of that, saying to the entire world that the US of A will not quit ever! We won't give up or give in, and we believe that anything is possible. What it means is that everyone will try a little harder. They will continue to do their work, their jobs, but now will give it 10%, 15%, 20% more effort. People will dream big, think big. Maybe, just maybe, even peace is possible.[138] If you've ever stood up against overwhelming odds and fought for what you believe in, then Trump's for you. On the other hand, if you voted against Trump in a battleground state, say, Colorado, and he loses that state, then you are a part of that and what happens next. What happens next will be nasty, ugly. When Trump called Hillary nasty to her face, he wasn't saying she was badass, just the opposite. He was saying that she was low-down capable of doing anything to ascend to power—cut any deal, sell anyone out—to satisfy her will to power and to exact revenge (on Bill, her father, who knows?). But make no mistake; she is not your champion. Hillary Clinton is bought and paid

---

[138] This seems to be happening now, May 15, 2018, with the stock market and economy booming, upcoming talks with North Korea, new trade deals, moving the US embassy to Jerusalem, but not if you are still listening to the thought leaders and experts.

for—the money's in the bank and that's going to cost you, not her. You are going to pay the bill.

Not too far in the future, there will be a massive migration of millions of people likely leading to a world war brought about by not global warming as much as human greed, selfishness, the will to power, and the need to survive. If Trump wins, he'll put the best people in the positions where they can do the most good. Pay to play will be over. Incompetence will be over. Submission, weakness, and cowardice will be dealt a blow. Struggle, strength, fearlessness, freedom, and triumph will be buoyed—in essence, Americanism.[139] If those are your values, Trump's for you. Trump doesn't carry grudges (if the fight was fair); he's a businessman. Maybe there'll even be a position for Hillary—ambassador to Iraq or special envoy to Syria, in charge of overseeing safe zones for the people. Or maybe she'll be just a civilian citizen working within the Clinton Foundation, focused only on humanitarian goals. Maybe she'll rise?[140] With Trump as president, there will be no more pay to play and corruption and special interests–dictating events. If Trump wins . . .

In thirty-six hours, we'll know who won.

---

[139] At some point in *this* story, it behooves *me* to talk of storytelling. There are conflicting narratives, stories, as to the history of America, the world, and of course, one's own story. What we (humans) tend to do is fill in blanks, regardless of whether the story is personal, group centered, or universal. We like/need stories. This is now known as confabulation or the tendency to fabricate in concert with others, or in one's own mind and memory, a compelling narrative that fits one's concept of self and reality. It's not abnormal or aberrant, but common. It has obvious survival value. We tend to put ourselves, our group, our nation/country, in a favorable light. To not do so is self-/group-destructive and abnormal. I do it, you (most of you) do it, Trump does it, Hillary does it, and the media does it.

[140] If that happens, it's certainly not now. She's written a memoir, *What Happened*, and is currently on book tour in foreign countries, continuing to make excuses and denounce Trump (see previous footnote).

Election Day

NOVEMBER 8, 2016

I woke up at 2:00 a.m. and couldn't get back to sleep, too excited, too much adrenaline. So I got up and made coffee and turned on the TV, all a buzz, and settled into the couch in my PJs. I pulled the throw over me and watched the shows, switching between the channels. The hosts were all a Twitter (literally), as were the reporters in the field, camped out in coffee shops and polling places in the various eastern battleground states. Last night, I watched Hillary Clinton's grand finale in Philadelphia with her star-studded lineup of endorsers. I almost felt embarrassed for them; try as they might, it seemed their hearts just weren't into it. They knew deep inside that they were twisting the truth to fit the narrative they were selling. It's hard to turn actual failures into a prelude for success, a reason to vote for her. It's just crooked thinking, fantasy, and/or delusion. It seemed like what they were doing was co-opting Mr. Trump's message as their own and asking us, the voters, to trust them. Really? "This time, we mean it. This time won't be like the last time. This time, we'll bring the change we promised. This time, we'll deliver on the hope for a better life and world. Trust us." As the saying goes, "If you do what you've always done, you'll get what you've always got." In other words, more of the same. To the contrary, a vote for Trump is "What have you got to lose?"

Trump's team was all over the airwaves, his children, his surrogates, and Trump himself even called in to Fox News. He seemed relaxed, confident, and aware. The pace he kept this last week was astounding, doing twice as many events and rallies as Clinton. It's hard to fathom how a seventy-year-old man can do that—five, six rallies a day in different states, from 9:00 a.m. to past midnight. I can't help but think, yes, this man will work his behind off. Maybe he really can fix all these problems or will die trying. What a contrast to our current president, Mr. Cool, President Smug, who talks a good game between rounds of golf but never delivers.

So today, Election Day, I'm going to do laundry, take a shower, and shave. I will wash my hair, put on fresh, clean clothes, settle in, and watch the returns come in. Maybe I will drink, maybe not. Consensus is, we'll know early[141] if it's going to be a long night or if Hillary's going to wrap it up early with wins in Florida and North Carolina. I can't see how anyone in their right mind could vote for her, but that's been my take all along. In fact, it appears that no one has changed their mind through this whole process since the two candidates locked down their nominations. What caught me this morning, watching the reporters interview voters in the coffee shops, was that some people—the deciders, the undecideds—still hadn't made up their minds on who they were going to vote for. That realization is frightening, that the *fate of the world* might hinge on the minds of people who can't make up their mind.

I thought to myself as I settled in, *Did I do all I could?* Then I answered myself, *Yes. I wrote and wrote and wrote and published and spoke up and out to make the case for Trump.* My so-called friends abandoned me, unfriended me on Facebook, both women and men. They bought what the media and the elites were selling. When I told Dad that, he said, "Then they weren't really your friends." True enough. How much of a hidden Trump vote is there? One in five? One in ten? That's why the ballot is secret so people may vote their true feelings.

I decided to drink. The world *is* a hostile place. Just because you want something to be true doesn't make it so. Maybe the only place it isn't hostile is in the womb if you are wanted. After that, it's up to the parents, not

---

[141]   The experts were wrong again. It was late before the election was called for Trump.

just the mother, to protect their children. The state's job is to protect the parents, the tribe, from outside threats. I am an atheist, if I haven't made that clear, but I get religion. I get belief and faith. It's a hostile world.

"I see you clucking, but I don't see any eggs," Dad would say. "Get out there and vote, Trumpsters! Don't be like them—all talk and no action."

Around 7:00 p.m. (MST), it became evident it was going to be a long night. Florida and North Carolina were too close to call. Never bet against the man who owns the plane. By 9:00 p.m. Florida, North Carolina, Ohio, Pennsylvania, Michigan, and Wisconsin all fell; but the experts wouldn't call the race. I am a college-educated white man, the only person I know who voted twice for Obama and now voted for Trump. There must be others! A vote for freedom from lies, from the snoots, and from the snobs, freedom to win, freedom to tell the truth! "Don't piss on my leg and tell me it's raining."

I went to bed at 12:00 a.m. (MST). They still hadn't called the race. For my part, I was confident Trump had won. Sleep was more important than what the experts thought and said—all the manufactured drama constructed for ratings or, said another way, for self-interest, i.e., money, sex and power. News and reporting no longer exist as they once did, back in the day, say, when Hunter Thompson reported for *Rolling Stone* in 1972 or David Wallace in 2000 with his essay *Up, Simba*.[142] Things have changed. This thing was over back in January (see "The Week the Election Was Won"). But then what about all the new postmodern elitists—those experts who told you what was what? The thought leaders, the smart people? I call them stupid, smart people. Trump, it was said, is superstitious—didn't want to claim victory until it was officially called. Hillary, for her part, would not concede. Seriously, this is not toughness or badassness; it's shock and denial, the beginning of the grieving process. Trump, for his part, believes in knocking on wood and the power of positive thinking.

---

[142] David Foster Wallace, *Consider the Lobster and Other Essays* (2006), 156–234.

Two Weeks After: Money, Sex, and Power

NOVEMBER 10–25, 2016

It's official. *Trump wins!*

I got up around 5:30 on Wednesday, November 9, and turned on the TV. Kellyanne Conway, Trump's third campaign manager, was speaking. She said, "A lot of people on the gravy train are scared to death." Steve Schmidt, John McCain's main man and a Trump hater said, "This is a giant primal scream. He [Trump] took out two parties." Both true; maybe three parties—the third "party" being the media. They are, the media, part of the scared party now—all riders on the gravy train. Watch as they scramble to keep the engine rolling. And then I saw and heard on *Morning Joe*, two esteemed men of color, elites, reporters for the *Washington Post* (see "Political Correctness," which speaks to the hidden Trump vote), "crying" (as was Jonathan Capehart, literally, which was caught on camera in London) that this is "white America's last stand" and that Trump is an "ill-informed racist" (see footnote 138 on confabulation).

News flash! These people, the elites (indeed, all people), need an enemy and are a great example of the ill-educated. I saw two racists on the set of *Morning Joe*, and they had dark skin. One of them, Eddie S. Glaude Jr., chair of the department of African American studies at Princeton University and a frequent guest on *Morning Joe*, stated his position in a piece in *Time*'s election-outcome edition (November 21, 2016). Maybe, more than anything, this short eight-hundred-word column sums up what is wrong, what was and has been gotten wrong about this election and America. He sees America through the lens of race, of black versus white. He thinks people are *motivated* by racial animus.

People, all people, are motivated by the same forces—money, sex, and power, i.e., survival. And by the same needs, for affiliation and achievement and power again. The "will to power," Nietzsche called it. For sure, these forces and drives are felt in different degrees in different people, different individuals. People are different. But these motivations are shared across race, across ethnicity, across gender. They *are* universal. (I read one account, by a feminist, who admitted that there *were* gender differences. She said, "Men will kill to protect/defend their mate, whereas women will kill to protect/defend their children." I don't disagree completely as both are capable of killing in service of protecting their family.) In this way, people *are* all born equal, just as every person needs food, water, and shelter.

Trump gets this instinctively, intuitively. The vast, *vast* majority of people get this too, intuitively. But leaders, thought leaders, use race and gender and religion and culture to divide people up into opposing groups so as to satisfy their own power and achievement motives, their own self-serving story. The struggle to survive, to compete against others (within and without one's own group or affiliation) to reproduce and thrive, is a universal trait. What Glaude and many of the other individuals and groups are doing is nothing more than a power play—trying to ascend to a higher level of status using any means available, in this case, the language of the victim and the oppressed, because they lost on the playing field (see "Despicable Democrats and the Media").

To his credit, Joe Scarborough challenged them. The segment blew through the sponsor break at the top of the hour. It was riveting TV, unscripted. This race wasn't about race. An argument could be made that the 2008 and 2012 elections were more about race than this one. But then again, it's not about racial animus but rather about power, for a race of people denied it for so long—about pride and achievement. It *felt* good to vote for Obama. This election was about money, sex, and power—the prime human motivators. Mika Brzezinski, true to form, was near tears (see "The Case against Trump"). Mika wants the world to be what it is not—not hostile, not chaotic—but awash with kindness, love, peace, and happiness. Scarborough said (to his credit), "People vote their self-interests."

Clinton, having gathered her composure, took to the public arena and spoke. She asked people to be open-minded and give Trump a chance. Then she went hiking with Bill (and the Secret Service) and bumped into another hiker, reeling with the shock of losing. Then they posed for a selfie. My eyes could not roll more, even as establishment Republicans, Never Trumpers, were falling over their Twitter accounts and congratulating Mr. Trump. Still, others were on their phones, calling Trump headquarters, touting their résumés. Indeed, on Saturday, November 19, even Mitt Romney came calling on the president-elect. Romney, earlier, was Mr. Trump's harshest, cruelest critic, saying not only was he, Trump, unqualified but also a fraud, a phony, and a con man—any and everything but a savvy businessman. Now, reportedly, Romney wants to be his secretary of state. It's enough to make your head explode. I'll leave the decision up to Mr. Trump. I trust his judgment; it's got him this far. He knows people and understands relationships. He may not know the issues or current policies, which drives people crazy, but he knows people and relationships, which, when you boil it down, is what matters. Put him in a room with people and a preferred outcome, and he'll figure it out.[143]

There is a reported four thousand jobs that "serve at the pleasure of the president," and currently fifty thousand résumés have been received at Trump Tower. Maybe, given his style, Mr. Trump can get even better results with just three-fourths of that. In other words, reduce the number of employees necessary to get the job done, a typical businessman's approach. But that has consequences. On the one hand, it reduces the expenses of the federal government; on the other hand, it increases the ranks of the

---

[143] Trump, first, chose Rex Tillerson as his secretary of state, then replaced him with Mike Pompeo. Much has been made of Trump's inability to fill some three thousand government positions. There are two reasons for this: (1) That would be impossible for anyone in the same circumstance, i.e., could you fill positions that you didn't know existed? Thousands of them? (2) There is an active resistance and opposition to *anything* that might contribute to Trump's success in achieving wins, also known as Trump derangement syndrome.

unemployed. In other words, it redistributes money from one class of people to another.

A business approach to government would be to hire the best person—regardless of race, age, gender, sexual orientation, religion—and pay them the least amount of money that they'll agree to work for and then invite them over for Thanksgiving dinner. Most Americans understand this intuitively. They get it and are grateful. This is the essence of conservatism—God, country, and family. This is the essence of tribalism. Mr. Trump gets it. Mr. Trump, so far, is exhibiting the exact same methods he used in business—identify your goals (see "Mr. Donald J. Trump's Platform 2016"), then find the best, most qualified, proven people to move you toward those goals. The specifics of policy will fall into place. Solve problems as they emerge. Think big. Be flexible but persistent. Have fun. He laid it all out in his bestseller, *The Art of the Deal*.

The Democrats and Hillary's supporters and surrogates were so confident of victory they were checking the real estate market in DC, bidding up the market. Now they are beside themselves with finger-pointing and blame. They seem to be settling on racism, sexism, and the Russians as the chief reasons for Clinton's defeat.

Listening to Hillary's speech, I thought, *She's a good loser, much better at losing than winning.*

Trump: "Once a choker, always a choker." True enough.

Trump: "I'm going to teach you how to win." He did.

A thought slid across my mind, a saying that I'd heard repeated again and again by believers: "Everything happens for a reason." And the addendum: "If it didn't happen, it wasn't meant to be." And so I thought, *Maybe there is a god? Maybe there is an invisible hand?*

The polls weren't wrong; the elites didn't tell the truth either because they don't understand statistical data (probably true) or because it wasn't in their self-interest (money, sex, power) to report accurately (most likely true). The margin of error accounts for the final vote (see "The Experts").

Obama? Can my eye roll still get more intense? (See "Something's Going On.") He's trying to protect *something* of his legacy. His strident campaigning for Hillary wasn't about her; it was about himself, his story. He said, "Ultimately we're all on the same team." True enough, but check the tape on what he said about Trump. He, Obama, thought he was backing a winner in Clinton, but he failed to understand, just as he's failed to understand from the get-go that the world is a hostile and chaotic place.

Obama is the epitome of all talk, no action. He gives great speeches. The best description of him was from an alt-right source (since banned) I'd followed on Twitter, who said Obama is a "rootless cosmopolitan." What does that mean? It means having no roots, no homeland, no territory, and no tribe and being comfortable in any urban place, regardless of country. In other words, Mr. Obama couldn't relate to the conservative values of God, country, and family. He, Obama, couldn't understand the world as it is—hostile and chaotic—and that most people need the assurances of God (a higher power), country (secure territory), and family (a tribe made up of people [who look] like themselves). In short, it is a world today that revolves around money, sex, and power. Mr. Obama thought/thinks the world revolves around him and his values, his worldview, which is very much a common trait.

People tend to think others are like themselves (projection) and are shocked when they're not. All people are egocentric and self-centered in that way. But reality doesn't match up. People are different. First, Mr. Obama threw his family, his tribe, under the bus, and then he did the same with his pastor Jeremiah Wright. (*Under the bus* means to sacrifice a friend or ally for selfish reasons.) He, Obama, is doing it again. Watch. He's in Europe now as I write this, trying to fortify his standing using the election as proxy. He, Obama, is trying to convince his transatlantic friends that he didn't fail, that his presidency was a huge success despite his policies being soundly rejected in the election. Mr. Obama still believes he's right, and eventually, people will come around to his point of view.

So I'm watching all week and reading everything available/possible because I'm writing this book. (I have no staff, no sponsor. I write not for money [though it'd be nice] but because that's who *I* am, a thinker, a reader, a writer, and a doer.)

So let's understand who we are. Can we? The media has lied to you. Hillary lied to you. The experts (nearly always) lie to you. Or to be kind, you are caught up in the cognitive distortion of confabulation. What *are* you going to do?

You want numbers, data?

Trump had 306 electoral votes; Clinton, 232 votes. It was a landslide in presidential elections. The polls didn't get it wrong. There *was* a hidden (shy) Trump vote because of the labeling of Trump as a sexist, bigot, and racist. You, too, were one if you supported him. People were afraid to show/ say they supported him. The media and the experts will twist that to/in their self-interest. In other words, blame anyone or anything other than themselves. That's their story. In practice, the fact is people are not rational but rather guided by their emotions. Most people are believers, are people of faith. So if you lie to them and/or don't deliver what you promise and if there is an alternative, they just might choose the alternative if they've a choice, which is what an election is. Because in reality, it *is* a hostile, chaotic world, and people know that. Most people, by nature, live in a state of fear or anxiety, though latent. That has served us well as evidenced by the fact that we're here and we dominate the planet. We (humans) live in a state of fear. We "whistle past the graveyard, put on a happy face." But it doesn't take much to get us to unite around the fear, the horror, of evil. We believe in evil—the evil empire, the axis of evil, the snake, the Russians, 9/11, global warming, terrorism, the billionaires, Donald Trump, the devil.

We seek relief.

For example, there is no proof of an afterlife, but the promise and belief is, there is, and it is better than this life, which is full of conflict and hazard—a struggle in a competitive, comparative, hostile world. To think/ believe it's not my fault, whatever *it* is, is comforting. We want them to take responsibility, to be accountable for what they have done, but us? The fault is outside of us (the fundamental error of attribution).[144] Doesn't matter if it is God's will or some other's. We are all vulnerable, and we seek relief.

And then along comes a man, with his name on a plane, who tells you he is on your side.

Trump: "What have you got to lose? I will not let you down."

"He's a demagogue!" they shout. "Don't believe him!"

Trump is unlike a normal person; he *is* fearless.

"He's a bully and a predator."

So what happened? Ask yourself. What am I? Where am I? Who am I? Why am I who I am? What *happened* to me? And what ought I to do?

It might be that you are a narrow-minded, weak and tender-minded, people-pleasing, neurotic introvert. And in being so, you are in complete opposition to Mr. Trump, who is an open-minded, strong and tough-minded, disagreeable, stable extrovert. You *are* vulnerable. In other words, it's not your fault. What are you going to do? Vote Trump? Or hate Trump?

---

[144] The tendency to overestimate other people's behavior as being dispositional and excuse our own as situational.

But you cannot ignore Trump. Even those who chose not to or couldn't vote know his name and what he looks like.

You've been ill-educated and yet told otherwise. You've been told you are well educated and are, at heart, a good and decent person. In other words, you've been bamboozled (see "Community"). This brings us all the way back to Freud (see "Freud on Trumpism"). But you might say Clinton won the popular vote. Yes, but take away Los Angeles, and she lost. Take away just five cities—Los Angeles, DC, New York, San Francisco, and Chicago—and Trump crushed her. Why are the cities and the urban centers one way and the rest of the country, the territory, another? The cities are where the young people go. The cities are where the immigrants go, legal and illegal. The cities are where the elites, the thought leaders, live. The cities are where the universities are. The cities are where the money is, where the power is, and yes, where the sex is.

In some ways, urban life is unreal. I recently listened to a podcast wherein several millennials talked about living in Los Angeles and what brought them there. The gist was that they could live there among people like themselves without working. There were jobs to be had for sure. They were jobs that didn't require working per se, but more like hanging out with friends. This stems from popular TV shows, like *Seinfeld, Friends, Parks and Recreation, Californication, Casual, You're the Worst,* and *Portlandia*—basically, shows about nothing. The (crooked) thinking of these millennials is that they can go to Los Angeles and perform, act, or write, just hang out and hook up (without consequence). These are not stupid kids; they're stupid, smart kids. One said, talking about the election, "I live in this insane bubble . . . with liberal, homo, hipster, comedic nerds." It's true. They get their news from fake news shows, like *The Daily Show* on the Comedy Central channel, and from late-night comedians and then complain that the election results were influenced by fake news posts on social media sites sponsored by the Russians. Now that is some crooked thinking.

Cities have their own zeitgeist and culture: New York, if you want to be in finance, news, or publishing; DC, if politics is your game; San Francisco, if it's social media and technology. (I don't know about Chicago. You like the wind?) Seattle, Portland, and Atlanta all got a specific attitude and culture. The fact that there *is* money there means people can exist by hanging out, getting coffee for people, waiting on tables, cleaning houses or pools or hotel rooms, landscaping, cooking for people, or parking cars. They do whatever it is people with money need doing, like delivering sushi and selling weed on the side or being nonspeaking figurants in TV commercials. Health care and well care (therapy) is big. They can do senior sitting, babysitting, pet sitting. The point is, it *is* an *insane bubble.*

Outside the bubble (and all cites are bubbles that have specialties that attract money and people with money) in the "flyover" country, people lost their jobs, their homes, their families, their kids, their towns, and their way of living, such as it was. They lost the pride and dignity that comes from work that creates a sense of self—achievement and accomplishment. *Lost* isn't the right word . . . *had removed?* All the while, the bubble people jetted from bubble to bubble with, perhaps, good intentions to help other people around the world better their lives. The bubble people even welcomed people into the country, legal or not, and offered them sanctuary. "Come on in," they told them. "We'll put you to work. Your dream awaits!"

The board of supervisors of the city of San Francisco, along with the mayor Ed Lee,[145] in response to the election of Donald J. Trump as president of the United States of America, passed a resolution that sums up the fear and hysteria that is driving the opposition to Mr. Trump becoming president. It is a good example of confabulation.

Summing up, the resolution calls Mr. Trump an "erratic, ill-informed racist and misogynist" and emphasizes a commitment to "Black Lives Matter and climate change [not a hoax], affirms LGBTQ and women's rights, and defies Trump's threats to revoke federal funding for sanctuary cities," and also emphasizes inclusivity, innovation, vigorous debate, immigrants, the homeless population, and internationalism.

And then there are Trump supporters, the "flown-over," the people in the rest of the country—the working class, who make and build and dig and cut and kill and drive and tend and grow things; the warrior class, who fight to protect the people, the tribe, from harm; and the small business class, who own and manage shops that sell the things people need to live and make life less stressful. Rural and small-town America is populated with people who used to understand life (with a capital *L*) and that life has gone away. To them, "Make America great again" is more than a slogan. They don't want to move to the city and compete with the kids and the immigrants or be retrained so they can sit in a cubicle or stand behind a

---

[145] Ed Lee died thirteen months later (December 12, 2017) of cardiac arrest. There is an election for mayor of San Francisco in June of 2018. There are four candidates—three women of color and an openly gay man.

counter and scan cheap goods made in China: "Did you find everything you need?" They like to make their own. They are outdoor people. They like to sit on their porches and drink whiskey and beer (not wine) and watch the sun set after a hard day's work. They want to eat supper and then maybe hook-up before hittin' the sack, get up before the sun, and do it all over again. They want to watch football and baseball on the weekends (not soccer), go huntin' and fishin', and stock the freezer with meat. That's the way it's supposed to be. They're not racists or sexists or homophobes or xenophobes; they're just people who believed in something and now are seeing it taken away. What has happened and is happening is that their values of God, family, and country are being demonized by thought leaders on the coasts and in the big cities. They have been mocked.

The people in the flyover country watched their dreams slowly evaporate and now are being called racists and bigots, white supremacists, Islamophobes, and homophobes. "Deplorables," Mrs. Clinton called them—stoking the fear factor for votes and, yes, pitting one group against another. She thought she had enough votes if she could just get all the bubble people to turn out.

She used fear and affiliation to motivate.[146]

"Lock her up. Lock her up," the flown-over people chanted.

"Build that wall! Build that wall!" became the rallying cry.

A bumper sticker dropped into my car's open window (with its line of "Trump. Make America Great Again" bumper stickers) declared:

> Trump for the White House
> Hillary for the Jailhouse
> Bernie for the nuthouse
> Obama for the outhouse

Driving back and forth across the western states of Colorado, Utah, Arizona, Nevada, and California, all through the summer and fall, I saw only Trump signs. I didn't see one sign or sticker for Clinton. Other drivers

---

[146] The actual vote totals are telling. It's true that Mrs. Clinton won the popular vote by some three million, but in California, she won by 4.3 million. That margin came from the cities. And San Francisco? That city has become a "private club for the superrich" (John Davidson of the Federalist), with its own caste system of the wealthy (median single family homes cost $1.5 million), the service class, and the destitute.

would flash their lights and give me a thumbs-up. When parked, they'd speak softly to me, telling me how brave I was. It was apparent in flyover country that there was a great feeling of suppressed joy just waiting to explode. At Trump rallies, it felt great to let the rage and joy out. The flown-over people felt betrayed by their government, politicians, and even their own children. You take away (remove) a man's opportunity to work and provide for his family and you strip him of his pride—and then you want his vote?

No, you (Hillary, Obama et al.) don't *care* about what he (and she) wants. You don't *care* about them. You've proven that. You've got enough votes, you think. Everyone who is anyone (the experts) says so. The thought leaders are telling and selling that God doesn't exist, that family (your blood), can be whomever one wants, that family is something one chooses, and that the country, *your* country, *and* its flag don't matter. The world should be open and free for anyone to go anywhere. And they're telling you that that's progress and that's science. And well, if you don't believe them, you're an ignorant bigot and so on and so forth. What you are told is that you are racist and sexist, too dumb and uneducated to know what's good for you.[147]

The thought leaders have pitted those people against the other people— not only the naive millennials but also the inner-city black people and the brown people too and the Muslim people, the Asian people, and the queer people. The thought leaders thought they could get the female vote on their side too—all females—because the bellowing orange-haired clown hated all women, viewed them only as sex objects to breed. You heard the tape, right? Saw the ads? Men don't talk like that, you were told, and you wanted to believe it. Only monsters talk like that.

---

[147] There is a psychological principle called the Dunning-Kruger effect, wherein one believes oneself to be superior to the other in any manner of skill, ability, and/or importance. It's another unconscious psychological mechanism, dating back thousands of years, humans share that was beneficial to our evolving just as we did, first recognizable in Aesop's fable "The Gnat and the Bull." It's a broad-based ignorance of awareness of self and the self's interaction with the environment. It's LeBron James pontificating about politics, and Laura Ingraham's response was "Shut up and dribble," meaning stay in your area of expertise, basketball. Of course, the media's response was Ingraham's a racist. See my illustration of the Dunning-Kruger effect on the following page: https://www.npr.org/sections/thetwo-way/2018/02/19/587097707/laura-ingraham-told-lebron-james-to-shutup-and-dribble-he-went-to-the-hoop.

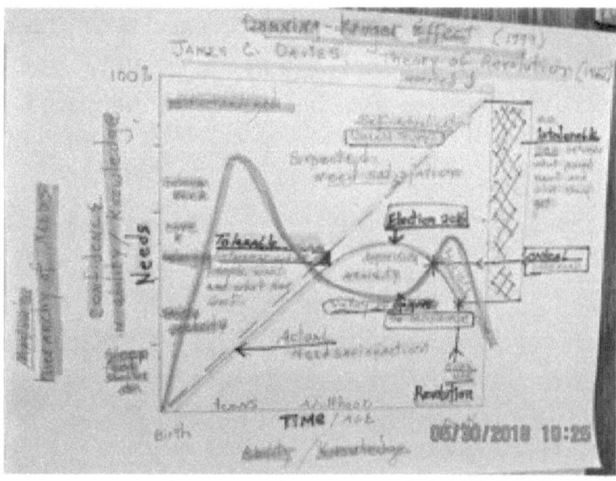

War or peace? Maslow's hierarchy of needs, the Dunning-
Kruger effect, and James Davies's theory of revolution
superimposed to show the coming crisis and critical crossroad

Above shows the Dunning-Kruger effect (the heavy gray line with two peaks), along with Maslow's hierarchy of human needs (highlighted on the left side) and with James C. Davies's "Toward a Theory of Revolution" (the lighter inverted j line), which, when combined, explain much of what I'm arguing here. Much of America's voting population and the thought leaders were sailing along thinking that they knew best, were right and good, and on the "right" course. But they were wrong, and the election happened, which upset their worldview and their *expectations*! Moreover, turned what might have been a tolerable gap between their wants and desires and what they actually had into an intolerable gap, into the "valley of despair," wherein they are now (June 2018), faced with a choice: turn their resistance into a full-out revolution or face reality and accept the fact that Trump, a self-actualized being whose accomplishments and achievements do match his expectations, *is* the president of the United States of America. And in doing that, they would help make America great again, get on with their lives, and work toward, again, their expectations of life, liberty, and the pursuit of happiness.

It sounds crazy, upside down, I know. But this is what the Democrats were selling: fear—fear of the other, fear of being dragged backward, fear of the planet's destruction, and fear that your world will collapse around you if you vote for the clown, all the while telling you it was Trump who was selling fear and dividing people by the color of their skin, their gender, their religion, or their sexual orientation. They even told you he would be coming for you. *Stalin-esque* was a phrase the thought leaders likened to Trump. The thought leaders filled you with hate and told you it was love.

"Love trumps hate" was the favored slogan.

They've filled you with fear, and you bought it. It's Machiavellian, and it almost worked.

Bernie Sanders is now telling you that he could've won, and some of you (Max and friends) are buying that. More than likely, Trump would have crushed him. The RNC had reams of oppositional research on him that would have completely disqualified him, except for those living in the "insane bubble." He would have lost the inner cities, as well as the working, warrior, and small business classes. For sure, the money classes would not have voted for him. Even some of the elite thought leaders would have turned from him. Maybe he would have got 30 percent of the vote and won four states: Vermont, California, Washington, and Oregon.

Who are you going to believe now? They will keep selling fear and hate and telling you it's love. Barack Obama will keep telling you what a great job he did. If that were really true, Clinton would not have lost. If Trump's supporters were racists, Obama never would have won in 2008 and again in 2012. Neither Obama nor Clinton had a remedy for the mess they helped create. They have no remedy for the people whose lives have been turned upside down because of globalization, technology, and self-interest. The Democratic leaders are clueless.

Trump: "Crooked Hillary." (My own nickname for her was Clueless Hillary.)

Trump: "What have you got to lose?"

She didn't lose because of hidden misogyny, which is what some feminists are selling. The most outrageous thing I read after the election was a column by a feminist in, I think, *USA Today*. I didn't link it because I don't think giving space to fanatics or hysterics is a good thing. The gist was, if you were a woman and voted for Trump, you are a vile fool (a disgusting, stupid woman, a disgrace to your gender). The author said you had internalized misogamy and had a hidden hatred of women. She, the author, used as examples Melania and Ivanka Trump, the president-elect's wife and daughter. If what she's peddling is not hate, it's envy or a reaction formation—hate that which you fear you need, such as the love of a man, the love of your father (see "The Missing Father"). What the author was doing was telling you that a woman who marries an attractive, wealthy, successful man; has children with him; and is successful in her own right, before and after, hates herself.

I don't even know how to discuss that in a sane manner, but I'll try.

Is the author suggesting that people (men and women) don't have preferences and make choices based on those preferences? That people don't sort people with regard to mating preference? Choosing the person they think will make the best partner—with regard to safety, security, health, children, success—whom they can possibly mate with? That like doesn't attract like? Is the author denying the real world? Maybe the author thought/thinks that an attractive, healthy, intelligent woman should mate with a forest-dwelling, sleeping-in-a-culvert schizophrenic? A troglodyte? A sort of postmodern *Beauty and Beast* tale? Or conversely, that a man of means (say, the Great Gatsby) should mate with an unattractive, unintelligent woman because "It's the right thing to do"? (See "Pussygate.") That that would be "fostering diversity," and it's being inclusive, "intersectional."

Again, it's a power play. Those lower on the hierarchy are trying to use whatever means available to advance their position and to seize power and/or gain status and money and then tell you how bad hierarchies and power are. Hypocrites.

I continue to read posts and columns by prominent women calling for other women to stand together and fight against the outcome of the election. Jill Stein, the Green Party's candidate, who received just over one million votes, less than 1 percent, has begun a campaign to fund a recount in critical northern battleground states, claiming the voting machines were hacked and rigged by the Russians. She's raised over four million dollars. Rebecca Solnit—a feminist, writer, activist—has hatched a conspiracy theory about Trump's victory, which also blames the Russians. Best-selling novelist Barbara Kingsolver has joined the chorus, likewise memoirist and advice columnist Cheryl Strayed. A female New York psychotherapist posted this on her Facebook page: "Many of my female patients are deeply triggered by the election results . . . so I'm doing two comp [free] support groups for women."

These are the comments:

"You're the best. Your patients are so fortunate to have you. xo"

"My therapist told me the same thing."

"Lovely."

"Wonderful."

(See "Malpractice, Victimology, and the Greatest Problem.")

Trump, in classic Trump (in a press conference with the *New York Times*), spoke, "But it's [the criticism] hard to explain. I don't care about anything having to do with anything having to do with anything other than the country."

This makes perfect sense to me, but his peculiar speech is used to frighten people.

The word *normalize* is making the rounds of the thought leaders. They are warning against normalizing Nazism and white supremacist thought, via the alt-right, by not standing up and fighting against Mr. Trump's election victory and not calling the alt-right neofascists. I've followed the idea of alt-right for most of this election cycle. The name popped up early on. The best discussion of it can be read here: http://www.breitbart.com/tech/2016/03/29/an-establishment-conservatives-guide-to-the-alt-right/.

The truth of the matter is that the alt-right is, in large part, *not* a group of racists and bigots but of naturalist conservative intellectuals and millennial jokesters. The following is a quote from the article.

> What little remains of old-school white supremacy and the KKK in America constitutes a tiny, irrelevant contingent with no purchase on public life and no support even from what the media would call the "far-Right." (Admittedly, these days that includes anyone who votes Republican.)

There *was* a group of white nationalists, 275 of them, who met in DC and heiled Trump and his victory, which was covered by fifty (50) journalists who gave it disproportionate coverage. Again, the fear factor was amplified by the media. The thought leaders, the elites, the bubble people, the stupid, smart people, led by the feminists, are in fact in practice, decrying that which they have done for the last twenty-five years—take something unordinary and uncommon and make it normal and acceptable instead of acknowledging its rarity and, thus, making it worse—making the uncommon common. In other words, since the cultural revolution began (in the '60s and '70s), alternative lifestyles have been pushed as "normal." But in fact, they are in opposition to that which is most common, therefore, abnormal. The best example of this would be the rise of single-parent households as "normal" and acceptable. Forty percent (40%, 4 in 10) births in the USA are now to unmarried women, and 58% of single-parent females are that way because of divorce or separation. Twenty-four percent (24%) of single-parent families have never married. The research data on how this family situation negatively impacts children is staggering. The thought leaders, the elites, in conjunction with the media and the entertainment industry, have normalized the dysfunctional family, which is partly responsible for the hatred (envy) of Trump and his family.

Donald J. Trump comes from a traditional American family: immigrants from somewhere else who establish themselves in America, work hard, raise a family, realize great success, and pass that opportunity on to their children. And here's where it gets very interesting. Fred and Mary Trump saw in their son, Donald John, a gifted boy but also someone who needed discipline and self-control, which was something, apparently, beyond their capabilities. So when young Donald was thirteen, they sent him off to the New York Military Academy in Upstate New York. There is where he learned about how the real world works (see pp. 72–3 in *Trump: The Art of the Deal*). What this man now is, is an excellent leader/warrior/family man—the right person at the right time to be president of the United States. He is fearless, aggressive, and tireless, yet with self-control (when necessary). In other words, the military academy taught him self-control and discipline (during his formative years), which he can call on when necessary (though his proclivity, granted, may be toward impulsivity and mischief—the midnight tweets).

And yet Hillary Clinton, the self-proclaimed champion of children and families, has done nothing to remedy the trend toward dysfunctional families in forty years (see "The Twenty-First Century So Far"). Crooked thinking. Crooked Hillary.

That a woman bears children and that is a burden (for her), in the least, a barrier/roadblock, to being equal in the working and/or warrior class and to being economically successful is just fact. That's a part of the real hostile and chaotic world we live in. Just as being queer is a barrier to the continuation of the species. It's true. The politically correct rail about equality and social justice, but the fact is, in reality, people are different and that, in practice, it takes all kinds (of people) to carry on. There is a place for everyone in society to contribute, but not everyone is equal. (See Hans Eysenck, *Inequality of Man*.) Not everyone belongs in college, not everyone can be a star, and not everyone deserves a trophy. But everyone does deserve a job, a way to contribute, and children deserve both parents. That is what's best for children and families.

In reading article after article, post after post, railing against the election of Donald Trump and how it will lead to the downfall of civil society, it seems to me most of the revulsion and rage deemed "necessary", the "apocalypse is coming" attitude is coming from female victims of sexual abuse and/or abandonment from one or both parents (see "The Missing Father" and "Freud on Trumpism"). To be clear, I am sorry. But neither the government nor the state can replace a *good* man with a job.

Another example of the politically correct, Left, progressive, postmodern movement's normalization of that which is harmful, in practice, is in regard to personal health. Someone, somewhere, decided that it was just fine to be grossly overweight, to be fat. Being large or a plus size is now normal. Bringing that to attention is taboo or fat shaming. The end result of this is a general population that is not physically fit, with a consequence of huge health-care costs and soaring insurance rates. Again, children suffer. With obese parents as role models, many children have no chance of having a healthy life for themselves. Long before they have reached maturity, they suffer from body image confusion, depression, anxiety, and eating disorders—none of which is really their fault but can be traced back to the normalization of an unhealthy lifestyle. Children are being overfed, overdosed, and ill-educated. Clinton as champion of children and families? Give me a break!

The real threat to our society comes not from the alt-right and Donald Trump but from the ultra-Left and their political correctness, hate and fear mongering, and Hillary's campaign that claimed that for forty (40) years, she has "fought for children and families." The reality is that children and families have never been more endangered than they are now, after twenty-five years of progressive policy. All that, hopefully, came to an end on November 8, 2016. The reign of the stupid, smart people, hopefully, is over, for at the end of the day, people, in general, are not stupid. In times of uncertainty and chaos, when you're up to your ass in alligators, you want someone who can drain the swamp.

Trump: "Drain the swamp."

"Drain the swamp, drain the swamp, drain the swamp" became a favored cry at his rallies. Trump would point at the pen where the media, the thought leaders, were confined, and the crowd would roar:

"Drain the swamp. Drain the swamp. Drain the swamp."

"Lock her up. Lock her up. Lock her up."

"Build that wall. Build that wall. Build that wall."

And yet the experts still thought there was no way Trump could win. He had no "path," they said. They were taking over/under odds on four hundred delegates for Clinton. (Check the tape on Steve Schmidt.) Clinton had twice as much money. She had the best "ground game" ever assembled. She had 360 newspaper endorsements (Trump had 11). She had most all the Hollywood celebrities. She had all the living former presidents. David Plouffe, Obama's boy-genius campaign manager went on *Morning Joe* and definitively told the world that she would win. He was "100 percent" certain.

Hillary Clinton won just 500 counties and 228 electors, but 64 percent of the money counties. Trump won 2,600 counties and 306 electors.

Trump won the people. Trump understands people and relationships. Trump understands money, sex, and power.

What's going to happen in the next four years? I don't know. What I do know is that people have not "evolved." People are the same as they've been for, I don't know, forty thousand years since the brain reached its current capacity, 1,300 cc. There are no new emotions or motivations and no changes in the way the body functions. People *are* bigger and live *longer* due to improvements in living conditions and technology (not everything is a horror show), but the needs and drives are still the same—money, sex, and power. The need to be "right" and the need to feel good dominate human behavior. The struggle between self and other, pleasure and pain, active and passive is still here and not going away. The struggle between the conscious and unconscious, between the known and the unknown, Maslow's hierarchy of motivational needs hasn't changed. We (most of us) live in a state of fear, and that fear will be used to influence behavior. And we will seek relief.

Trump: "All talk, no action."

He might well have won if that's all he ever he said.

The Recount

DECEMBER 3, 2016

Well, well, well . . . where are we now? In October, during the heated campaign, Trump said when asked that he reserved the right to challenge the results of the election, but only if the results were not clear. In other words, if the vote tally were within, say, a margin of error, he might well call for a recount—an investigation into if, in fact, the result accurately represented the will of the people. Trump also joked that if he won, no problem.

Here are some quotes, regarding Trump's assertion, from before the election:

Dana Milbank: "The refusal to accept this bedrock principle of democracy was shocking."

William M. Daley: "He [Trump] really has no appreciation for our history, which most of the world looks at with great admiration, as opposed to some banana republic."

Hillary Clinton: "He [Trump] refused to say he would respect the results of this election. Now, make no mistake, by doing that he is threatening our democracy."

Nancy Pelosi: "Donald Trump once again threatened the foundation of American democracy."

John McCain: "A concession isn't just an exercise in graciousness. It is an act of respect for the will of the American people."

Andrew Sullivan: "His refusal to accept the results of this election disqualifies him automatically from any office in the United States."

These are the thought leaders of the ultra-Left (and establishment Right), leading you down a road to nowhere. *And now* the defeated are trying to entice you to circumvent democracy altogether and sign a petition imploring the Electoral College (538 persons) to vote to elect Hillary Clinton as president of the United States. The hypocrisy (claiming to have moral standards or beliefs to which one's own behavior does not conform, i.e., pretense, lying) is enough to make one's head explode. My friend (of over fifty years) Gerald L. Kirstein[148] posted daily (on Facebook) about this. I thought for sure *his* head would, yet as I finish this book and Trump's been in office for over eighteen months, he's still carrying on about the fraud that he asserts was the election of 2016. He's not alone. They just won't let it go.

Here's the real story: The thought leaders, the elites, the media all were in agreement and told you, went "on the record," and predicted that Donald J. Trump was a joke, a farce. He, Trump, was just messing around and is not a serious candidate for president of the United States! And then via the election, they were all proven wrong! And so they either have to admit they were wrong (do not have any authority and/or credibility with regard to that which matters, the lives and loves of people) or find fault with you, the system of democracy, the apparatus of counting votes, or something other than they don't know what they're talking about and have no claim to authority! In other words, they are not deserving of the large amounts of money you pay them for their counsel, advice, direction, and leadership. They are the fraud.

Think about that.

Think about the fact that the media, the Fourth Estate, got it wrong from the get-go. They told you Trump was a joke and that he was just

---

[148] Gerald lives in the Pacific Northwest, is sixty-something, and is single with two young adult daughters. Gerry is, like me, a military brat. We absorbed the assassination of president John Kennedy (in 1963) together, as friends, in middle school, at Travis AFB. Gerry went on to get a BA in political science at the University of California in Berkley.

playing with you. In the beginning, they said he wouldn't and/or couldn't do this and/or that, that he had a "ceiling" of 10%, 20%, 30%, 40%, and so on and so forth. He can't win this, that, whatever. And they were wrong! Now what?

I'll tell you what. They will do everything in their power and purview to persuade you that they are right and you are wrong, unless you agree with them.[149]

Think about that.

They don't have an argument when it comes down to that which is: People are different. People are selfish. People are tribal.

---

[149] "Research shows we [humans] like compliments more than sex or money." Eric Barker, *Barking Up the Wrong Tree: The Surprising Science Behind Why Everything You Know about Success Is (Mostly) Wrong* (2017), 143.

This idea, that being right, is the driving force behind the media's, experts', thought leaders', elites', need to somehow undo the election, supported by both motivation and personality research beginning, perhaps, with Abraham Maslow's theory of the hierarchy of human needs, where the esteem needs (self-respect, achievement, status, dignity, validation, etc.) were ranked higher up than all others, except for the need for self-actualization, which, Maslow concluded, very few people (1 percent) reach. The esteem needs are where most of successful people wind up. Compliments, flattery, validation (earned or not) received boosts one's self-esteem, which reinforces one's belief (however erroneous) that they are a good person and worthy of their status as expert, thought leader, person, etc. In essence, Trump's victory shattered these people's self-esteem!

Into the Wild

DECEMBER 11–31, 2016

This is from Marco V. Morelli's project: www.infiniteconversations.com. "Thoughts on the Election" (November/December 2016)

My buddy Marco was so distressed he put out a call for and encouraged all the people he knew to express themselves in a reasoned manner on his website's open forum. He pleaded for "an open-minded and creative *conversation*, not merely personal rants or recriminations." He wanted to "avoid the rancor" of the popular social media sites. "I want to know what you really think and what you really feel like [or we . . . as a cooperative community] can really do.[150]

Marco invited me to participate as, perhaps, the only person he knew who actively supported Trump. He and I watched the first debate together at my apartment, you'll recall. What follows are excerpts from the conversation.

---

[150] Infinite Conversations is an online and cooperative project started (2015) and maintained by my Colorado pal Marco V. Morelli. It is ongoing, and I encourage you to check it out.

Marco Morelli: Our "information diet" (*us*, generally speaking, but of course, the *us* is generally problematic) seems to be a big part of the problem. I know it is for me, something I struggle with and against.

I don't know who or what to trust, what's "nutritious" and what's poison. I've come to feel that entire dimensions of the noosphere[151] are toxic, laced with deliriants, tranquilizers, nerve gas. Social media is some kind of date-rape drug. We wander around dazed in the nuclear blast zone, nibbling hungrily on irradiated rations. It's all search engine optimized.

This is a deliberate effect, I'm coming to believe. At the very least, it's a useful one. It's not a matter of fake news versus real news. (It's funny how occult a word for "the plural new" might be.) It's utter disorientation regarding fundamental ontological distinctions, a state of stupefaction, psy-ops reality. The invasion is already well underway. What antidotes do we have? What good, healthy victuals might embolden us to create the future again? Or is it the case, as it's been said, the poison is the gift? To this, I would only reply, dosage is everything. At the same time, no one said waking up wouldn't hurt. I think you're (J. Dockus and anonymous) right to point to art and the *primacy of immediate experience* (i.e., everyday human reality in the analog mode) as good medicine. At some point, we just have to snap out it. Get back to ourselves. Get out!

"Only a fool fights in a burning house."

But then, in my view, we need to regroup—realize what's hit us, study the situation with due sobriety, and take appropriate action.

---

[151] Noosphere is a new "layer" of the earth, reversing biological evolution via technology and the power of the mind (consciousness). It is first introduced by Pierre Teilhard de Chardin (1922).

"This is a time for artists to get busy. . . There just needs to be a productive use of energy which pushes back toward our humanity . . . I speak of actual concrete individualism."

Indeed, this could be an entire discussion. *Who am I?* is still a darn good inquiry. Regarding the politics, I would say it's not identities that are ever threatened or that need to be protected or that need promotion. It's actual people, both individuals and groups of people, their cultural knowledge and social practices, art and ritual, the wholeness and integrity of the human. For example, at Standing Rock, it's not identities that are opposing the pipeline: the battle lines go so much deeper . . . to the very nature of our relations. Oddly enough, actual concrete individualism may require a new tribalism of anti-identityism, lest we allow ourselves to be atomized into a thousand narrow conceptual categories. Marketers are very interested in our identity. Political operatives want to know our every belief and predilection. The state is especially interested in questions of identification. (We are likely already, most of us, ridiculously detailed in various centralized databases involving highly accurate facial recognition, etc.) This is all said and done, well and good. It just tells me we need new ways of encoding our communications and constituting culture.

Me here at my computer on a Sunday morning, before dawn, spitting into the hurricane . . . "Open to learn, closed to protect."

I like this a lot. It's simple too, middle way—not too hard, not too soft, just right. Also, it's life-based, reality-based. Common sense. With this one thought, it seems to me, you could heal the so-called political divide.

In the meantime, however, it appears we have the opposite principle in ascendency, something more like, "open to exploit / closed to forget." Can this change? IMO, as we said, re: Iraq and Afghanistan, it's about hearts and minds. But I also think "open to learn, closed to protect" points to a general design principle. It's something a healthy organism (including a social organism), which is interdependent with other organisms and is constantly interacting with its environment, must do—failing which it will cease to exist. Perhaps "open to learn, closed to protect" could be a social meditation of sorts—a heuristic koan, sublingual, suggesting common ground for how boundary-level decisions are arrived at.

Mark: I haven't read (yet) all the replies, but I wanted to put my two cents in at the request of Marco immediately. I'm 90K words into a book I'm writing about this event. So Briefly, Trump won because that's what he does—win. He has a philosophy and a worldview, an ethos, that was perfectly suited for the times. One could say, "Everything happens for a reason, and if it didn't happen [Bernie or Hillary winning], it wasn't meant to be." The elites, including the mainstream media, did not and do not understand Trump. They decided early on he was a joke. They were wrong. He is anything but a joke. He's a very serious man who has fun. He laid out his philosophy in his 1987 memoir, *The Art of the Deal.* Apparently, no one read it, or if they did, they didn't get it. It's all there. That's what he did, what he's doing, and what he will do. They fed you a false narrative from the beginning and then doubled and tripled down because they have been humiliated. They are the experts, and he proved them stupid. And they can't stand that. Trump is none of the things they defined him as. So in short, don't worry, it'll be fine—great, in fact, if (big *if*) you all will get behind him and let "Trump be Trump." He understands people better than all the experts. He understands that at our core, we all want the same thing—to be loved and to love, to be respected and valued (except a few sickos). Everything they've told you about him is untrue. They hate him, but you don't have to. Don't let others lead you down the path of bitterness and despair. It's the law of attraction, folks.

Trump gets it.

Marco: Ha! Well, @Mark_Jabbour, every ointment needs its fly, every card deck needs its trump, and every checkerboard amphibian needs its Cheshire Cat. (Yum.) Yeah, sure, I'll come to your housewarming. Make it an inauguration party? Maybe you can make that salsa again. It was damn good! I'll bring some beer, and we can open up your green medicine cabinet too. The real wild card here, it seems to me, is the possibility (likelihood?) of some kind of game-changing event—e.g., a dirty nuke attack or climate-related catastrophe or accidental military confrontation w/ China—something where events spin out of control and Trump is forced to respond to a crisis, which I expect will be with disproportionate force, provoking a wave of reactions and protests, which turn violent, followed by countermeasures (an alpha strongman needs to demonstrate his strength), which all spirals out control. And then we really learn the consequence of allowing a police state infrastructure to build up, almost literally under our noses, over the past couple decades. This is the WWIII scenario I can see precipitating. On the other hand, we might just get the logical continuation of capitalism. Lots of deals, a temporary economic boom, which eventually (sooner rather than later, I'd wager) overshoots planetary limits once and for all: we hit the tipping point and actually, undeniably even by Fox News, start seeing rapid sea-level rise, superstorms, etc. in real time.

Yum, indeed!

Standing Rock will be Trump's first major test, imo. Energy Transfer Partners wants Trump to force the Army COE to push the project through. If this happens—which can only happen violently—the opposition movement will explode, and things will get ugly fast. If, on the other hand, Trump is able to strike a deal that makes both sides happy, then we're in business, and your more optimistic scenario gains some credibility. However, I'm not betting on it at this point.

Mark: I think your second scenario is most likely. We're already seeing the capitalists and foreign markets responding with optimism.

All these problems that you speak of are solvable, including the rising seas and super storms. Our (humanity's) greatest asset is, after all, our ability to adapt to a changing environment. The major problem is, however, that heretofore we have adapted by moving or migration. Migration was the cure-all, even for person-to-person and tribe-to-tribe conflicts. However, we've run out of room. There are too many people. "Build that wall!" (And then some sea walls.) We've become too successful, and nature always finds a way to solve that problem. And nature doesn't care. The earth will be fine. It'll go on spinning and wobbling its way around the sun for billions of years more. We are our own problem. Trump's a problem-solver. "Render therefore to Caesar the things that are Caesar's," Jesus (allegedly) said that sometime, a few years ago. The hysteria from the Left is a power play. They are playing the fear card, using reverse Darwinism to gain control, as in the OJ trial, where the defense used jury selection (in nature, it is known as sexual selection) to select the uneducated so they would dismiss the sophisticated (DNA) evidence and nullify the truth: OJ committed the murders. Here we have the Left who have failed to solve the problems when given the chance, now playing the fear factor—the race card, the woman card, the sky-is-falling card—in the hope of not losing, which they did, and in the hope of not being known for what they are, losers. PS. I'm not moving till after the inauguration. Maybe we can have two parties!

I'm glad you brought up Standing Rock—the world in a grain of sand. The resolution is simple, and yet the passions are high enough to bring forth war. First, Trump sold his stock in the company. Second, respect the rights of individuals and tribes. There is no need for conflict. Trump understands this. Let's make a deal (otherwise known as politics) where everyone gets something of what they want, but maybe not everything. We all can have clean water and air (life), and also people can make money. Here's the solution: Create a paid position of watcher of the water (a paid position for, say, $50k a year, times three, with access to the wheels [see below] and decision-making power) and also create shutoff values on the pipeline (i.e., if oil leaks/spills, which are inevitable). There is a big wheel (two) where one can shut off the flow of oil. So there's a temporary interruption to the status quo, but it's remedied quickly. There's no need for all this drama and hysteria, except for people's pride and whatever. (*Errg!* People, *sheesh!*) Trump gets all this. He's a problem-solver. Give him his due, his recognition, i.e., let Trump be Trump, and we'll all be the better for it. Watch him, challenge him, but be respectful. And we might just emerge on the other side. He wants what you want—love, respect, recognition, and solutions to problems. He gets it.

Marco: I hope you're right on this, Mark. But my concern is that a deal implies the expectation of fairness (lest it merely be a pretense for theft), which is extremely difficult to achieve with such an asymmetrical distribution of power. One side has all the guns and money; the other side has only their bodies, prayers, and potential popular moral appeal. The Native Americans have made many deals with the US government, and where has it gotten them? Your proposed solution involving monitoring of the pipeline, I would assume, is already what's done (per regulations). And yet spills remain a not-infrequent occurrence. But let's see what happens. Like I said, to me, this situation is Trump's first big test. One can easily find reasons to not feel confident about the outcome. But what do I know? I'm just another loser. Pass the salsa.

Mark: I have to admit I haven't followed this closely because, frankly, who ya gonna believe? Why did it ever come to this point? If there was a conflict about where the pipeline was being laid, it should have been resolved long before any digging began. Don't you have to get all the permits and easements approved *before* the project begins? Anytime you build anything, you have to get it all approved. If not, why is there an EPA? Why are there engineers? Why are there architects? Why are there government agencies and inspectors? Who dropped the ball on this one? Who "played ball"? Obama's administration. I've seen pictures of pipe in an open ditch. And then I've also seen a squiggly line on a map that shows the route of the pipeline and that it does not cross onto the reservation but goes above it, where it then crosses the Missouri River. So the tribe really does not have a case. Their case is, what if it leaks into the river and pollutes the water supply of the reservation? Okay, you monitor it closely. At the first sign of leakage, you shut it down until it's fixed. Done. Which makes me think it's all political, i.e., a bunch of crapola. Another example of outrage that is outrage for the sake of outrage. It's all crap. This is the swamp that Trump wants to drain—bloated bureaucracies and phony outrage! All, so people can score a paycheck or feel better about their sorry-ass selves. I'm so sick of this (another reason why I voted for Trump). Trump, being an international builder and developer, knows how the crapola game is played.

John Duckus: Mark Jabbour, these words of yours are a little more sensible to me. Very glad for 'em. After reading this, you seem like a decent dude, not just trolling but sharing your sincere thinking and beliefs. I'd hang out with you and like to try that salsa Marco mentioned. Your quirky originality is definitely welcome to me. Only I still don't get your thing for Trump. I kinda understand your angle. Since he's the president-elect, it is what it is and one must work with it. A certain way of handling this would only work the thorn in deeper, causing more, not less, pain and agony, possibly leading to infection.

But Trump has quite a record and history. A leopard cannot change its spots, and a tiger cannot change its stripes. A wolf is a wolf, even if it comes disguised as a sheep. I don't expect when I see a hippopotamus, that it will suddenly leap up on its hind legs and begin dancing like Baryshnikov. That only happens in Disneyland or in Trumpland. It's not going to happen in reality. One must choose between Trumpland and reality, and I emphatically choose reality. Trump yells "I'm a winner!" over everything, no matter what it is, no matter who challenges him with facts. Facts, of course, don't matter to him, only results. The ends justify the means. He yells "Pathetic! Loser!" over anyone who displeases the spoiled child in him. By a kind of charismatic bullying, he convinces many that a rundown jalopy is a Rolls-Royce, that a pile of [dung] is gold (see Trump University), and it's sad and frightening to me that he actually succeeds in breaking so many down and getting them to submit to him by nothing more than aggressive propaganda and relentless self-promotion. That's what *the* Donald does.

A sucker is born every minute. And the more suckers whom he "pulls one over on," eyes riveted to the spectacle he creates, the rawer and more irrational the better, deliberately stirring up controversy to keep attention fixed on himself, the more his "occult" power and love for himself grows. That's where he gets his narcissistic supply. He's made himself into a brand, stamps his name on as many things as he can, multiplies his image, presenting himself as a golden idol. Many indeed worship and fetishize him. When he looks into your eyes, he's not seeing you but really looking to see a reflection of himself so that he can admire himself. Puncture that illusion and make yourself feel too much in your concrete individuality, too different from him, and he immediately sees an enemy to be conquered or suppressed. The sociopathic part is what I do think is his nature. He's not aware that he does this, creature of impulse that he is; he can't help being as he is, in the same way that a spider can't help spinning a web, catching flies, and sinking its fangs into them, sucking out their guts.

Trump lacks a conscience, like someone color-blind can't see colors, and that's not his fault. Conscience is just not part of Donald Trump's recipe for success. The kind of well-considered and measured reasoning Marco displays here—sensitive to detail and nuance, open to debate and fair play, with deep feeling and respect for concrete individuality, extending beyond his own to include others in reality, not just abstracted and hoarded into stereotypes—is foreign and even contemptible to Trump. To him, conscience is for suckers and weaklings, to be treated rudely and trampled underfoot, and too much reasoning undermines action. In extremis, this is true (see *Hamlet*), but Trump leapfrogs over everything and goes straight for immediate gratification, grabbing first prize without doing the training and actually running the marathon, pandering to the basest instincts, something one could say is a major contributor to the erosion and collapse of civilization in the first place. He cuts out all the middle stuff of work, the difficulties and complexities, the patience required to process matters thoroughly, and always leaps straight to conclusions, asserting success and proclaiming victory no matter what.

I myself feel the appeal of this. He taps into a machismo in us, and many of his followers feel galvanized and energized by that and are acting out on it, beating on their chests and throwing their weight around. Trump really scored the mother load of narcissistic supply by tapping into all the real frustration and anger in this country, all the people who have been screwed over by policies, which have served mostly the rich and well-to-do through the years. It has finally reached a head, no longer able to be contained and endured, and exploded. And now all the parasites feast in an orgy on the carcass of the old body politic, engorged and intoxicated on its blood, and soon there will be a call for more blood, with Trump brandishing his sword and leading the way.

Marco Morelli: Which is to say, the market is going to do what it's going to do. So why the faith in President Trump when the market will trump Trump anyway? Because he "gets" it? He's going to find a way to win one way or another?

Mark: Yes, that's been his history.

Marco: I'm all for winning. But doesn't it matter how we win? Can we look critically at the underlying rules of the game, maybe change the game itself? Or has that been tried already (communism, anarchism, etc.) and failed, so we should just get with program. The Trump Train is leaving the station!

Mark: In a word, yes, and no to the first question.

Marco: Let's grant your wet dream that the United States of America is now a fully owned and managed subsidiary of *Trump Enterprises*. Hostile takeover complete.

Mark: You got it!

Marco: The United States is rebranded *Trumpland*.

Mark: Exactly! Trump = USA. He has crossed over into a world that we "normals" only experience in our dreams.

Marco: Time is now subsidized, so 2017, by executive order, is retroactively renamed the "Year of Trump Natural Spring Water," while 2018 is slated as the "Year of Trump Golf." Cue the Left going nutso—but who's listening to them crybabies anymore, anyway?

Mark: Unfortunately, it's an echo chamber, i.e., a bubble. And apparently, they learned nothing. It is a complex of politicians + lawyers + academia + the Media—or PLUM. Thus, it is, as you point out, "the samizdat."

Marco: You stick out your tongue there in your bachelor condo in your gated community and mock the @JDockuses of the world (and the rest of us "concrete individuals"). *Na na na na na na!*

Mark: You got me. Nailed me. I have always been a fish out of water, a Trump-like creature but not quite. And so in our, his and mine, golden years, *he* takes over the world. I just move to a newer, nicer gated community—my version of Trump Tower.

Marco: Is this the world we want to live in? Does it matter anymore? Don't we know where this way leads, from a book (*Infinite Jest*) we once read?

Mark: Which ending? The book's, which is back to the beginning, or the author's? Which is so sad. It has always been my contention that he was misdiagnosed and, thus, misdosed from the get-go.

Marco: I see where you're going with this, buddy! It's all about art and life! We are witnessing the entertainment! The samizdat is here!

Johnny Gentle 2016 and 2020 ("Year of the Trump Executive
Briefs in Boxer and Bikini Styles, Made with All-American
Cotton") and 4EVA! You call Trump a mutant, which I think is
actually technically and philosophically accurate, but he's so much
more, isn't he?

Mark: It's true!

Marco: He's a monster of our own imagination.

Mark: No, he's real. He's part Robin Williams, part Teddy Roosevelt, part
Jack Welsh, part Hugh Hefner, and part Mickey Mantle.

Marco: He's the culmination of an underlying logic, the effect of an
algorithm. He's the personification of a force that delivers us to
our destiny.

Mark: Maybe. But "destiny" begs the question: Determinism versus free
will? The first chapter of my book is titled "Gods, Heroes, and
Men," and I roll from there. Trump's MO is founded on the
principle of the power of positive thinking, which is closely aligned
to the law of attraction.

Marco: He's practically a god, let's be honest. At the very least, he's *an*
avatar of one, an apotheosis. And well, hey, if you can't beat 'em,
join 'em, right? Become one with your god. I thought of a great
Tantric exercise that our lefty, spiritual-type, empathic friends
might put to use in their contemplative disciplines (crazy wisdom
stuff, this):

Sit quietly, upright, with your eyes closed, and ring a bell
to begin the meditation.

Focus on your breathing, and let the muscles of your
mouth relax.

Imagine yourself performing fellatio on Donald J. Trump.
Visualize it completely.

Keep at it. Imagine him berating you while you lick and
suck. He is moaning "Yeah, baby, make America great
again" over and over. Time stretches out endlessly, year
after subsidized year, rolling off your tongue.

Keep going. Keep working on *the* Donald's "little hand" until he's so excited. He's winning so bad he ejaculates in a torrent of verbal abuse, "You're fired! You're fired! You're fired!"

Return to your breathing. Feel the breath going down the front channel and up the spine, let it circulate while you visualize Donald Trump's "seed" dripping down your face, burning ecstatically into your skin.

Congratulations! You're now enlightened.

(Did that help, @Mark_Jabbour?)

Mark: Definitely! We should put together a list of the elites and send them your remedy. It's much better than what I'm seeing and reading.

PS. Regarding "false hope," that's been America's foreign and domestic policy since the get-go, no? Promise(s) followed by abandonment and then death and/or genocide. Maybe it is the only thing that is certain. For example, Syria and Obama's redline, Bush 43's "we'll be greeted as liberators"; Bush 41's promise to Iraqis after Desert Storm, and Kennedy's Bay of Pigs fiasco. You want to talk about the USA's promise to the first Americans? Or again, Obama's promise of hope and change? How about Chicago? Obama may go down in the final analysis as the worst American president ever! Followed by Bush 43, then Clinton, followed by Bush 41, and then followed by Carter. Can it get any worse? And then along comes Trump: "What have you got to lose?"

I went to one of the rallies. The love and hope and joy was contagion at its finest, better than any drug-/alcohol-fueled rock concert. That joy is still going on with his thank-you tour. Watch! (They're live streamed.) Watch the faces. The joy his supporters feel is reflected in their faces, and it is *so* hopeful. However, the elite hate it—hate that they got it wrong, hate that they may be irrelevant. They now hate hope. Ironic.

At Trump's last thank-you rally in Mobile, Alabama, he brought out on stage Hope Hicks, his spokesperson who's been with him from the jump. She was just a girl working for the Trump Organization's real estate division and his daughter Ivanka when Trump selected her to be his press secretary, which is his wont to promote from within and recognize innate talent. The twenty-seven-year-old took the stage and spoke publicly for the first time, with a big smile, "Hi. Merry Christmas, everyone! And thank you, Donald Trump."[152]

If there is reality in the power of positive thinking and the law of attraction, then buy a ticket on the Trump Train. (Wall Street, the market is.) This *is* a contest between forces, a test of the human condition, the human animal, "the third chimpanzee." Are we just another animal, or are we something more? Is there such a thing as choice at all?

Did we succeed with an open-minded, creative conversation? No one's position moved, only hardened. What's the point?

---

[152] Ms. Hicks went on to be communication director before resigning after being questioned, for nine hours, by the special council investigating the Russian collusion with the Trump campaign.

December 13, 2016

The "stop Trump" movement is reaching fever pitch from all the usual public persons to the everyday man on the street. The recount effort flopped. Trump actually picked up votes in Wisconsin, and the other two states stopped the process. The movement now is citing "evidence" that the Russians threw the election to Trump.[153] I have no idea anymore what's true and what isn't. The CIA doesn't have a good track record, as President-Elect Trump points out. Why have spooks running around subverting governments, snatching people, selling weapons, and doing psy-ops when you can just sit down with governments and do business deals, where each side gets something of what it wants, but not everything. Isn't that better than war? Just asking. I see now where some are accusing Trump of treason and calling for his execution. Really? Seriously?[154]

---

[153] July 28, 2018, still no "evidence" of the Russian/Trump collusion, but the beat goes on. Sad.

[154] July 19, 2018, Trump just returned from a meeting with Russian President Vladimir Putin. It's as if nothing has happened in eighteen months—we are in some sort of time warp. The thought leaders, the elites, the Left, are saying what they said right after the election. But a lot has happened, as I noted in other updates. What happened this week in Russia is a good thing. It was two alpha males (each with enough nuclear firepower to blow up the world several times over) feeling each other out and trying to figure out a way to

I just scanned the Electoral College's electors' intentions and found five of those who are pledged to vote for Clinton, saying they cannot vote for her, and one of Trump's not following the pledge. I guess we'll find out on December 19.

---

make peace, not war. I think Trump did exceptionally well, got the upper hand, so to speak, as evidenced by the soccer ball gift from Putin. Trump, much as Bill Belichick (another alpha male) did, dismissed the gift (trophy) quickly, tossing the ball to his wife, Melania, and saying to Putin, "I'll give it to Barron" (Trump's twelve-year-old son), all the while smiling and thanking the Russian president. (See footnote 107, being presidential.)

December 14, 2016

Donald Trump named Rex Tillerson as his secretary of state. Tillerson is the former CEO of Exxon Mobile and, even more so than Trump himself, has done business and made successful deals all over the world, including with Russia and Vladimir Putin. This is driving the Left still crazier, if that's possible. Trump is doing exactly what he said he would do—*hire* the toughest and smartest people he could find to do the jobs that need doing. Mr. Trump also cancelled a presser concerning his business and potential conflicts with his job as president. Instead, he tweeted out that he would make no future deals for his company and turn over the operations of it to his sons, Donald Jr. and Eric. That's it, folks; that's all there is. That's his style. The rest, all the questions the press is dying to ask him, is irrelevant. They, the press and the media, are both coming close to irrelevancy. And of course, they're screaming bloody murder, trying to *prove* their importance.

Trump is continuing to bring the movers and shakers, the real players, into private conference at his headquarters in Manhattan, a.k.a. Trump Tower. Today, Trump's having a high-tech summit with many of the CEOs of the megatechnological industry, all of whom voted for Hillary and many of whom helped her to raise great sums of money. Trump beat them all and has been critical of many of them. Now he wants to know what they think, how and if they will help him make America great again. Trump's agenda has been rock-solid since day 1. He wants to bring back high-paying jobs for American workers and make America safe, strong, smart, and rich. He wants to bring back pride in achievement and accomplishment. It's simple. Trump told Chris Wallace of Fox News that he didn't need an intel daily briefing unless there was something new to note. Again, they are going crazy. All Trump is doing is what he said he would do, which is what he has always done—that which needs doing to be successful, guided by his ethos that has served him well for fifty years. It's simple.

At the forefront of the news today is the horror that is Syria—destruction, demolition, and genocide, i.e., war. And they want to know: What will Trump do? He's already said and demonstrated that he's not going to say or broadcast what he will or will not do. Such is counterproductive, he's said.

Now we here go into the wilderness—into the wild—because ever since the advent of modern communication systems and news as a commodity, the expectation has become that the people should be informed as to the intentions of the generals. But that's a losing formula, which is, by the way, antithetical to Trump's ethos.

Now, however, I am faced with this: my children (one bio and two step) were all Bernie supporters who voted for Hillary and are now going bonkers with hatred for Trump. One gave money to Jill Stein's scam (seriously, Trump actually gained 100+ votes in Wisconsin); another is stuffing envelopes with form letters, stamped, and sent to electors to disavow their duty and not vote for Trump (which is, in essence, asking the electors to ignore the democratic process, the bedrock of America—that your vote matters! One person, one vote!). I am at a loss as to what to do.

From almost the get-go, I understood what was going on. I thought, *This is a no-brainer. Trump will win in a landslide.* I thought the people would see what I saw, but I was wrong.

I thought there was a good probability that Trump would win all fifty states, and thus the popular vote by a two-to-one margin. Oh my word was I wrong! Oh, the tenacity with which one is capable of *clinging* to one's beliefs (as David Foster Wallace wrote in *Infinite Jest*: "Everything I've ever let go of has claw marks on it.") is *mind-blowing*!

December 20, 2016

The Electoral College has voted. Trump lost two votes, and Clinton lost five. The final official (to be certified on January 6, 2017) tally will be Trump 304 and Clinton 227. And yet "What the hell is going on?"
(News update: The Chinese pluck an underwater USA surveillance drone from international waters. There was an assassination in Anchor, Turkey, of the Russian ambassador to Turkey at an *art gallery*! And then moments later, a big rig pinballed through an outdoor Christmas mall in Berlin, Germany, killing twelve and injuring forty-eight. The DOW is up, hitting all-time highs. And President Obama is taking a seventeen-day vacation in Hawaii with only thirty-five days left in his presidency. He's informed of events while playing golf.)

The media's consensus is congealing around the idea that it was the Russians and the FBI's James Comey who duped some (uneducated/stupid or "useful idiots") Americans to vote for Trump. The elite agree.

I check in to Facebook.

Ah, another podcast from some of my LA friends (different ones, not millennials but older, more experienced, one would think). I learn that as a Trump supporter and defender, I am an "idiot and subhuman." My middle-aged writer, teacher, sexually abused mother friend says repeatedly, "Oh my god. I mean, you know . . . 538 . . . climate change, Obamacare! Oh my god. I mean, you know . . . facts. Truth. Oh my god . . . Nazis."

Michael Moore—yes, *that* Michael Moore, the author of *Stupid White Men: And Other Sorry Excuses for the State of the Nation* (2002)—keeps imploring his followers to keep resisting and to keep fighting that it, Trump becoming the forty-fifth president of the United States, is not official until January 20, 2017. Until then, Moore says, there is still a chance. This is after he posted he would pay any fine incurred by electors if they switched their pledged vote. Isn't that bribery?

Michelle Obama, the First Lady of the United States, tells Oprah Winfrey that "hope is gone."

Ta-Nehisi Coates, on *The Daily Show*, said (seriously) that Donald Trump only had to be "rich and white, that was it" to become president.

During the Electoral College's vote, a female protestor screamed out, "You have just elected Hitler."

Rachel Maddow, in the crooked and twisted way she thinks, explains in a twenty-minute monologue/story/confabulation of political terror and genocide spanning decades how the election of Trump threatens security around the globe and concludes with this:

> And the Gong Show / Star Wars bar scene quality of the Trump transition, particularly on national security issues, honestly, to me, most days it is usually something approaching funny, but it is national security and it is hard and dangerous and fraught with peril even in good times. But right now, what they are inheriting, these are not good times.
>
> On national security, I am literally praying that the transition gets better than what it is right now.

I can make sense of this from a psychoanalytic perspective. The reaction, catastrophic and hysterical, of supposedly smart and decent Americans, including my own children, to the fair and normal presidential election of 2016. But *that* is depressing me, a normally optimistic person. I have no friends anymore. My father died. Relief comes only through escape into an alcoholic haze or through dreams. I dreamed I was tending bar and served an unspecified beverage to an attractive middle-aged woman who then turned away and walked toward the door. Suddenly, she collapsed in a heap. I shouted out for help and sprinted out from behind the bar, knelt down beside her, and placed my hand on her chest, where her heart was beating fiercely, violently, straining to burst out of her body. And then . . . I saw she had no head.

December 28, 2016

I think what partly upset people and got them on the verge of revolution, personal and/or political, is that there *are* two worlds—one is real and the other illusory. Donald J. Trump lives in and has been extremely successful in the real world. The real world is the world of gravity; it is a competitive, chaotic, hostile, Darwinian, Hobbesian world. The unreal world is the one of peace, wherein everyone is equal and free, everyone matters, and everyone is entitled to life without struggle and failure—a noncompetitive, nonjudgmental, noncomparative la-la land of rainbows and unicorns, and one in which Mother Earth nurtures and cares for everyone. (Sorry.)

Here's the story: The fairest, largest, longest-lasting, most rigorous, most scrutinized election the world has ever known was just conducted in the USA. And Mister Donald J. Trump won. He was not a politician and had never run for political office before. Before June 16, 2015, he was a real estate developer and private businessman. The United States of America has the most powerful military in the world. It has the largest economy in the world. It has the finest and most prestigious universities in the world. It has the finest hospitals and medical doctors in the world. It has the largest banks and stock exchange in the world. It has the largest and most profitable companies and corporations in the world. The United States has the largest and freest media in the world ever. By all measures, save two—landmass and population size—it is the most powerful and prestigious country and nation the world has ever known. And Donald J. Trump is now the freely and fairly elected leader of that nation.

Not a single "expert" (or astrologer, that I know of) gave him a snowball's chance in hell of winning that election, which indicates he accomplished the most remarkable, *amazing* feat a single individual has ever accomplished in the history of the world, arguably. And that is driving many people—the people he defeated, the people on the other side, the experts, the overly self-righteous people, the envious people, the jealous people, the vulnerable people (for whatever reason)—flat-out clinically insane. But for all the talk of truth and facts, for all the lamenting of their loss, that is the fact and truth of the matter. So here we are on the brink of a brand-new year, heading into unknown territory, a place never before imagined or visited— heading *into the wild*. I say, enjoy it!

Trump Derangement Syndrome

JANUARY 8, 2017

Trump derangement syndrome, which is really a reaction formation (see "Freud on Trumpism"), is a hatred for that which you fear you need, which is some powerful stuff—hate and fear. In this case (TDS), what is hated and feared is a strong father. The problem is, of course, that hate and fear are such powerful emotions and, as such, play out in the real world with hurtful consequences.

Consider this:

Thursday, January 6, while standing on an old, old garden bench in my walk-in closet, stretching out to my right, reaching for a folded sheet, the bench's loose legs torqued counter to my lean and collapsed inward, causing me to flail widely and foolishly grab for the nearest handhold, which happened to be a loose 2 × 10 wooden shelf, spanning built-in vertical closet dividers. The shelf dislodged from its perch and followed me to the floor in a heap and landed with a thud on my head just above my left eye. My glasses bounced from whence they were, so I couldn't see clearly the tangled mess that was me, shelf, bench, and sheet. My head hurt, and I felt for blood with my fingers and was relieved feeling none. This, being 2017 (the age of instant sharing), I got up, located my spectacles, found my phone, and snapped a shot of the debris and destruction. I sheepishly shambled into the dining room to the bar and tossed down a shot of tequila, wandered over to the fridge, took out a beer, popped the cap, and swallowed a long drink of the bubbly, refreshing brew. With that, I sat down at the table, clicked on my phone, and uploaded to Facebook the picture with a brief comment explaining what had happened—how I could have died—and waited, drinking. Three days later, I'm still here waiting, sober now, and have surmised this: No one cares about me. I am alone.[155]

Not a single person commented. No one liked my post. Not even a crying or worried emoji posted. No one cared; not even my children. This, I think, is the manifestation of Trump derangement syndrome in real time, in the real world, in real life. In all probability, what my friends and family secretly felt deep down was a wish that I *had* died, because I deserved to, because I was a horrible person, my true nature having been revealed by my support of Trump. I was/am really a racist, sexist, homophobic, xenophobic bigot, with whom the world would be a better place without. *Good riddance*, they nod, *justice delivered*. "Let's divide up his money and property, redistribute it, and celebrate good karma."

This is Trump derangement syndrome.

---

[155] Validated months later by my psych girl, a licensed clinical psychologist whom I pay $2.50 a minute to tell me that which I (mostly) already know, and also doesn't care. But for the fee she pretends to, which in a bizarre way comforts me.

The Zen of Trump

JANUARY 19, 2017

On the day before the inauguration, it appears the Trump derangement syndrome has not abated but intensified. Over sixty Democratic Congress persons have pledged to boycott the inauguration, and there are hundreds of thousands who have said they will protest in their respective cities by marching on Saturday. The hysteria is a psychological disorder, now regarded as a single definite condition, whose symptoms include conversion of psychological stress into physical symptoms, selective amnesia, shallow and volatile emotions, and overdramatic or attention-seeking behavior. The term has a controversial history as it was formerly regarded as a disease specific to women. It seems beyond understanding, but it's real. It seems now that the disorder is *not* specific to women but can affect both genders and anyone in between. I submit that the condition, TDS, reflects a partial personality construct that is not uncommon across gender, race, ethnicity, and/or culture.

Personality is a very complex formulation, but let's stay with the construct of the Big Five or OCEAN (openness, conscientiousness, extroversion, agreeableness, neuroticism), specifically the domains of conscientiousness and neuroticism. At the high extreme of conscientiousness are obsessive and control dictates, and at the low end of the spectrum is impulsivity. In the middle of the continuum is flexibility, where one is not obsessed with control or always acting without forethought. One is flexible. At the extremes of neuroticism are obsessive worry and fearlessness. In the middle of the continuum is reason, where one examines the situation and responds with due regard and judgment as to one's overall health and well-being, and beyond that, the health and well-being of one's family and tribe, and beyond that, all persons regardless of affiliation. (The latter condition does not exist in the real world but is sometimes pretended.)

Trump is flexible and completely stable with regard to being fearless. He is fearlessly flexible or completely transactional, and that triggers hysteria in some persons, especially the highly neurotic obsessive-compulsive personality who needs order, predictability, and control to avoid panic attacks.

Trump cares but doesn't care. That's the Zen of Trump.

The Inauguration and the March

JANUARY 22, 2017

I woke up excited. *This is fun,* I thought. *He did it. Trump won against all odds. That cannot be denied. He cannot be stopped.* The swearing in happens early, as opposed to Election Day, which happened late with a lot of waiting, watching, and not knowing. I had thought I might remain in my robe and boxers, eating donuts and drinking coffee, but it didn't go down that way. I did shower and shave and got dressed out of respect. What bothered me, worried me, was not what Trump would say or not say or do or not do but what the Resistance would do, all that negative energy put forth out into the universe—not carbon pollution but people's mind pollution.

I learn, via Facebook, that my son is flying to DC to protest.

Trump's inaugural address is very tough. He reiterates his campaign promises. His policy is "America First." No exceptions. "We will shine." Now is "the hour of action." The days of "all talk, no action" are over. He refers to the American landscape that he saw during the campaign as being one of "rusted-out factories, like tombstones, scattered across the landscape." It is a fearless, aggressive speech. To win, he had to take down both establishment parties represented by the Clintons, the Bushes, and the Obamas standing behind him on the dais and, in addition, the entirety of the mainstream media, the fourth estate—all of whom laughed and guffawed at not only his candidacy but also him as a person. It was pure moxie and perfectly Trump.

I feel as though my son went off to fight in a war I think is undeserving, unjust. I am sad. My Facebook friends are posting apocalyptic messages. Their closed-minded, obsessive-compulsive, introverted, people-pleasing neuroticism is coming through. (Now deemed normal, i.e., average.)

Trump took no prisoners, stating clearly that there is a new sheriff in town and that business as usual in Washington is over. No more getting rich on the backs of the middle and working classes. The forgotten man will no longer be forgotten but served.

One female Facebook friend inadvertently posts truth (it was snowing where she lived) as metaphor, "There are snowflakes falling out of the sky." I laugh out loud.

I sleep well (after inauguration day), get up, and turn on the TV and the coffeepot. The crowds are massive all across the nation. There are pink hats (pussy hats) everywhere; yesterday, the hats were red, the "make America great again" hats. The TV reporters are beside themselves with glee. I think that they, the protesters, had two years to get their act together, and yet they lost the election. *Respect the peaceful transition of power. That's what makes America, America.*

My son posts a picture of a poster being held up (there were more signs than I've ever seen in my life—hand-painted signs, creative signs, vulgar signs, signs of all kinds—almost all anti-Trump): "Hey, patriarchy, bye." That *is* the main theme, the big idea behind the protest. My son is a keen observer. He writes below another picture post of the massive crowd, that he is "nervous in crowds, but a tyrant with no capacity for empathy or compassion makes me more nervous. So this crowd is worth it." I am, again, sad. His thoughts are a product of being surrounded by man-hating women. He names them all: mother, sisters, nieces, aunts, cousins, grandmothers, teachers, girlfriend, coworkers. They are "women who helped shape me," mistaking their hate-bonding, their misandry, their collective animus, for love. This is a perfect example of how information, accurate though it may be, does not tell the whole story and so, therefore, has deleterious consequences. I know most all the women he mentions as shaping him. There is not one (that I know of) who is in a stable, traditional marriage. These are never-married, multiple-divorced, lesbians, childless, and bisexual women. These are women with an axe to grind or who have been so ill-parented and/or ill-educated that they can't have but a distorted worldview.

There's nothing I can do or say. I am silent, but I wonder, *does he consider his grandfather and his father, persons with no capacity for empathy or compassion?* We both supported Trump and are not unlike him in some (many) ways. Nevertheless, this is their day, and I hear them. But what I see is fear and failure—an explosion of pent-up, suppressed rage, manifested in an outpouring of joy and glee, fueled by the surprise of their numbers, of a resistance to the patriarchy and white supremacy. They are man-haters (including men) with a target, a symbol for their own fathers, grandfathers, brothers, uncles, cousins, boyfriends, bosses, and coworkers who have and had neglected, abused, and abandoned them. It is misguided. It is transference.

I get it. But this is the negative energy that will poison the ether, and *that* will bring us all down. Trump owes his astounding success to his belief in the power of positive thinking. That has been his creed his whole life. I believe in it too but am not as good as he is in practicing it. The thing is, its opposite is also true—negative thinking/energy has power. It's the law of attraction. You attract to you that which you focus your energy on. If there is a massive amount of energy in the form of negative thoughts and emotion of an apocalyptic future, that future might manifest. Follow Trump and his belief in peace and prosperity through strength and traditional conservative values, and *that* future just might manifest. If there is equal opposing energy, it'll be a long, hard slog to get anything but more of what we've had—a world divided between us and them, a world wherein the amity/enmity complex reigns supreme, a hostile, chaotic world. Maybe that's just the way it is, the way things are. Trump believes we can mitigate that by making deals with our friends *and* enemies. Trump believes in a transactional world wherein everyone gets something of what they want, varying degrees of love and happiness for all.

The protestors, with the help of the mainstream media or major media outlets (as the intersectional feminists and their allies prefer to call them) and the social networks have concocted a story, a confabulation. This is that story:

Trump is an illegitimate president. He won the election with interference from the Russians and their leader, Vladimir Putin, who broke into the DNC's computers (echoes of Richard Nixon and the Watergate break-in), stole, and then leaked damaging information to undermine and discredit Hillary Clinton and helped Donald Trump get elected, because they can control Trump, because they have debt and dirt on him, so he will do their bidding, thus restoring Russia as a great superpower. Trump is a pawn, a puppet, a shallow, stupid, bungling, abusive bully. *Finally,* now, with their (the man-haters) united protest, they will right all the wrongs and triumph over evil—the evil that is the patriarchy and white supremacy.

But wasn't it Bill Clinton whom the Russians paid $600K to for a speech in Moscow in 2010 when his wife was secretary of state, and then later, the US State Department approved the sale of US uranium to Russia? Yes, it's been fact-checked. But never mind that.

Trump, to the man-haters, is the ultimate symbol of men's subjugation of women as nothing more than sexual objects—good for only breeding and housekeeping. And so it is that the small-minded, introverted, obsessive-compulsive, passive-aggressive, neurotic, domesticated female is finding joy in coming out in large numbers (stronger together) and believing that they really did win! But again, the irony is that they (*have*) won, having elected a black president who gave them a diverse cabinet of minorities and women (nonwhite men, the patriarchy) and have passed laws that legalize (and subsequently normalize) abortion, interracial marriage, gay marriage, transgender/sexual beings, female soldiers, female politicians and CEOs, open borders, free birth control, single motherhood, marijuana, and blacks and queers all over TV. They (feminists/progressives/liberals) did, in law and culture, kill the patriarchy and white supremacy but failed to alter reality or the natural world and so *failed* in the universal quest for happiness—the desire of which we all aspire to and which Trump has mastered. Trump gets *it*, has achieved *it*, and now wants only credit/validation for that, which necessitates recognition for the ultimate achievement, the presidency of the United States. To deny him that is not a victory but bitter pettiness, resentment, envy, jealousy—a reaction formation against a successful, powerful man and a beautiful family.

I knew a person, a young girl, who could not be happy in and of herself but, as part of a family, had to make everyone else miserable, which then made *her* happy because that control satisfied her desire for power and control over others. *Schadenfreude.* But that state of power and control was only temporary, and the satisfaction/relief wasn't long-lasting because it didn't resolve the underlying needs of the girl. The next time she entered into a family, she might again encounter happiness and joy unrelated to her, and that angered her. So then the melodrama would repeat itself. There is no progress, no resolution, no moving forward. And now, many years later, the girl is grown up, has aged, but not matured in the sense of having grown emotionally or psychically; and so she repeats her juvenile behaviors—finding satisfaction in undermining others' happiness and success. She gets off on poking people in the eye; she experiences joy in disrupting other people's happiness. She basks in the glory of taking the disadvantaged and "saving" them. And then she presents her achievement publicly, shouting, "Look at me! Look at what I have done!" Not that much different than building tangible, concrete things like buildings and golf courses and putting your name on them for all to see. She loves the recognition and the spotlight.

Trump does too but doesn't pretend it's something other than what it is—pride in achievement. This is the essence of the March on Washington—the transfer of power from the authority (the competent father) to the self-identified victim, the oppressed. It is selfishness disguised as compassion. In the long run, it is destructive to the natural order of social beings because it is a false narrative. It is a fiction, a fairy tale, being sold as reality, which is bound to end badly.

People need order. A society that reproduces sexually needs strong, smart, competent men—protectors and providers—in a world that is chaotic and hostile and unpredictable, so as to be able to continue on.

First-Order Narcissism

JUNE 9, 2017

I left the Del Mar Beach Club, and I was sad. The beach club is a private, gated housing complex that sits on a bluff above the Pacific Ocean (32° 59′ N 117° 15′ 37″ W) in the small city (pop. 13,000) of Solana Beach in Southern California. My father and mother lived there for sixteen years from its, the DMBC, opening in 1973 until 1989. Dad called his condo the Paradise Hotel, and it *was* paradise visiting Dad and Mom in Southern California for some forty odd years. I was sad because we had just had Dad's final service at Riverside National Cemetery. He was ninety-six when he died, and I had rented an oceanfront condo at the beach club for the week, well, just because it reminded me of him and the good times we'd had. It was a *great* week!

The service was spectacular with the whole shebang that the US military is capable of—honor guard and gun salute, taps blown, by a former student and officer under Dad's command. Another retired colonel who had served under my father spoke elegantly about Dad and his leadership abilities. His pastor and good friend also spoke. We laughed and cried. My son was there, the finest son a man could be blessed with, whom Dad said "owed his fine qualities to the grace of his mother," my ex-wife, who was also there. My son said his grandpa "taught me how to take care of people." My older brother was there, Dad's number 1 son, who did a fantastic job of putting the whole service and subsequent party together, as well as being a great big brother for the week. My dear cousin June Bug hosted the party and was her witty and adorable best self. My two nieces were there—gorgeous, helpful, and supportive as always. My oldest best friend forever also came. He is that rare man, a true, good, hard-drinking, hardworking buddy and conversationalist—one who never lies or lets you down.

Concurrent with our week of celebration was the San Diego state fair, held at the Del Mar Fairgrounds and racetrack right across the street. Big brother took us all to the fair, as well as out to dinners, shopping, and of course, down to the beach. The fair was grander than I ever remembered, the food exquisite, and the ocean its most beautiful, reassuring, comforting, calming self. The weather was perfect—not too hot and not too cold, just right, a constant sixty-five degrees. The Batmobile, my ride for fifteen years, performed flawlessly. The accommodations at the beach club were first rate—big league. Just as I remembered, it is paradise. Thank you, Dad! One last gift from a sometimes-generous man.

Because my father lived so long, I was fortunate to have him in my life for sixty-seven years. Not many men can say that. People sometimes said to me (my son, ex-wife, girlfriend), "You're just like your father." And they didn't mean that in a good way. He was a first-order narcissist—the kind who'd score a 10 on a test for narcissism and boast about the perfect score. (Me? Maybe I'd score an 8?) I would answer defensively, "I'm not *that* bad."

Maybe I'm a second-order narcissist—the kind who denies it or pretends he's not. However, I wasn't as good as Dad either. Dad was fun. When he came into a room, peopled smiled. Often, he'd enter singing. And like I said, he was generous, but there were conditions—strings, I called them. You had to appreciate his generosity, his singing, and his jokes. He *was* funny. (Walking down the hallway of the apartment complex where he spent the last best years of his life before moving into assisted living, he'd say, "Welcome to the hardware store, nuts on the left, loose screws on the right."

And he was honest, sometimes brutally so. He took no prisoners. There was no pretension about him. What you saw is what you got—a man in love with life and himself and proud of it.

Dad wasn't one of a kind, though. There are other narcissists about—Donald J. Trump, our president, for one. He, Trump, is like my father in many ways, which is why, maybe, I wasn't shocked or surprised he won. First-order narcissists are winners. They hate losing and losers—quitters. They're competitors and believe they're always right, but they're also flexible. If you can present an idea in such a way that demonstrates its (the idea's) rightness, they will change their opinion or mind. You just have to know how to present it in such a way that they can then take credit for coming up with the idea. It's a trick for sure, maybe a little dishonest, but will gain you respect with the narcissist—the big guy. I understood that about my father, and in his later years, he would ask my opinion about things and say to me, "What do you think? You were always the smartest of us." Maybe he knew all along what I was doing but played along because those were the rules—the protocol of the narcissist.

Being right isn't a valued trait unique to narcissists. It's a trait shared by all people; it's universal. It's just a matter of degree. The stick-to-it-ness, the "never give an inch" part of being right, that is so dominant in narcissists is what separates them from ordinary folks. It (being right) is a survival mechanism to be right, to not give in or up, to not quit until you're proven right. "There's water in this direction [true, if you don't give up], I know it. Follow me or die trying." Those that don't quit will succeed. Those that believe in themselves will win, unless they don't have the stamina or the talent. That is the law of natural selection, the law of the jungle: never give up or in, never quit, and keep fighting. Narcissists are the best! First-order narcissists that is. My father *never* quit. He lived to be ninety-six and believed he'd earned it! He was flirting with the nurses three days before he died! *And* he was entitled to a long life because he was a winner, *the best*!

Another universal trait (shared by all in degrees) is the need to feel good. To feel good and to be right is heaven on earth. And to be right makes a person feel good. And so to be wrong makes a person feel bad, which is why so many people hate Donald Trump. He proved, without a doubt, that they were wrong and he was right. Trump, like my father, is a first-order narcissist; and I love and understand them. They are a gift.

Thank you, Dad. And thank you, Donald J. Trump. You make me smile. You make me feel good. And I was right.

Further Readings

Ardrey, Robert. *The Territorial Imperative: A Personal Inquiry into the Animal Origins of Property and Nations.* 1966.

Aronson, Elliot, Timothy D. Wilson, and Robin M. Akert. *Social Psychology: The Heart and the Mind.* 1994.

Barker, Eric. *Barking Up the Wrong Tree: The Surprising Science behind Why Everything You Know about Success Is (Mostly) Wrong.* 2017.

Benjamin, Lorna Smith. *Interpersonal Diagnosis and Treatment of Personality Disorders.* 1996.

Byrne, Gary. *Crisis of Character: A White House Secret Service Officer Discloses His Firsthand Experience with Hillary, Bill, and How They Operate.* 2016.

Clinton, Hillary. *What Happened.* 2017.

Crichton, Michael. *State of Fear.* 2004.

Eysenck, Hans. *The Inequality of Man.* 1973.

Eysenck, Hans, and Michael Eysenck. *Mind Watching: Why We Behave the Way We Do.* 1989, 1994.

Freud, Sigmund. *Civilization and Its Discontents.* 1930.

Goldschhneider, Gary. *The Secret Language of Birthdays: Personology Profiles for Each Day of the Year.* 1994.

Gosling, Sam. *Snoop: What Your Stuff Says about You.* 2008.

Jabbour, M. E. *Attachment: A Novel of War and Peace.* 2006.

Junger, Sebastian. *Tribes: On Homecoming and Belonging.* 2017.

Kaplan, Robert D. *The Coming Anarchy: Shattering the Dreams of the Post Cold War.* 2000.

Lasch, Christopher. *The Culture of Narcissism: American Life in an Age of Diminishing Expectations.* 1979.

Low, Bobbi S. *Why Sex Matters: A Darwinian Look at Human Behavior.* 2000.

Maslow, Abraham. *Motivation and Personality.* 1970.

———. *Towards a Psychology of Being.* 1968.

Matthews, Chris. *Life's a Campaign: What Politics Has Taught Me about Friendship, Rivalry, Reputation, and Success.* 2007.

Milkman, Harvey B., and Stanley G. Sunderwirth. *Craving for Ecstasy and Natural Highs.* 2010.

Moore, Michael. *Stupid White Men: And Other Sorry Excuses for the State of the Nation.* 2002.

Morris, Dick. *Rewriting History.* 2004.

Nettle, Daniel. *Personality: What Makes You the Way You Are.* 2007.

Obama, Barack. *Dreams from My Father: A Story of Race and Inheritance.* 1995.

Reeve, Johnmarshall. *Understanding Motivation and Emotion.* 1992.

Russell, Arlie. *Strangers in Their Own Land: Anger and Mourning on the American Right.* 2016.

Schweizer, Peter. *Clinton Cash: The Untold Story of How and Why Foreign Governments and Businesses Helped Make Bill and Hillary Rich.* 2015.

Tolstoy, Leo. *War and Peace.* 1869.

Trump, Donald J. *Crippled America: How to Make America Great Again.* 2015.

Trump, Donald J., and Tony Schwartz. *Trump: The Art of the Deal.* 1987.

Tur, Katy. *Unbelievable: My Front-Row Seat to the Craziest Campaign in American History.* 2017.

Untermeyer, Louis. *Aesop's Fables.* 1965.

Wallace, David Foster. *Consider the Lobster and Other Essays.* 2006.

———. *Infinite Jest.* 1996.

———. *Oblivion: Stories.* 2004.

———. *The Broom of the System.* 1987.

———. *The Pale King.* 2011.

Webster's New World College Dictionary. 4th ed. 2001, 2000, 1999.

Westover, Tara. *Educated: A Memoir.* 2018.

Whittlesey, Lee H. *Death in Yellowstone: Accidents and Foolhardiness in the First National Park.* 1995.

Wilson, E. O. *On Human Nature*. 1978.

Wolff, Michael. *Fire and Fury: Inside the Trump White House*. 2018.

Zimbardo, Philip, and Michael Leippe. *The Psychology of Attitude Change and Social Influence*. 1991.

Index

tribes, 133, 138, 140, 142, 147–48, 150–
    52, 155–56, 189, 200, 204, 259,
    268, 273, 276
Truman, Harry, 172
Trump, Donald, xviii, xxi, 18, 20, 29,
    39, 90–91, 97–99, 105, 111, 139–
    40, 144–45, 174, 284, 301–2
  credo, 192
  memo to the *Washington Post*, 111
  platform, 67–69
  slogan, 136, 276
Trump, Fred, 283
Trump, Ivanka, 105, 280
Trump, Melania, 139n61, 194n107,
    304n153
Trump derangement syndrome, 271,
    312–14
Tur, Katy, 176, 262

V

value, 141n62
victimology, 59, 98
Vincent Peale, Norman, 99, 140

W

wall (between the US and Mexico), 86,
    89, 91, 94, 111–12, 117, 119, 163–
    64, 184–85, 205, 219, 225, 257
Wallace, Chris, 254, 306
Welsh, Jack, 300
Westover, Tara, 42
Whittlesey, Lee H., 187n97
Williams, Brian, 263
Williams, Brian H., 186, 189
Williams, Robin, 65, 300
Wilson, E. O., 189
Wolff, Michael, 213n118
Wright, Jeremiah, 273

X

Xavier Johnson, Micah, 154

Y

Young, Neil, 175

Z

Zarqawi, Abu Musab al-, 50